Space, Place, and Violence

Direct, interpersonal violence is a pervasive, yet often mundane feature of our day-to-day lives. Paradoxically, violence is both *ordinary* and *extraordinary*. Violence, in other words, is often hidden in plain sight. *Space, Place, and Violence* seeks to uncover that which is too apparent: to critically question both violent geographies and the geographies of violence. With a focus on direct violence, this book situates violent acts within the context of broader political and structural conditions. Violence, it is argued, is both a social *and* spatial practice. Adopting a geographic perspective, *Space, Place, and Violence* provides a critical reading of how violence *takes place* and also *produces place*. Specifically, four spatial vignettes—home, school, streets, and community—are introduced, designed so that students may think critically how 'race', sex, gender, and class inform violent geographies and geographies of violence.

James A. Tyner (Ph.D., University of Southern California) is Professor of Geography at Kent State University. His research interests include political, population, and social geography. He is the author of 11 books, including *Military Geographies: A World Made by War* (Routledge).

Space, Place, and Violence

Violence and the Embodied Geographies of Race, Sex, and Gender

James A. Tyner

NEW YORK AND LONDON

First published 2012
by Routledge
711 Third Avenue, New York, NY 10017

Simultaneously published in the UK
by Routledge
2 Park Square, Milton Park, Abingdon, Oxon OX14 4RN

Routledge is an imprint of the Taylor & Francis Group, an informa business

© 2012 Taylor & Francis

The right of James A. Tyner to be identified as author of this work has been asserted by him in accordance with sections 77 and 78 of the Copyright, Designs and Patents Act 1988.

All rights reserved. No part of this book may be reprinted or reproduced or utilised in any form or by any electronic, mechanical, or other means, now known or hereafter invented, including photocopying and recording, or in any information storage or retrieval system, without permission in writing from the publishers.

Trademark notice: Product or corporate names may be trademarks or registered trademarks, and are used only for identification and explanation without intent to infringe.

Library of Congress Cataloging in Publication Data
Tyner, James A., 1966-
Space, place, and violence : violence and the embodied geographies of race, sex, and gender / James A. Tyner. – 1st ed.
p. cm.
1. Violence. 2. Social psychology. I. Title.
HM1116.T96 2011
303.6–dc22
2011015652

ISBN: 978-0-415-88083-1 (hbk)
ISBN: 978-0-415-88085-5 (pbk)
ISBN: 978-0-203-80212-0 (ebk)

Typeset in Adobe Caslon Pro and Copperplate Gothic
by Prepress Projects Ltd, Perth, UK

Contents

Preface · VII

Acknowledgments · XIII

Chapter 1 Everyday Geographies of Violence · 1
   Violence as Subject 5
   Towards a Geographic Understanding of Violence 11
   Making Space, Constructing Place 14
   Place as Disciplined Space 18

Chapter 2 Home · 25
   Home as Refuge? 27
   Constructions of Home 29
   Intimate Partner Violence 34
   Same-Sex Domestic Violence 50
   Home, Nation, and Violence 59
   Conclusions 67

Chapter 3 School · 69
   Discipline In/Of Schools 71
   School Subjects and Violence 83
   Conclusions 94

Chapter 4 The Streets — 97
Modernity and the Serial Killer 99
The Serial Killer as Urban Redeveloper 104
(Eliminating) Sex on the Streets 113
The Streets of Ciudad Juárez 120
Conclusions 128

Chapter 5 Community — 131
Communities and Sovereign Geographies 135
Shifting Borders, Shaping Communities 140
(B)ordering Communities 150
Communal Belonging and Losings 155
Conclusions 160

Chapter 6 Violence and the Pedagogy of Impunity — 163

Notes — 173
Bibliography — 201
Index — 217

Preface

On September 3, 1944 Recy Taylor, a married woman living in Abbeville, Alabama, was gang-raped while walking home from church. A woman of African-American descent, Taylor, then 24 years-old, was abducted and assaulted at knife-point by seven white men; later, six of the men raped Taylor and left her for dead. Twice, two all-white, all-male grand juries failed to bring any charges for indictment. During the proceedings, Taylor herself was presented as a whore, certainly not deserving of any justice. Sixty-seven years later, on March 30, 2011, the Alabama House of Representatives approved a resolution expressing regret for the failure of the State of Alabama to prosecute crimes committed against Recy Taylor.

What does the story of Recy Taylor say about space, place, and violence? I maintain that her story says a lot, but perhaps not what we might expect. One reading might conclude that her tragic ordeal is a product of a particular time—and place—in the history of the United States; that her violent rape was the result of a society that no longer exists, a geographic and historic era that disappeared with the elimination of segregated drinking fountains and public urinals. And yet, how far removed are we from the brutal events that took place nearly seven decades ago? Racism and sexism have not disappeared;

and the accusations of women's worth remain remarkably similar. Rape victims are still blamed for being attacked—for dressing provocatively, for being in the 'wrong place' at the 'wrong time'. A case in point is the recent media coverage of an 11-year-old Hispanic girl from Cleveland, Texas who was gang-raped repeatedly by upwards of 19 men between September 15 and December 3, 2010. The initial *New York Times* story of the incident in effect *blamed* the girl, quoting unnamed sources that she wore heavy make-up, dressed inappropriately, and hung out with older boys. Even more egregious: the story quoted a woman who was concerned that the rape 'destroyed the community' because the alleged rapists would have to live with it for the rest of their lives.

Violence is pervasive—the numbers are quite clear. In the United States, over 10,000 people are murdered each year; nearly 70 percent of these people are killed by firearms. Approximately 90,000 women are forcibly raped each year. An estimated 25 percent of all elementary school children and 40 percent of all middle-school children report being bullied *at least once every week*. And each year, hundreds (if not thousands) of men, women, and children die while attempting to cross the border between the United States and Mexico. These statistics, however, fail to capture the daily tragedies—and politics—that stem from such violence. Indeed, we can become numbed through a litany of numbers; we may forget that these are real people: our fathers and mothers, brothers and sisters, sons and daughters. They are people like Recy Taylor or the 11-year-old girl of Cleveland, Texas.

Some acts of violence do stand apart, often because the victim is a celebrity. In March 2009, for example, the beating of singer Rihanna by rapper Chris Brown brought domestic violence into the spotlight. And yet, the approximate 1.3 million *other* women who are beaten by their partner or spouse every year go unnoticed or uncommented. We do not hear of Theresa Still, the 43-year-old Altoona, Wisconsin woman who was killed by her live-in boyfriend in December 2009.

Space, Place, and Violence confronts this paradox: that violence is both everywhere and nowhere. When we listen to the nightly news, or read the morning papers, we are confronted with a seemingly endless litany of violent events: beatings, murders, rapes, and so on. And yet, violence can become so pervasive, so prevalent, that we don't always 'see' violence—unless, of course, it affects us personally, or a celebrity. *Space, Place, and Violence* seeks to provide some clarity—to open up new paths for exploration—to these uneven geographies of violence.

A second and related paradox is also considered, namely that we too often teach our students about structural and institutional violence, to the neglect of direct violence. Students, it is presumed, can readily recognize certain events as violent: murder, rape, beatings. Other forms of violence, such as the structural violence resultant from neoliberal practices and structural adjustment policies, are less recognizable. Hence the paradox: by focusing on structural violence in our classes, we tend to lose sight of the most obvious—indeed, graphic—forms of direct, interpersonal violence. And while it is true that interpersonal violence dominates most popular discussions, to the neglect of structural forms, we should not be confronted with an either/or choice, a false dichotomy between 'structural' or 'direct' violence. Rather, this book addresses head-on the question of violent interpersonal geographies *within the context of structural and institutional parameters*.

Although of interest to all levels, this book is designed and written with the undergraduate student in mind. Note that I do not explicitly direct this book to *geography* students; rather, I hope to speak to a broader audience. Simply put, as a geographer, my goal is to demonstrate the usefulness of a geographic perspective to our understanding of direct, physical interpersonal violence. Why? For the simple reason that violence is a social and spatial practice; that direct violence is an act to regulate people through a discipline of space.

Space, Place, and Violence is built around four case studies—four spatial vignettes—organized largely around different 'scales' of analysis: home, school, street, and community. Our emphasis is on how institutions and structures provide a context for understanding violence and, in the process, we understand that direct violence is not separable from pervasive structures of race, sex, gender, class, and so on. This book is different, therefore, in that it explicitly addresses the spatiality of interpersonal violence—a subject that is too frequently overlooked. In Chapter Two, we first consider intimate partner violence, but as informed by shifting concepts of 'home' and 'family'. We will see how the home is a site of potential, if not actual, violence and how this violence is often used to repress certain identities (e.g., gender, sex, and ethnicity) that are perceived as challenging or transgressing dominant (heteronormative and patriarchal) ideals.

Chapter Three directs attention to school-based violence, but not the attention-grabbing headlines of school shootings. Instead, we focus on the banal, mundane, everyday violence of bullying and teasing. Here, similar to our discussion of the home, we think how school violence reflects dominant cultural attitudes and expectations, where, for example, young boys are encouraged to 'stand up' for themselves while simultaneously bullying those children who fail to conform to prevailing gendered expectations. More broadly, we explore the 'meaning' of education and how schools—as hegemonic institutions—reflect pervasive attitudes toward the 'place' of children within society.

Although women are more likely to be assaulted within their own home, a wide-spread belief is that women are more at risk from 'stranger-danger' while walking in a public space—on the street. Chapter Four begins with this paradox but questions more broadly the 'place' of women in society. Through a critical engagement with serial killers, street prostitutes, and urban redevelopment, this chapter explores how misogynist attitudes of female respectability contribute to and excuse the brutal murder of women. Comparisons are drawn between the de-industrialized cities of North America with the industrializing city of Ciudad Juárez in northern Mexico.

In the penultimate chapter, we break-down and challenge the concept of 'community' and examine how ideas and ideals of 'popular sovereignty' provide insight into the policing of the U.S.–Mexico border. We engage directly with the intersection of 'race', class, and the *valuation* of humanity as we see how certain groups of people are literally hunted down and/or allowed to die because their presence is seen to threaten the fabric of community. Throughout, in this chapter and the preceding chapters, we focus our attention on how political and economic processes infuse violent practices.

Space, Place, and Violence is the first book-length treatment of geography and direct, interpersonal violence. It thus stands apart in its aims and goals. This text, though, is neither exhaustive in its scope nor definitive in its conclusions. Rather, as an initial foray into a diverse and difficult terrain, I want to encourage students (and instructors) to think through the intersection of space, place, and violence. I want readers to confront difficult issues and events—topics that are uncomfortable, yet of vital importance in our daily lives. Consequently, this is a critical text rather than a prescriptive text. When finished, I hope that students have been challenged to think through their common-sense understandings of violent geographies and to conceptually understand not only how violence works *in* place, but also how violence *produces* place.

Alabama's resolution reads, in part, that "such failure to act was, and is, morally abhorrent and repugnant." Action, then and now, is required. One place to begin is by asking questions—and by not forgetting.

Acknowledgments

Jessica, my youngest daughter, asked me to write a book about mermaids. This is *not* that book. In the pages that follow, you will encounter no mermaids or unicorns, faeries or elves. You are, however, encouraged, much like John Lennon so long ago asked of us, to imagine a world less violent—a world, perhaps, where little girls can dream of mermaids without nightmares of bullyings and beatings, rapes and murders.

This has been a difficult book to write—but I have been fortunate to have been assisted along the way with the help of many friends, colleagues, and family members. First, I thank my editor at Routledge, Steve Rutter. He took a chance on this project, and offered invaluable insights and critical feedback when necessary.

Over the years I have benefitted from my interactions with colleagues; through their insights, they have helped form my thoughts and clarified my understanding of politics, violence, geography, and life in general. Thanks are given to Michael Dear, Mona Domosh, Colin Flint, Pierrette Hondagneu-Sotelo, Larry Knopp, and Laura Pulido. Special thanks are extended to Stuart Aitken, Joshua Inwood, Joe Nevins, Melissa Wright, and two reviewers, Gail Hollander at Florida International University and Joshua Barkan at University of

Georgia—all of whom read various drafts of this manuscript, in whole or in part. This book would not have been possible without their help. At Kent State I have been fortunate to work, and often collaborate, with a remarkable group of graduate students, many of whom provided critical comments and suggestions for this book along the way: Gabriela Alvarez, Steve Butcher, Alex Colucci, Alex Peimer, Stian Rice, Andrew Shears, Dave Stasiuk, and Dave Widner.

Closer to home, literally, I thank my parents, Dr. Gerald Tyner and Dr. Judith Tyner, for their continued support. I thank also David Tyner, Karen (Tyner) Owens, and Bill Owens. All of these remarkable individuals have helped provide a solid moral foundation for my life. And as always, I thank my now 10-year-old puppy, Bond, and my 12-year-old cat, Jamaica. Late at night, while reading or writing, I can always count on these two to keep me company—even if they are both snoring. Most importantly, however, I must thank my immediate family—mostly for putting up with me: Belinda, my friend, partner and wife; and Jessica and Anica Lyn, our two daughters. Throughout the course of this project, they have kept me relatively sane, and have provided always the silver lining, to see the positive in life. And it is with their blessings that I dedicate this book to the girls and boys who can still find room in their hearts to believe in mermaids.

1
EVERYDAY GEOGRAPHIES OF VIOLENCE

We often think of the 'everyday' as those mundane, banal, even trivial activities that occupy our daily lives. We wake up and brush our teeth, shower, eat and expel our bodily wastes. We work and go to school. We eat (again) and go to bed. And there is a familiar regularity—a comforting routine—to our everyday. Strangely, this routine is often perceived as boredom. Indeed, according to Philip Wander the everyday becomes "the grey reality enveloping all we do."[1]

Violence is also part of our everyday life. As Hille Koskela explains, "Being too afraid to take a path across a dark park is a practical question of everyday life."[2] Likewise, according to Elizabeth Stanko,

> If any of us takes measures to try to guarantee our safety—such as staying alert on the street, resisting arguments with our intimates because their bad tempers might lead to a beating, or avoiding certain public places that make us feel uneasy—we are automatically taking violence into account as a possible occurrence in our lives.[3]

However, we don't even have to leave the confines of our homes to be exposed to violence. Simply watching the latest Hollywood blockbuster movie or television show is also a part of our everyday life. And these shows are increasingly violent. Indeed, *35 years ago* Timothy Hartnagel and his colleagues found that 80 percent of all prime time television shows included violence, and that the frequency of violent episodes was eight per hour.[4]

Consequently, "most of us are exposed to violence in one form or another on a fairly regular basis. Being exposed to violence means you can either be witness to violent behavior or be victimized by violence."[5] According to recent surveys, there are an estimated six million children abused or neglected each year in the United States; moreover, studies indicate that nearly 40 percent of boys and 50 percent of girls saw someone else being slapped at home. And this exposure to violence is not limited to the home. Other studies report that as many as eight out of ten children report that they have seen someone else threatened with violence, or beaten up, at school.[6]

The role of violence in our everyday lives is paradoxical. On the one hand, violence, and here I mean *actual, physical violence*, is pervasive. Indeed, the number of violent acts committed every day is staggering. According to a *World Health Organization* report, world-wide approximately 4,400 people die every day because of intentional acts of self-directed, interpersonal, or collective violence. In the year 2000, for example, an estimated 1.6 million people died a violent death. About half of these deaths were suicide, a fifth were war-related, while one-third were homicide-related.[7] Untold thousands more are injured or suffer other non-fatal consequences as a result of being the victim or witness to acts of violence.

Despite (or because of?) these statistics, we often don't associate violence as a mundane feature of our existence. Instead, violence is that which interrupts our day-to-day activities. We are *confronted* with violence; violence is something that happens, that occurs, that disrupts our normal routines. We are shocked when we learn that a close friend has been physically assaulted; we are saddened and horrified to hear on the nightly news that a teenager shot and killed a number of his classmates. These out-of-the-ordinary, or *extraordinary*, events may give us pause, and a chance to reflect on our lives, but beyond this, are viewed as separate from our lives. Indeed, it is something that happens to someone else, someplace else; not us, and certainly not here.

On the other hand, even extraordinary violence has become mundane and banal. Indeed, violence has become so common-place that it often recedes into that 'grey envelope' of the everyday. This claim was recently brought home on the streets of New York City. On April 18, 2010, a 31-year-old homeless man was stabbed after attempting to help another woman who was being mugged. The man, Hugo Alfredo Tale-Yax, crumbled to the sidewalk and lay in a pool of blood. And yet while he lay dying, at least 25 people walked past Tale-Yax; none of the people stopped to offer assistance. Incredibly, one person did pause to photograph the dying man.[8]

Commentators were quick to offer explanations for this outwardly callous behavior. Perhaps everyone assumed someone else called the police. Perhaps people were scared to get involved. Perhaps they assumed he was drunk (and thus, not 'worthy' of assistance?). Despite the many excuses forwarded, the fact remains that many people did not waver in their day-to-day activities; it was as if the crumpled body of Tale-Yax was simply a part of their everyday landscape.

How do we make sense of this paradox—that violence is both ordinary and extraordinary? How do we make sense of violence as part of our day-to-day existence? How does violence shape our perceptions and conceptions of particular places? In turn, how do these places—homes and schools, streets and communities—inform our understanding of violence? Is there a lesson to be drawn from these questions?

At this point, let me quickly note what this book *is* and *is not*. It is not a text book on the definition or explanation of violence. My shelves and perhaps yours also, are filled with books on the subject of violence.[9] Likewise, hundreds of academic journals regularly publish thousands of articles on violence. Many of these books and articles are exceptionally insightful and indeed provide some guidance to my own work. However, the existing literature does not present the story that I want to tell. As a geographer, I am interested in the twin concepts of 'space' and 'place'. And I believe that these two concepts are intimately related to violence. Consequently, I want to better understand 'space' and 'place' (or, simply, geography) from the standpoint of violence; concurrently, I want to better understand violence from the standpoint of geography.

That said, there are many different ways of approaching violence from a geographic perspective. We can for example map out distributions of violence (i.e., where murders occur) and seek causal explanations to account for these patterns. We might also 'step inside' the minds of violent people and try to understand how they perceive the world around them—their spaces and places and how these environments influence their actions. Here, however, I pursue another direction. My concern is on interpersonal violence *in the context of broader political and structural conditions of violence*. I want students to think through and understand how direct violence informs and is informed by broader social processes, such as capitalism, patriarchy, sexism, and nationalism. I want students to understand, also, how these broader structures and processes frame our thinking about violence—frames that make some types of violence visible while obscuring others.

Note that I do not attempt to 'explain' violence; instead, I hope to provide some level of understanding. The difference is not as subtle as it might appear. To 'explain' something implies a level of knowledge that permits predictions to be made. Following Dan Flannery and Randall Collins—two preeminent, but very different, scholars of violence—I do not believe that we can ever 'explain' and thus 'predict' violence. It is possible, however, to provide a level of understanding. Flannery, for example, notes that "we have yet to develop any foolproof way of picking out who will act violently toward others and when, and under what circumstances violence will occur." Otherwise, Flannery continues,

> If we were so good at predicting who would become violent, we would do a better job of picking out school shooters, individuals who randomly shoot at motorists at gas stations and on highways, and those who kill their coworkers over some workplace dispute.[10]

Randall Collins agrees. He writes that "It is a false lead to look for types of violent individuals." Collins explains that though there are some statistical correlations between some variables (e.g., poverty, ethnicity, and age) and certain kinds of violence, these fall short of predicting most violence.[11]

The philosopher Wilhelm Dilthey (1833–1911) considered that while we *explain* nature, we *understand* social life and human intentions.[12] Consequently, Dilthey proposed that we seek *verstehen*, a German word which roughly translates as a cross between the English terms 'understanding' and 'empathy'. In other words, *verstehen* seeks to understand why people do what they do, in terms of their own personal theories; it is an appreciation of context rather than an attempt at prediction.[13]

Space, place, and violence. These are the main characters in the stories that follow. In the four substantive chapters that comprise this book, I present four spatial vignettes that capture some of the many ways in which our characters relate. I do so comparatively, in an attempt to understand how violence informs both space and place and, concomitantly, how space and place inform violence. First, however, it is necessary to introduce our characters. I begin with an overview of violence as an academic subject. This is complemented with a brief discussion of the concepts of 'space' and 'place'. Combined, these components provide the foundation for geographic understanding of violence.

Violence as Subject

Violence surrounds us … And we know it. It lurks in dark alleys and empty parking lots. It hides in our homes and our schools. It peers at us from our television screens, movie theaters, and now even our electronic game consoles—as our 'entertainment' activities are increasingly saturated with images of violence. And it roams across our football fields, race-car tracks, and other sporting venues.

But what is violence? The word itself provides little in the way of understanding. We routinely speak of tornados, earthquakes, and other 'natural events' as being violent. We also describe both car crashes and collisions on the football field as violent. In recognition of these many and varied usages, Richard Mizen laments that the "word 'violence' tends to be used in such a loose and broadly defined way that its use as a precise term of description or as a clear concept is severely limited."[14]

In *Space, Place, and Violence* I approach direct violence[15] from the standpoint forwarded by the World Health Organization:

> The intentional use of physical force or power, threatened or actual, against oneself, another person, or against a group or community, that either results in or has a high likelihood of

resulting in injury, death, psychological harm, maldevelopment or deprivation.[16]

As Etienne Krug and his colleagues explain, this usage (attempts to) encompass all types of violence and, more significantly, reflects both the context and 'nature' of violence.

Violence, following this approach, is further sub-divided into three categories: self-inflicted, interpersonal, and collective. Self-inflicted violence includes both suicide and self-abuse. Interpersonal violence, conversely, includes violence committed by one person toward another and two broad types are recognized: family/partner and community. The former type of interpersonal violence is distinguished primarily by life-span and living arrangement (i.e., domestic violence, child abuse/violence, and elder abuse); the latter includes 'acquaintance' and 'stranger' violence. Lastly, collective violence includes group forms of violence, and may include warfare or gang behavior.

As with any definition, the above categories are neither mutually exclusive nor necessarily exhaustive. Moreover, as detailed later in this book, many of these terms are likewise subject to debate. The term 'community', for example, is a heavily laden term that influences our understanding of violence. Consequently, specific chapters will revisit our definition of violence.

Although my focus is to provide an understanding of the relationships between space, place, and violence, it is necessary to briefly consider the purported causes of violence. It is common-place for academics to note that violence cannot be attributed to a single cause; that any given act of violence is both contingent and context-dependent. To this end, a useful starting point is provided, again, by the World Health Organization. Here, four 'levels' of factors are thought to increase the likelihood of one becoming either a victim or a perpetrator. The most proximate level is *biological*, or personal, which would include the 'body' itself. Key characteristics include demographic factors (e.g., age, sex/gender, education, income), personality disorders, and drug use.[17] In the United States, for example, young men are statistically more likely to be both victims and perpetrators of physical violence. Indeed, *world-wide* the differences between male-on-male violence and female-on-female violence are immense and, according to Daly and Wilson, these are universal. In their meta-analysis of 34 same-sex homicide studies around the world, they conclude that there is no known human society in which the level of lethal violence among women even begins to approach that of men.[18] This suggests that there must be a strong *biological* component to violent behavior—a component that nevertheless can be (and has been) modified by societal factors (e.g., laws, customs, and other practices). Many social scientists, however, are reluctant to consider the role that biology plays in violent behavior. As Alvarez and Bachman explain, because of their academic training, social scientists have tended to focus on social factors and have often ignored biological theories.[19] Indeed, many social scientists remain indignant to any explanation that speaks of biology.[20]

The body, however, must remain central to our understanding of violence. Bodies commit violent acts (e.g., people yell, punch, kick, shoot, and engage in other 'harmful' acts); and violence is commonly enacted on bodies. However, the body–violence linkage is not so simple. Too often we take bodies, including our own, for granted. By this I don't mean that we forget to eat properly or exercise regularly. Rather, I mean that we don't always question how our bodies—and other people's bodies—influence our daily activities. We know, of course, that our bodies come in different sizes, shapes, sexes, and colors. We know, also, that these *physical traits* provide meaning to other people. And often these meanings are beyond our control. Tall people are often assumed to be better leaders; obese people are perceived to be lazy. And the meanings attributed to skin color (e.g., race) are well established.

Physical traits, or, more precisely, the meanings attached to bodily traits, go a long way toward 'explaining' some (but not all) violent acts. Both hate and sex crimes, for example, are obvious sets of violent acts that are precipitated largely on the basis of physical appearances. Consider the tragic death of Pamela George.[21] On April 17, 1995 Pamela George, a mother of two, was brutally raped and beaten to death by two young Caucasian men. George herself was a member of the Saulteaux (Ojibway) nation in Regina, Saskatchewan, Canada. On Easter weekend, two 19-year-old university student-athletes, Steven Kummerfield and Alex Ternowetsky, decided to celebrate the end of the term. They began the night drinking and then decided to cruise 'the Stroll', a part of Regina known for street prostitution. Initially the two young men attempted twice to lure an Aboriginal woman into their car; when these efforts failed, Ternowetsky hid in the trunk of their car. Appearing to be alone, Kummerfield was able to convince George to enter his car, whereupon he drove to a secluded spot near the airport. Kummerfield then let his friend out of the trunk and the two men forced George to perform oral sex on them. They then beat George, before leaving her for dead. Two days later, when questioned what he did that night, Kummerfield replied, "Not much. We drove around, got drunk and killed this chick."

The murder of Pamela George raises many disturbing elements that will be explored in the remainder of this book: her 'position' as a poor prostitute; her being a woman of color; her assailants being supposedly upstanding Caucasian men. However, it is more than outward bodily traits (i.e., sex and skin color) or occupation. Rather, it is important to consider also how, and where, our bodies *relate* to other bodies. This directs our attention to the second level toward understanding violence, namely that of *interpersonal* relationships. Specific types of relationship violence include stranger violence, such as the relationship between George and her two assailants. Other relations include, but are not limited to, co-worker (workplace) violence, spousal/domestic partner violence, child abuse, and elder abuse. At this level, in short, the chance of becoming either a victim or a perpetrator is based on particular *social* relations and where these social relations take place.[22]

Violence, again, does not have to be directly experienced. Indeed, the witnessing of violent social relations may have a particular bearing on the socialization of (future) violence. To this end, social scientists employ a variant of social learning theory. This approach suggests that violence is learned, similar to our ability to learn to read and write, or to ride bicycles. Accordingly, social learning theory "asserts that people learn through conditioning, reinforcement, and imitation and modeling."[23] Consequently, people (but especially children) learn from both direct experience (i.e., being beaten), or vicariously, as when they watch (and learn) from others being violated—whether in the home, the schoolyard, or even television. As Alvarez and Bachman explain, one of the most consistent findings is that those who witness or experience violence and abuse as children are more likely to perpetrate it as adults. This is known alternatively as the 'intergenerational transmission of violence theory' or the 'cycle of violence' theory. However, these approaches are often insufficient, in that they fail to account for the observation that most children who witness or experience violence do not always or necessarily grow up 'violent'.[24] More succinctly, context matters.

A third level, therefore, consists of *situational factors*. As Collins argues, we should be concerned less with 'violent individuals' but rather with 'violent situations'. He proposes that

> If we zero in on the situation of interaction—the angry boyfriend with the crying baby, the armed robber squeezing the trigger on the holdup victim, the cop beating up the suspect—we can see patterns of confrontation, tension, and emotional flow, which are at the heart of the situation where violence is carried out.[25]

As we will see shortly, Collins' situational approach aligns most closely with my immediate concerns of space and place. Where we differ is in his tendency to consider space and place (the situational factors) as backdrop for human behavior, as opposed to space and place as active participants.

Lastly, a fourth level considers broad *societal* or cultural factors. Included here are cultural norms that impact gender roles or familial relations (e.g., parent–child relationships), criminal justice systems, social welfare programs, and exposure to media-based forms of violence. Growing up within a 'culture' of violence, for example, has been proposed as a reason why some people engage in violent behavior. Indeed, numerous studies in the United States have identified the existence of a 'gun culture' to explain the prevalence of (mostly male) violence. Statistics, to an extent, tend to bear out this relationship: compared to other industrialized societies, such as England, the Netherlands, France, and Norway, households in the United States far-and-away possess more guns than their counterparts in Europe. Furthermore, the 'normalcy' of gun-ownership is more pervasive in the United States than elsewhere. Do these characteristics lead to greater rates of violence? The evidence is mixed.[26] Consider the aforementioned observation that violence (and especially homicide) is largely perpetrated by males. This holds across societies and for different historical periods.[27] Such findings seriously undermine the forwarding of *exclusively* sociological explanations. As Buss notes, one glaring shortfall of social learning theory is that "it cannot explain why even in cultures without these media influences men kill much more often than women, why sex differences in murder are universal across cultures, not unique to modern Western culture."[28] Simply put, the existence of a 'gun culture' in the United States (which I do not deny exists) fails to account for the widespread occurrence of male-on-male violence that is prevalent in other societies that do not exhibit a 'gun culture'.

Another important societal factor consists of group identity and, more specifically, how particular groups interact and relate to each other. According to Iris Young, a social group is a collective of persons differentiated from at least one other group by cultural forms, practices, or way of life. More precisely, groups are expressions of social relations; groups exist only in relation to other groups. Susan Opotow suggests that norms, moral rules, and concerns about rights and fairness govern our conduct—and thus affect our relations and behavior—toward other people. However, as Young elaborates, many groups (bodies) find themselves *socially* and *spatially* excluded; not every person (or group) is necessarily included in the scope of justice. Indeed, it is not uncommon for a whole category of people to be expelled from useful participation in social life and thus potentially subjected to severe material deprivation and even extermination.[29] This is seen most clearly in the context of genocide; but it is also apparent in the home and on the schoolyard.

Moral inclusion and exclusion are pivotal to our understanding of the geographies of violence in that it sets parameters around social relations. Susan Opotow explains that "inclusion in the scope of justice means applying considerations of fairness, allocating resources, and making sacrifices to foster another's well being." Conversely, moral exclusion "rationalizes and excuses harm inflicted on those outside the scope of justice. Excluding others from the scope of justice means viewing them as unworthy of fairness, resources, or sacrifice, and seeing them as expendable, undeserving, exploitable, or irrelevant."[30] In short, moral exclusion works to *legitimize* violence.

The idea of moral exclusion is particularly important for our subsequent discussion of space, place, and violence. Moral exclusion underlines the socio-spatial practices that marginalize and subjugate certain bodies; this is seen most clearly in the prevalence of 'us–them' thinking. According to social psychologists, the *relational* practice of 'us–them' thinking originates with social categorizations and these mental constructs—man/woman, black/white, citizen/noncitizen—are cognitive tools that segment, classify, and order our social environment.[31] The process of social categorization is thus foundational to the evocation of place. As James Waller explains, "Not only do social categorizations systematize our social world; they also create and define *our place in it*" (emphasis added).[32]

Who, or which group, is granted or denied access to certain places? What activities are deemed appropriate or not? What relations of power are maintained when 'place' is invoked? And who has the authority, the ability, to define (and enforce) those places? It becomes clear that the processes leading to moral inclusion or exclusion have a *geographic* component, one that is infused with power. In particular, place becomes a site of contestation, the locus of social control where ideologies of racism, sexism, classism, and so forth are enacted. Consequently, there may emerge a *moral* obligation (or perceived necessity) among some individuals to maintain these places against the intrusion of unwanted Others. And when policing these places, it matters little whether the perceived intrusion was intentional or not. To better understand these relations, therefore, it is necessary to understand the geographies of violence.

Towards a Geographic Understanding of Violence

Many people live with a fear of violence, a fear of being robbed, mugged, raped, or murdered.[33] Consequently, we may alter our behavior in response to a pervasive, albeit latent, fear of violence. We might, for example, avoid particular places at certain times of the day or night.

We might also decide where or where not to live based on our perception of violence. In short, as Stanko finds, "Places, as well as specific or types of people, become labeled as potentially hazardous." Indeed, she concludes that "Images of danger become subtly woven into our perceptions about a place."[34]

Geographers have provided crucial insights into the perception of fear.[35] The pioneering efforts of Gill Valentine, Rachel Pain, and Hille Koskela are especially notable for their insights into the geographies of fear. These scholars have highlighted, in particular, the salience of gender toward people's fear of both public and private spaces and how a fear of violence impacts social mobility and interactions.

Unlike the scholarship of geographies of fear, the study of *direct* violence—and specifically direct, physical violence between two people—has been mostly tangential to the field of Geography.[36] Indeed, compared to war and other forms of organized (mass) violence, geographers have been somewhat silent on the centrality of interpersonal violence to everyday life. Why is this? I believe, in part, it relates to another paradox surrounding violence: violence so dominates our *popular* discussions that we tend to focus on other, less-well-known forms. For example, students are likely to understand both rape and murder as forms of violence. And certainly these topics are well discussed on radio and television talk-shows, news accounts, and other forms of media. Students however may not necessarily view environmental destruction as violence; nor are students likely to perceive economic practices (e.g., predatory lending) as forms of violence. These topics, moreover, are less likely to be considered in any great detail in the media or other popular forums. Consequently, geographers and other social scientists have provided valuable insight into the study of institutional and structural forms of violence. And here lies the paradox. In addressing the lack of coverage on, say, structural violence, geographers have not always contributed to the discussions of interpersonal violence as much as they could. It is not that geographers have avoided violence; rather, it is simply a matter that there is too much about violence that needs to be said.

Consider, for example, the recently published *WorldMinds: Geographical Perspectives on 100 Problems*.[37] According to the editors,

"Academic work is often popularly satirized for its lack of practical import beyond the comforting walls of the ivory tower." However, they note, "the momentum of contributions by geographical scholars has created a remarkable effervescence of conceptual and methodological practices that have enhanced the discipline's relevance in scientific and social discourse."[38] Consequently, entries include discussions of non-point sources of pollution, global climate change, water resources, drugs, cancer mortality, and illiteracy. These are forms of violence that typically go unnoticed. And yet, *WorldMinds* is conspicuously silent on interpersonal violence. Neither homicide nor rape, for example, are addressed as 'problems'; nor is there an engagement with intimate partner violence or school bullying. There is no discussion of related problems, such as gun control or the arms trade.

Likewise, the edited volume *Violent Geographies*, while providing a needed understanding of the political structures of violence, is seemingly lacking in its engagement with interpersonal violence. To be sure, this volume is more limited in scope, concerned as it is specifically with political violence. However, while specific chapters address suicide bombings and terrorism, militarism and global warfare, the volume as a whole does not consider the *politics* of everyday violence of spousal abuse, school violence, or (again) rape and sexual violence.[39] For example, it would be beneficial to consider the underlying politics behind gun control and how this impacts homicide rates in the United States. Conversely, it would be helpful to consider the politics surrounding women's rights and the implications for intimate partner abuse.

Lastly, consider the edited volume *The Geographical Dimensions of Terrorism*, published in the immediate aftermath of the attacks of September 11, 2001. Apart from contributions on 'insurrections' and 'drug production, commerce, and terrorism', one finds discussions of 'the need for a national spatial data infrastructure' and 'data modeling for emergencies'. To be sure, this latter volume was a product of a particular historical moment. As the editors explain, "In the days following September 11, 2001 ... [m]any of us who are geographers felt an urge and a need to see if we could find ways to apply our knowledge and expertise to make the world more secure."[40] But this was a missed opportunity, for it limited the discussion of terrorism to that defined by state agencies. Alternatively, a geography of terrorism *might* have broadened the discussion to include the use of drones and aerial bombardment as acts of terrorism on the everyday lives of people living in Pakistan, or (again) of rape and sexual violence as forms of terrorism. In other words, terrorism is not limited to large-scale events, but can in fact be found within our homes and schools—and perpetrated by our supposed friends and families.

I highlight these omissions in *WorldMinds, Violent Geographies*, and *The Geographical Dimensions of Terrorism* not as a critique against the editors or contributors, but rather to emphasize that Geography, despite its remarkable contributions to social justice and the study of violence in recent years, remains an unfinished product: our geographical accounts of the 'everyday' too often neglect the centrality of direct, personal violence. This constitutes a broad omission, not simply within Geography, but for the study of violence in general, for 'geography' must lie at the center of any discussion of violence. This is not meant as some glib statement, such as 'all activities, including violent acts, *take place*'. For one thing, this statement is a truism—what doesn't take place?—and thus provides no help in understanding. For another, it is incomplete, for it fails to consider what 'place' (or 'space') actually means to people experiencing violence.[41] Accordingly, in the following section I provide an overview of the twin concepts of 'space' and 'place' with an eye toward a geographic understanding of violence.

Making Space, Constructing Place

In Nigel Thrift's memorable phrase, 'space' is often regarded as the fundamental *stuff* of geography.[42] That said, space is often treated as the elephant in the room. We all know it's there, but we refuse to acknowledge its presence. And when we do, we often speak past ourselves. We use the same word but fail to realize that the word has multiple meanings. On the one hand, we might think of space as that 'emptiness' of a room, a street, or schoolyard. These usages imply an *absolute* conception of space. On the other hand, we may consider the notion of *relative* space; here, concern lies with the distribution of phenomena across space. With relative space, the focus is on the spaces—the distance—between objects; with distance being measured in terms of transport costs or travel time. To take an obvious example, the 'distance' between Los Angeles and New York City is relatively closer when traveling by airplane than the distance between Los Angeles and San Francisco when walking.

Both absolute and relative conceptions of space are widely used. However, recent years have seen the forwarding of yet another conception of space, namely that of *relational space*. Now, rather than viewing space as an inert backdrop, or a stage on which humans operate according to abstract physical laws, space is increasingly understood as an actor in its own right. The forwarding of relational space suggests that that space, in effect, is produced; but so too does space produce. This reconceptualization may not be immediately obvious and requires some elaboration.

It is common to say that an individual 'made' history. Implicit in this statement is the understanding that 'history' (i.e., time) was made figuratively; that through one's actions, events were affected. The United States president Abraham Lincoln, for example, *made history* in the sense that his actions significantly affected the course of events in American society. Rarely, though, do we hear of someone 'making' geography (e.g., space). Such a notion, however, lies at the core of a relational understanding of space.

Doreen Massey writes that space is constituted through social relations and material social practices. Let me illustrate. Imagine that you are sitting in a university classroom. The room has a particular area, or floor *space*. There are desks and chairs, chalk boards and trash cans, and these have a particular spatial arrangement. When classes are not in session, such as on weekends, or late at night, the room may be considered to be empty—despite the presence of chairs, desks, and so on. However, throughout the day, when classes are in session, the room becomes a *place*. But depending on the students, the room is a different place. In the morning, for example, the room might be occupied by a mathematics class, while in the afternoon it is occupied by a geography class. The room may stay the same, but the social relations and interactions are very different. This is because the interactions among the students and the professor vary. Likewise, playgrounds, streets, and shopping malls all become different places depending on who occupies those spaces and when. In short, we begin to understand that space is given meaning through social relations and interactions. In the process, spaces become places.

The French theorist Henri Lefebvre contributed much to our understanding of the production of space. Throughout his career, Lefebvre wanted to understand the interaction between spatial arrangements and social organization at different historical moments. How, for example, are cities organized? Hence, he might ask, how were feudal cities organized compared to 'modern' industrial cities? Lefebvre's insights, and especially how he understood social and spatial organization, provide some guidance toward our understanding of the spatiality of violence.

Lefebvre proposed that every society produces its own space. In other words, space is not *something* that simply exists, waiting to be inhabited. As Roger Matthews succinctly writes, "Space is ... never neutral."[43] Instead, space comes into being through social relations and interactions, manifest in competing claims, usages, and material practices. To clarify his argument, Lefebvre introduced the concepts of *spatial practices*, *representations of space*, and *representational spaces*. Spatial practices include the arrangement of buildings and pathways, but also the rules and regulations that constrain behavior within these spaces. The concept of 'spatial practice' therefore highlights the material, or concrete, routines of everyday life.

Both *representations of space* and *representational spaces*, as the terms suggest, relate to non-material, or ideological, spaces. Representations of space are spaces that are "purposefully representational of certain societal ideas, and therefore the holders of these ideals attempt to control its use."[44] We are taught and socialized to understand these spaces, of who is permitted access to any given space, and what behaviors are acceptable. We are taught, for example, that public parks are spaces for children and families. Teenagers who attempt to appropriate these spaces for their own use—to just 'hang out'—are shunted away by authorities. Representations of space, likewise, may be physically visible on the landscape. Walls, fences, and other barriers might be erected; signs may be posted. Over time, we internalize these socio-spatial lessons and learn appropriate behavior; and through repetitive (daily) actions, these representations of space become naturalized and normalized. Based both on who we perceive ourselves to be, as well as how we are perceived by others, we tend to avoid some spaces, while gravitating to others. And we begin to associate certain people—and certain behaviors—with particular spaces. The dominance of representations of space, of course, is far from complete and never uncontested. People do in fact challenge the norms and regulations of established spaces. These alternative understandings are termed *representational spaces*. These are the spaces of resistance and transgression (see below).

These elements—spatial practices, representations of space, and representational spaces—operate simultaneously, in terms of both 'time' and 'space'. Think again of the public park (or even our earlier discussion of the university classroom). With respect to the spatial practice of the park, there are certain objects present: playground equipment (i.e., swing sets, slides), benches, walking trails, bike paths, dog runs, restrooms. These objects both enable and constrain people in their interactions at the park. Concurrently, there are certain rules and regulations designed to control and limit certain behaviors. A posted sign, for example, may indicate that the park closes at 10:00 pm. Another sign specifies where dogs are or are not permitted and warns park visitors to 'clean up' after their dogs. Still another sign cautions that bicyclists must stay on marked paths. On any given day (or night), however, these *representations of space* may be challenged, either intentionally or not. A dog owner may not in fact 'clean up' after his dog; and older teens may 'hang out' at night, long after the park officially closes. Other illegal activities, such as drug use, might occur in the stalls of the restroom. Of course, such *representational spaces* need not necessarily be illegal nor carry negative connotations. The park, for instance, may be the site of a public protest against nuclear proliferation; alternatively, a couple may be married there.

Already we can begin to see how a relational conception of space might provide some understanding of violence. The contrast between representations of space and representational spaces, for example, suggests that activities deemed legal or not legal have a spatial component and that these may be contested. Certain behaviors might be legal in particular areas and at particular times, but illegal (i.e., criminal) at others. In short, we understand that space, far from being an inert stage upon which people act, is itself an active participant. And it is through this working of 'space' that we derive an understanding of 'place'.

'Place' like 'space' means many things to many people. For some, 'place' may suggest ownership or an emotional connection or attachment between a particular person and a particular location (i.e., a home or an apartment). Conversely, 'place' may suggest privacy and belonging (i.e., this is *my* place, not yours), or a position in a social hierarchy (i.e., putting someone in their 'place'). 'Places', likewise, are inscribed with various qualities, thereby emphasizing their uniqueness (i.e., this is a *nice* place, this is an *evil* place, or this is a *warm and humid* place with an average rainfall of 38 inches).[45]

More recently, geographers and other social scientists have come to see 'place' as "a crucial actor in producing affects because, in particular, it can change the composition of an encounter" between two or more people.[46] Place, in other words, operates as an active participant in social relations. Indeed, as Paul Adams and his co-authors write, most academics today do not interpret 'place' as having some primordial essence but instead write of the *becoming* of place.[47]

Places, in short, do not exist without people. As Cresswell explains, place "needs to be understood as an embodied relationship with the world. Places are constructed by people doing things. ... Place is constituted through reiterative social practice—place is made and remade on a daily basis."[48] Places are lived and embodied spaces.

Place is thus a human construct; it exists as a concept that is made real. By this I mean that place as a concept is defined, understood, and given meaning through human interactions and behaviors—including violence. Our understanding (*verstehen*) of violence is therefore closely tied with our trying to understand how other people and groups envision both space and place and, more fundamentally, how their meanings of space and place are maintained. To do so requires us to consider both discipline and violence as human spatial behaviors.

Place as Disciplined Space

At this point, it is necessary to consider more closely the concepts of 'violence' and 'discipline'. Discipline, according to the French theorist-philosopher Michel Foucault, is a type of power; it entails "a whole set of instruments, techniques, procedures, and levels of applications."[49] In other words, disciplinary power should not be thought of as something that is possessed, or claimed, by one individual, group, or institution. Rather, disciplinary power is fluid, conditioned by specific and particular social relations. For Foucault, power, including disciplinary power, exists on two conditions, the first being that 'the Other' is recognized and in a position to make choices, and the second being that, faced with a relationship of power, a whole field of responses, reactions, results, and possible interventions may open up. Power is thus not a matter of consent; but neither is it a renunciation of freedom. When a parent disciplines a child, for example, that child may still resist; likewise, there remains room for negotiation and compromise.

Viewed from this perspective, disciplinary power is relational; it is exercised only between two or more 'free' subjects. As we will see shortly, this contrasts with 'violence' which, for Foucault, is a totalizing practice. When violence is applied to people, their subjugation is complete. Violence removes the possibilities for active subjects to reinscribe themselves; it removes the possibility for resistance.

Disciplinary practices are neither inherently negative or positive, nor repressive or constructive. A well-known example is the discipline meted out by parents to their children. Children must be taught to look before crossing a street, to not touch a hot stove, to not eat cookies before dinner, and so on. Notice also that these disciplinary lessons 'take place'; that children are taught appropriate behaviors with respect to specific spaces. The child, therefore, is not allowed to cross the street 'at will'. Moreover, children are taught that they should not go to certain places without a 'responsible adult' present. For the most part, these examples indicate a 'positive' form of discipline. The basic point, however, is to consider the context and contingency of disciplinary practices.

Although disciplinary practices permeate societies, there (almost) always remain opportunities for challenges. Cresswell explains that one way to illustrate the relation between place and behavior is to look at those behaviors that are judged as inappropriate—thus requiring discipline—in a particular location. Some inappropriate actions are intentional. A child, for example, may cross a street when her parents aren't looking. These 'acts of resistance' imply intentionality—a purposeful action directed against some disliked entity or rule. The 'lunch counter sit-ins' during the Civil Rights era in the United States, for example, were acts of resistance. Other actions, termed 'transgressions', are not intentional. As Cresswell writes, transgression is judged by those who react to some behavior at some place; to have transgressed means to have been judged to have crossed some line that was not meant to be crossed.[50] Gang activity provides another good example. It is common that gangs will lay claim to particular areas, such as streets, clubs, or bars. Newcomers to the area may not be aware of the unwritten codes of conduct. Their presence, their transgression, may unknowingly signify a challenge to members of the gang, resulting in harassment and/or physical violence.

As Nigel Thrift explains, all of the different ways of thinking about space and place are attempts to rethink what constitutes *power*, that is, once we no longer think of power as simply command and control.[51] Spaces are produced through social relations and interactions; we are socialized into an understanding of these spaces which, in turn, become natural and normal. These spaces, however, are coded by dominant embodied conceptions of 'race', sex, gender, and so on. In short, these socially produced spaces become disciplined; they become, through discipline, places. Stated differently, *places are disciplined spaces*. Consequently, we recognize that both acts of resistance and perceived transgressions may constitute a threat to the construction and maintenance of a *place*.

Direct violence emerges as a crucial behavior in this process of disciplining space and producing place. And to understand violence as human behavior, we need to return to our conception of place as defined by social relations. For our present purposes, we need to understand first that violence, like discipline, is both 'individual' and 'relational'. Violence is individual in the sense that individual people can and do engage in violent behaviors: taunting, slapping, kicking, raping, shooting, stabbing, and so forth.[52] Violence, though, is also relational in that these acts are perpetrated by one individual against another. There is the husband who beats his wife; the stalker who murders his ex-girlfriend; the teenage boy who shoots his class-mates. In any of these cases, we can identify extenuating factors, contributing causes, and trigger mechanisms. But in the final analysis, we are left with one individual who engages in violent behavior against another individual.

Second, we must acknowledge that while humans have the capacity for violence, not all humans are violent in every situation.[53] As Collins writes, "even people that we think of as very violent—because they have been violent in more than one situation, or spectacularly violent on some occasion—are violent only in very particular situations."[54] Thus, David Smith explains, "every organism has a behavioral repertoire, a set of potentials that lie dormant until or unless they are triggered by something in their environment."[55] In other words, the situational context (e.g., the structural and cultural conditions) is important. Thus, we can surmise that in a society that promotes the 'husband' as breadwinner and provider (i.e., a cultural factor), a man's unemployment (i.e., a structural condition) might result in feelings of humiliation and inferiority (i.e., a relational attitude), and he may subsequently engage in violent behavior in an attempt to reassert his authority.

And third, we need to understand that violent behavior—from the perspective of the perpetrator—is a rational behavior.[56] Granted, many violent actions may not on the surface appear 'normal' to most members of society—the murderous activities of serial killers is an obvious example. This, however, should not detract from our understanding of violence as purposeful behavior. Even the most apparently 'insane' violence has a rational meaning to the person who commits it.[57] As Alvarez and Bachman write, "many perpetrators of crime and violence see themselves as being justified in their actions and often define their acts as a legitimate response to some behavioral or ethical breach on the part of their victim."[58] Consequently, we can understand violence as a controlling behavior to achieve specific goals: ascending social hierarchies, creating a reputation that deters encroachers, protecting and keeping our mates and families, escaping from abusive relationships, gaining access to new lovers, and many others.[59] In other words, according to Alvarez and Bachman, the perpetrator perceives his or her violence as a form of *social control*.[60]

Such an understanding is consonant with our *spatial* understanding of discipline. In other words, what I will argue in the following chapters is that the idea of 'rationality' has a geographic component. The justifications for violence forwarded by perpetrators correspond to broader social norms and processes. Acts of direct violence, whether these may be rape, murder, or battery, are situated within larger contexts of power, knowledge, and space. In the case of intimate partner violence—a subject discussed at length in Chapter Two—many men often engage in hyper-controlling behaviors that are meant to socially *and* spatially restrict their wives' activities. Such behaviors might include hyper-surveillance (e.g., monitoring phone calls, or unannounced 'visits' to the wife's place of employment) or prohibitions against having friends. When these disciplinary techniques are insufficient, these men may utilize more violent actions, such as verbal or emotional abuse, slappings, beatings, or even murder.

What I hope to argue in this book is that there is an underlying *spatiality* to violence. Violence is a practice of both social and spatial control. Humans are social animals; their households, communities, and societies (however defined and embodied) are constituted through social and spatial relations. Concepts of place come to be defined through these relations; and disciplinary practices are utilized to establish, maintain, and protect these 'places'. When more 'benign' disciplinary practices are insufficient, violence may result.

My intent, and hopefully yours, is to open a *critical* dialogue, to engage in broader discussions of space, place, and violence. The notion of 'doing' critical geographies, as Kitchin and Hubbard explain, has become a central theme within human geographic study.[61] That said, confusion abounds as to what constitutes 'critical' learning broadly stated, and critical geographies more specifically.[62] Nicholas Blomley, for example, warns against an 'uncritical critical geography'. He notes that, while "critical scholarship can offer rigorous, compelling and persuasive social science," it can also become uncritical and offer little in the way of insight, understanding, or direction.[63]

A critical approach to space, place, and violence is one that addresses the forms of oppression and inequality wrought by structural and institutional processes; works to overturn the socio-spatial processes that regulate and reproduce social exclusion; remains sensitive to the life experiences of marginalized groups; seeks to be empowering and emancipatory; and promotes political and social change.[64] To be critical is to be normative; but this requires a deeper sense of reflexivity. Critical scholarship—and critical learning—entails a commitment to change. In other words, it is not simply enough to 'study' violence; the point is to challenge violent practices, to counter those social-spatial practices that permit, facilitate, and legitimate violence.

The challenge is not easy. As Olson and Sayer rightly argue, "we cannot escape questions of ethics and what constitutes human flourishing or 'the human good.'"[65] They continue that "To decide what constitutes flourishing and suffering involves a kind of judgement, indeed a kind of valuation." Indeed, to "reject judgement and critique is to create a space for dogmatism rather than refuse it."[66] Do we, for example, condone the abusive husband because he lost his job? Do we condone the schoolyard bully because she herself was abused at home? Do we neglect the murdered prostitute because she was a prostitute? Do we mistreat and violate migrants because they cross a border without authorization? In the chapters that follow students are confronted with these questions, and are encouraged to think about the social relations and interrelations of violence, of the spaces and places that both form and are formed by violence. Ultimately, students are encouraged—while engaged in their daily lives—to think *and act* differently about the geographies of violence.

2
HOME

> *My dad would beat up my Mom, and me or one of my sisters would call the police if it got really bad. Or if my mom told me to call, and then they would come. I was really scared, for her and for me, because it was really obvious that if he was going to hurt her, he would hurt us too ...*[1]

Home. The word seems simple enough: Home is where we live. And yet, as Linda McDowell notes, "'home' must be one of the most loaded words in the English language."[2] What does she mean by this statement? Is she referring to the fact that some people live in 'apartments' while others live in 'houses'? That some people 'own' their homes while others lease or rent? Or are we missing something when we focus too much on the physical structure that we call 'home'?

For many of us, we may not think too much about 'home'. But when we do, we often think of home as a place of shelter, of security. Home is a place where we eat, sleep, and interact with family and friends.[3] Home, in other words, has its own *spatial practice*. You'll recall from Chapter One that Henri Lefebvre developed the idea of 'spatial practice' as the arrangement of buildings and pathways, and the rules and regulations that constrain behavior within those spaces. The spatial practice of our home, therefore, would include the neighboring homes (or apartments)—what we might conveniently call a *neighborhood*.

However, the home itself—the spatial arrangement of bedrooms and bathrooms, kitchens and garages—likewise has its own spatial practice. Children are taught to eat in the kitchen (or dining room) but not in their bedroom. Bicycles are kept in the garage and not the bathroom.

At this point you might be wondering what any of this has to do with violence. And this is a good question. To answer, let's consider the following scenario. A young boy (we'll name him Johnny) is caught eating cookies in his bed late at night. This is not the first time Johnny has been caught. In fact, just last week Johnny was sent to bed without supper for disobeying the family rules of not eating in bedrooms. Now, Johnny is caught again. What happens? Do his mother and father yell at him (again)? Previous attempts to *discipline* Johnny have clearly not worked. Sending him to bed without supper hasn't worked. Perhaps Johnny should be grounded? Or perhaps Johnny's father resorts to … violence. Maybe Johnny is spanked. Or maybe Johnny is beaten.

The 'home', as it turns out, is some *place* and not simply a dwelling to be lived in. We are taught what behaviors are appropriate within the home: where to eat or not to eat, as Johnny is learning. But we are also taught about appropriate *social roles* within the home. And in the process, through the repetitive, day-to-day learning, we may come to expect these behaviors as natural and normal: just the way things are.

It is for this reason that McDowell finds the term 'home' so loaded. Far from being a simple little word that refers to our dwelling, 'home' is viewed as a site—a place—in which broader structures influence and are influenced by the social relations that circulate in and out of the home. In this chapter we will step inside the home and see how dominant structures of capitalism, patriarchy, and heterosexuality (among others) work to discipline the spaces of home. First, we will consider the long-standing assumption of 'home' as a safe place, followed by a lengthy discussion of home as a 'social construct'. These two sections are necessary in that they provide the foundation, so to speak, for a more in-depth look at three specific forms of interpersonal violence that are mostly (though not exclusively) contained within the home. The first of these forms of violence is that of intimate partner violence. I highlight how violence within the home is linked to the maintenance of patriarchal social orders but caution that an over-emphasis on patriarchy risks overlooking other crucial components—namely racism and capitalism. Next, we consider same-sex violence and, especially, the intimate partner violence of lesbian couples. This focus serves, in part, to counter the essentialization of intimate partner violence as exclusively male-generated and male-dominated. Lastly, we think through the racialization of intimate partner violence, with a focus on mail-order brides. Combined, these three forms of home-related violence speak to the multiple ways in which interpersonal violence is part-and-parcel of broader social processes and practices.

Home as Refuge?

It is both tragic and ironic that for many women and children, violence is most often experienced at 'home'.[4] Indeed, although women learn to perceive danger from 'strange' men in 'public' spaces, in actuality women are most vulnerable to acts of violence in their own home, and from men they know.[5] In her study of everyday violence, for example, Elizabeth Stanko quotes a young woman who explained, "[I] was aware of crime but it was literally down across the tracks or some place up the country or off, in wherever, up in the hills. It was contained in another place."[6] But for this woman, that 'place' turned out to be her home; the assailant was her husband.

Despite a voluminous literature on intimate partner violence,[7] the topic remains hidden in plain sight. As Stanko explains,

> Whilst our attention is continuously attuned to that which happens in public places, there is a stony silence, almost a denial of the extent of violence that happens in private, usually between those who already know each other. ... To the extent that it is acknowledged at all, we assume that this private violence is normal. Real violence, that which is committed by strangers, is abnormal, an affront to public safety.[8]

Violence in the home has been hidden, in part, because of our dominant *representations* of home. Early writings on 'home', for example, were both uncritical and highly masculinist, reflecting the prevailing 'common-sense' understandings of the term.[9] The geographer Yi-Fu Tuan, for instance, portrayed 'home' as a place of refuge and solace, a place where one could escape the drudgery of everyday life.[10] According to Tuan, home is "that special place to which one withdraws and from which one ventures forth."[11] Related to this view of 'home as refuge' is the idea that it is a private, often familial realm, clearly differentiated from public space and removed from public scrutiny and surveillance. The private realm of the home is therefore understood as a place that offers freedom, security, and scope for creativity and regeneration.[12]

Such a myopic (and overly benign) understanding of home is no longer tenable. As feminist writers in particular have noted, Tuan's writings, among many others, were indicative and symptomatic of an entrenched masculinism that pervaded (and in some respects, continues to pervade) academia and the broader society. Thus, Tuan would write that "the owner of the house has the freedom to establish *his* world, *his* scale of values and meanings" (emphasis added).[13] More than just gender-blindness, Tuan's conception of home as *man's domain* played into the dominant representation of home that typified Western societies since at least the industrial revolution. Furthermore, this masculinist thinking underscored the prevalence and justification of 'domestic' violence and contributed to a situation whereby law enforcement agencies maintained a hands off view of this violence.

Research on the meanings and experiences of 'home' have proliferated in recent years, with substantial contributions made within the fields of Anthropology, Architecture, Geography, History, Philosophy, and Sociology.[14] Home is now understood as an ambivalent *place*, one that is simultaneously a spatial and social unit of interaction.[15] As Linda McDowell explains, "the 'reality' and the symbolic meaning of the home combine to produce the construction of a particular version of a home in different ways in different societies."[16] Peter Saunders and Peter Williams concur, writing that "the home is a place invested with special social meaning and significance where particular kinds of social relations and activities are composed, accomplished and contextualized."[17]

The contested meanings of 'home' are important for our geographic understanding of violence. The home becomes a site where appropriate roles, behaviors, and expectations are both taught and learned. These roles, behaviors, and expectations, furthermore, are gendered, sexed, aged, and even raced. In many societies, for example, the gendered and sexed home is manifest as a heterosexual and patriarchal *place*. However, given that home as place is derived through social interactions and relations, home also produces and reproduces a plurality of overlapping and, at times, contradictory identities. 'Home' is raced; 'home' is aged; 'home' is 'classed'; and so on. As Nicky Gregson and Michelle Lowe argue, "a multiplicity of meanings suggests that rather than seeing things in terms of a single ideology of home, we need to think of home in terms of dominance and resistance."[18] This is a key point and, as detailed in this chapter, one that becomes crucial to our understanding of space, place, and intimate partner violence. It is the activities that are performed in these domestic spaces at given times and in given relational contexts that reflect and/or subvert particular ideas about gender, age, sexuality, and so on.[19]

Constructions of Home

The 'home', both literally and theoretically, does not exist in isolation. Rather, it must be conceptualized within a broader context, namely that of political economy. Consequently, we must situate our understanding of home—and the violence that is part of the home—within a larger societal setting.

Every society produces its own space, and this socio-spatial production is, in large part, derived from the existing *mode of production* that is prevalent at the time. Simply put, a mode of production includes both 'forces' of production and 'relations' of production. The forces of production include those elements that constitute the productive capacity of the economy—the 'instruments of labor'—including, for example, land and machinery. Relations of production, conversely, include the social relationships between different economic actors and include property relations, work relations, and the ideological and political framework in which people produce and exchange goods.[20] Furthermore, according to Richard Peet, these social relations are "characterized by a dialectical interplay between co-operation and competition, collaboration and struggle."[21] Such an understanding coincides with our understanding of 'place' as coming into being through *social relations* and *social interactions*. Consequently, places (including homes, but also schools, grocery stores, prisons, and so forth) are intimately associated with the overall mode of production and the corresponding *material* and *ideological* parameters of that mode of production.

Henri Lefebvre, whom we encountered in Chapter One, postulated that every "society to which history gave rise within a framework of a particular mode of production, and which bore the stamp of that mode of production's inherent characteristics, shaped its own space."[22] As such, dominant economic systems, such as feudalism or merchant capitalism, would be manifest both on the landscape and in the various constitutions of home and family. In pre-capitalist, agrarian societies, for example, both productive and reproductive work was carried out within the household or family.[23] The rhythms of work were regulated by need and the amount of labor used in production was equivalent to the amount of labor needed for reproduction.[24] There was, however, no 'universal' family; social arrangements reflected local customs and different geographical and historical contexts. The *family*, for example, might include both immediate and extended kin, servants, apprentices, and even slaves. Indeed, as Aitken explains, the "Latin root of the word 'family' is *famulus*, or servant." Aitken continues that when 'family' was first used in English in the fifteenth century, it was derived from *familia*, in reference to the domestic servants who lived and worked in the home. Only rarely was *familia* used for the entire household. It was not until the middle of the seventeenth century that the term narrowed to include only groups of related people.[25]

Depending on the society in question, therefore, the household (or 'family') was composed of both kin and non-kin members. There was a customary division of labor, with women largely responsible for reproductive tasks (i.e., the processing and preparation of food, house cleaning, gathering firewood, fetching water, tending to the fields) and men mostly engaged in harvesting.[26] There was considerable variation, however, and social relations did not always imply a rigid hierarchy in importance. In most pre-capitalist societies, work arrangements were mostly based on satisfaction of immediate needs. Under other systems, such as feudalism, families typically produced some goods as commodities or as recompense to their feudal lord.[27]

These socio-economic relations and practices underwent a significant transformation throughout Europe after the fourteenth century, transformations that would significantly impact the structure and meaning of both 'home' and 'family'. Although subject to debate, there is growing consensus that the transition from feudalism, through merchant capitalism, to industrial capitalism in Europe was the result of a "phase of economic, demographic and political 'crisis' [that] brought about the combination of steady population growth, modest technological improvements and limited amounts of usable land."[28]

Under the evolving system of merchant capitalism, the widespread introduction of money and of waged-labor ushered in crucial changes in labor arrangements. Consequently, there emerged a reallocation of work effort between women and men and among family members in household production and reproduction.[29] Three key transformations stand out among all others: the separation of the producers from their means of production and subsistence; the formation of a social class which has a monopoly of the means of production (i.e., the capitalist class); and the transformation of human labor-power into a commodity.[30] Combined, these changes would have a profound effect on the household as a unit of production and consumption. As productive tasks shifted from the needs of the household to those of the market, the household per se no longer had access to the means of production. Familial needs, including the provision of food-stuffs and (increasingly) clothing, were provided through an exchange of labor-power for wages. In turn, work-for-wages became distinct from work in the household.[31]

There emerged a gradual but notable separation between 'work' spaces and 'living' spaces, a *spatial* separation that carried with it important *social* dimensions. As Saunders and Williams write, men and women, children and adults, enjoyed different capacities for action and encountered different constraints on their actions within the home and beyond.[32] Women, for example, continued to work in the home, engaged in such activities as childcare and food preparation; however, these 'jobs' came to be defined as being qualitatively different from *men's work*.[33] Consequently, as Aitken concludes, women's work became invisible and spatially isolated from the public sphere.[34] It was also during this transition that the idea of the 'family' underwent an important ideological shift. By the late seventeenth century, according to Aitken, as the control of the means of production moved away from the private sphere, servants were no longer considered part of the family.[35]

In time, the division of family labor began to assume a new spatial dimension, one in which (most) women and children were confined to the domestic sphere, separated physically and ideologically from men's activities in the public sphere.[36] As explained by Domosh and Seager, the development of these 'separate' spheres served very particular purposes, among which was the reproduction of capitalism itself.[37] As more and more components of social reproductive tasks, including education, health, and manufacturing (e.g., food processing and cloth making) were transferred away from the household, the home became recognized as a separate place in which the labor force could be indoctrinated with appropriate values and attitudes of discipline and service.[38]

A reconfigured spatiality of everyday life translated into a gendered ideology of *familialism*. As Elizabeth Eviota explains, this ideology centered on "the extension of women's procreative functions to women's responsibility for the home" and included such constructs as feminine nurturance, masculine protection, maternalism, self-sacrifice, and emotional and financial security.[39] In short, the home became a place of patriarchal control and discipline.

Andrew Sayer and Richard Walker render these constructs into three basic forms of patriarchal control.[40] First, embedded within capitalism is the control and appropriation of women's labor. Whether as wives or daughters, women's access to the products, benefits, and income has been decidedly unequal. Women, for example, were increasingly excluded from the better-paying industrial occupations, as men recognized the dangers of competition from female labor.[41] Indeed, as Aitken explains, women in the public sphere were viewed as threats to the newly constituted modern family as well as society as a whole. By the end of the nineteenth century, in fact, the presence of women in the public sphere was increasingly seen as unnatural and even dangerous.[42] A second form of control hinges on women's child-bearing abilities. Thus, women are represented as "crucial economic assets who hold the key to future labor power and male heirs." And last, male prerogative extends into the control over women's desires and affections. To be sure, as Sayer and Walker note, women have throughout history been overwhelmingly consigned to child-rearing, household upkeep, and family nurturance; however, under capitalism the cultural artifact of home and work, the private and the public, became particularly acute.[43]

The separation between 'work' and 'home' was not, however, as clearly demarcated as is conventionally thought.[44] Rather, the home continued to be a *fluid* place, one where different living and working relationships both produced and were produced by different social relations. Nevertheless, a particular ideology emerged, one that presupposed a *hetero-patriarchal* social system. The family was the means by which labor was reproduced; consequently, the family came to be identified almost exclusively in terms of biological reproduction. Heterosexuality was the unquestioned norm. It was widely understood and promoted that the natural purpose of sex was for biological reproduction and that sexual identity was linked inextricably to the individual's role in the reproductive family.[45] Marriage as an institution was thus predicated on procreation and the family was to ensure a proper upbringing based on strictly defined gendered and aged roles. The husband/father figure came to be identified as both primary provider and disciplinarian; the wife, consequently, was seen as both subservient and complementary in that she was the fundamental care-taker and spiritual center. Children, as the saying went, 'were to be seen but not heard'.[46]

Many women, however, were well aware of the reality of housework, its tedium and repetitiveness, and the extremely hard work involved in housework and childcare.[47] For these women, the home was certainly not a haven from the drudgery of everyday life; rather, it was their everyday life. And it was far from being a refuge against oppression and exploitation. Indeed, home became a contested place, one where the hegemonic and gendered representations of space clashed with the realities of daily life, one where the man's dominion was challenged.

Within the home, the husband/father figure assumed a dominant position and was seen as the ultimate arbiter for rules enforcement. Significantly, the emerging state apparatuses also worked to facilitate the hetero-patriarchal foundations of the home and family. The legal system, in practice, favored men. According to McDowell, the idea of 'home' as a private place for personal relations contributed to an official tolerance by the state of men's control over women. Thus, for example, domestic violence was not defined as grievous bodily harm like other forms of interpersonal violence; instead these violent acts were considered justified for the maintenance of a properly ordered society. Consequently, police*men* were reluctant (or unwilling) to intervene in what were seen as private disputes between a 'man' and *his* 'wife'.[48] Domestic violence was a problem to be dealt with *inside* the home; men in fact were generally allowed to beat their wives as long as they did not kill them or the violence was not 'extreme'.[49] Furthermore, because of women's financial dependency on the male 'provider', coupled with a dearth of safety nets, many women were unable to escape their violent partner. And divorce in many societies was not a legal option.[50] In short, an ideology of hetero-patriarchy was woven into the larger fabric of society, an ideology that was reaffirmed and reproduced in marriage practices, legal systems, and property relations.[51]

The notion of the male-dominated nuclear family permeates many societies. Indeed, as Maggie Wykes and Kirsty Welsh explain, "our everyday notion of the family, and perhaps more crucially the role of heterosexual, paternal masculinity within the family, is repeatedly presented in both factual and fictional texts and unproblematic, even when the evidence is to the contrary."[52] Not surprisingly, these social relations pre-figure our discussion of violence within the home.

Intimate Partner Violence

A good wife always knows her place.[53]

In Chapter One I suggested that place is 'disciplined space'; that we as human beings are socialized into an understanding and expectation of the appropriate uses of space and, in turn, these actions contribute to the making of place. Thus, we may assert that home is "an expression of lived space, of human meaning and of being-in-the-world."[54] Home, in other words, becomes a *place* through lived social relations. I further noted, however, that places are fraught with competing conceptions and uses, both of which may be actively resisted or inadvertently transgressed. Dominant meanings of home, therefore, are continually contested and 'require' discipline. Discipline though is never complete and, as such, threats or acts of violence are often invoked in an attempt to (re)establish control.

Within many discussions of 'home', the widespread nature of violence within families is often overlooked.[55] Indeed, it is not uncommon for people to presume that the home is a 'space of violence' only insofar as it is vulnerable to threats from the outside.[56] Consequently, we barricade our homes with dead-bolts and bars; we hire armed response security services and install surveillance cameras—all in the hope of keeping *strangers* out.

And yet for many people—but especially women—the home is the most dangerous place to be found—and not because of strangers.[57] Women in the United States are nine times more likely to be *deliberately* injured in their homes than on the streets; indeed, violence in the home accounts for more injuries than car accidents and muggings, combined. Furthermore, domestic homicides account for approximately one-third of all female homicides per year.[58] By way of comparison, only 3 percent of men in the United States are murdered by their female spouses.[59]

Over the past decades, approaches to violence within the home have changed from viewing it as limited to a few problematic marriages, and disbelieving and blaming battered women, to recognizing the prevalence of serious levels of physical violence and psychological abuse in many, and many different forms of, intimate relationships.[60] In the 1970s and 1980s, for example, terms such as 'wife abuse', 'battered woman', and 'domestic violence' were introduced. These terms, however, reflected an initial focus on the physical violence experienced by married, heterosexual women. In time, as awareness grew of other forms of abuse, including violence within lesbian and gay couples, violence among unmarried, cohabitating and dating couples, and of violence toward women in the process of separation and divorce, newer theoretical conceptualizations were forwarded.[61] 'Intimate partner violence' has emerged as the main conceptual tool with which to understand these forms of violence.

Despite widespread usage, however, there is little consensus among academics and activists on exactly how to define the term 'intimate partner violence'.[62] For many researchers, intimate partner violence is an inclusive term used in reference to physical, psychological, emotional, and/or sexual violence perpetrated in the context of an intimate relationship. The National Violence Against Women (NVAW) Survey, for example, defines intimate partner violence as those practices that include rape, physical assault, and stalking perpetrated by current and former dates, spouses, and cohabiting partners; both same-sex and opposite-sex cohabitants are included.[63]

Regardless of definitional problems, researchers are in general agreement that intimate partner violence is a widespread problem. In fact, researchers estimate that on average approximately 25 percent of all intimate relationships in the United States involve at least one incident of physical abuse; this figure holds both for married heterosexual couples and for same-sex partnerships.[64] Findings also indicate a global prevalence of intimate partner violence. A recent survey conducted by the World Health Organization (WHO) found that between 15 and 71 percent of women surveyed in ten countries reported experiencing some physical or sexual violence at some point in their lives by a current or former partner.[65] Other studies reflect similar patterns. In the Philippines, for example, one study found that between 11 and 26 percent of married women reported some level of physical aggression by their partner; in Bangladesh an estimated 35 to 42 percent of married women reported being abused; and in Turkey, nearly 58 percent of women indicated that they have been subject to violence by their spouses.[66] More specifically, a community-level survey of women in a London borough found that more than one in two women had been in a psychologically abusive relationship during their lives; one in four women had been in psychologically abusive relationships in the past year; one in three women had suffered physical and sexual abuse requiring medical attention in their lives; and one in nine women had suffered physical and sexual abuse requiring medical attention in the past year.[67]

Intimate partner violence is predicated on domination, intimidation, and coercive control.[68] As Barrie Levy explains, the principal technique used to establish control is the micro-regulation of everyday behaviors—those same social behaviors and relations that constitute home-as-place. Most commonly, these disciplinary techniques are associated with stereotypic female roles and expectations, including the manner in which women dress and behave, cook, clean, and even perform sexually.[69]

Similar to most crimes, there is an underlying 'rationality' and 'legitimation' of the violence on behalf of the perpetrators. Indeed, the "justification of wife abuse occurs in every society, with significant variations depending on the sociocultural context."[70] And studies throughout the world indicate that many abused women believe that their partner was justified. In Vietnam, for example, studies have found that violence against women is considered to be a socially acceptable behavior of Vietnamese men, who use violence to punish their wives for transgressions from their traditional roles (i.e., disrespecting or talking back to a husband or his family, disobeying, or being unfaithful). Both men *and* women believed that violence in these settings was permissible.[71] Similarly, throughout the Middle East and North Africa, sizeable proportions of both men and women believed that domestic violence (against the woman) was justifiable in certain settings. In Israel, 60 percent of Palestinian women agreed that nagging or insulting the husband constituted legitimate grounds for a husband to beat his wife; large proportions of women in both Egypt and Jordan also excused spousal abuse when violence was used against 'transgressing' women.[72] In other words, these acts of violence may be understood within a *spatial* context of gendered role expectations and enforcement, all of which are underlain by ideologies of patriarchy, masculinity, and sexism.

It should be quickly noted, however, that there are other interpretations for women's seeming acquiescence to male-on-female domestic violence. As Liz Kelly and Jill Radford write, women are often systematically encouraged to minimize the violence they experience from men; in both law and practice, women (and children) have been unable to speak about their experiences of sexual abuse, coercion, exploitation, and assault.[73] According to Kelly and Radford, women often dismiss certain forms of violence, as if 'nothing really happened'. Consider the following quotes provided by Kelly and Radford:

> "I was kerbcrawled too, earlier this week. I hate this sort of thing. It happened again later in the day, when I was walking home. I was in tears by the time I got home, nothing happened, just comments, but I was intimidated."

> "I've been frequently harassed by kerbcrawlers. It happened even when I was pregnant. There were several incidents about a fortnight ago, though nothing actually happened. The assumptions men make—their arrogance. It makes me sick and angry. I don't go out much alone now. I resent that enormously."

> "A stranger, a man passing in the street and pulled a contorted face and hissed something at me. Nothing happened, but I was unsettled for a while. It was pure menace, out of the blue. You wander along thinking your own thoughts and suddenly this invades your space, your life with menace. I have the right to daydream in the street sometimes. One can't live in a constant state of alertness, awaiting the violence of men."[74]

These three comments highlight that although the women were routinely harassed and intimidated, they downplayed the violence as if 'nothing really happened'. Of course, as Kelly and Radford correctly identify, all of these women understood that something did happen, that their personal spaces were violated. However, these women also understood that their experiences of 'something' were unlikely to be validated. As one respondent explained,

> "I didn't tell the police, they would have gone over and over it, asking me all sorts of questions about what I was doing[,] making out it was all my fault, and then in the end tell me nothing happened and I'm silly to make a fuss over nothing."[75]

What constitutes 'violence' is contested. There is, in other words, an underlying politics that surrounds our understanding of—and our response to—violence. This politics of violence, moreover, is played out both individually and institutionally. Hence, many women downplay or minimize violence because they understand at a certain level that authorities often do not consider these women's experiences, or the men's behaviors, as a form of violence. Kelly and Radford stress that "When women say 'nothing really happened' they are making a statement about how much worse it could have been. When the law says 'nothing really happened' it implies that a woman has not been violated/abused."[76]

Attempts to downplay sexual and other forms of violence are not confined to public spaces. Indeed, Kelly and Radford find that while the phrase 'nothing really happened' does not appear as frequently or as explicitly in women's accounts of 'private' sexual violence, forms of denial and minimizing can also be discerned. In fact, they suggest that the 'naming' of violence within intimate relationships is often more difficult, as "many women have an investment, at least in the short-term, in not defining men's behavior as abusive." For example, according to Kelly and Radford, some women may be "influenced by romanticized public representations of intimate relationships which encourage them to view abuse as an, albeit distorted, form of caring." Likewise, other women may perceive "practical and material reasons for dismissing the abuse they are experiencing."[77] The following quotes are illustrative of these attitudes:

> *"I remember my first responses were dismissing it and disbelief. I nearly did it again today, because I'm still at the point where I think 'well it's not really violence.' Then I think 'come on be straight with yourself.' It did start out in minor ways with pushing and it wasn't till near the end of the marriage that he got into things that you think of as being attacked. That went a long way before I thought this is violence—a hell of a long way."*

> *"I kept quiet about it partly because of this business of not accepting it as violence—and there was a very strong sense that because you were married you didn't say anything. I was depressed for a long time, I accepted that label, that it was my personality and nothing to do with the marriage, the violence."*

> *"I didn't think of it as—it wasn't until really late on that I thought there was violence. … I can't remember any major acts of violence until about four years ago, any real sort of injuries but the threat was there."*[78]

Women's inability, or unwillingness, to name violence when it is experienced is, in fact, part of patriarchy. And it is for this reason that patriarchy must be considered as both a source of, and 'excuse' for, violence against women. Although insufficient by itself for an understanding of intimate partner violence, patriarchy is a key contributor to understanding male-on-female violence. That said, patriarchy as a concept has many different interpretations, depending on the theoretical and disciplinary orientation of the writer or speaker. For many feminists, patriarchy is a political concept, and refers specifically to a relational and gendered process of dominance (by men) and subservience (by women). This dominant-subservient relationship involves three basic forms of power: men's control over women's labor, men's control over women's reproductive abilities, and men's control over women's affection. Consequently, theories based on the idea of patriarchy as a system hold that accounts of violence against women should center on gendered social relations and the uneven distribution of power. However, as Gwen Hunnicutt finds, this seemingly straightforward understanding is problematic for at least five reasons. First, it simplifies power relations, with explanations too often neglecting the importance of other social integuments, such as 'race', sex, and class. Second, conventional uses of patriarchy as a concept often imply a false universalism, suggesting that patriarchy is both ahistorical and aspatial. Third, traditional theories of patriarchy cannot account for violence committed by women against men, nor for violence committed by women against other women. In other words, patriarchy *is* important for understanding *some* forms of violence, but it is too often incomplete when considering other forms of violence. Fourth, patriarchal explanations too often cast 'men' as a singular group. Such a move, however, downplays the salience of other social and cultural factors and thus risks overlooking other contexts that enable violence to continue. Fifth, traditional accounts cannot explain why only a few men use violence against women in societies characterized as patriarchal. For example, if ideologies and practices of patriarchy are so dominant within a given society, why aren't all men in that society violent toward women?[79]

Hunnicutt argues that understanding violence through the lens of patriarchy requires a sensitivity to a range of patriarchal manifestations; that to understand male (violent) behavior, it is necessary to reveal how men are situated in their own scheme of domination. Indeed, we must be mindful of how these men understand their own misogynist and violent behaviors. As Jeff Hearn and Antony Whitehead write, "Men who have been violent to known women exert power in specific, embodied ways; they embody men's power and their own violence." They caution also that it is incomplete to attribute male violence solely to patriarchal motivations. They explain that

> it may seem absurd to assume that the individual man who batters his female partner is motivated by an ideological choice to cause her to conform to the gender category 'woman' within patriarchal social relations. What is being described here may be better understood as a potential effect of violence, rather than a motivational cause of violence.[80]

Hunnicutt warns that varieties of patriarchal ideology—while often coincident with structural conditions—may in fact exist apart from these structural conditions. Indeed, incidences of patriarchal violence may actually increase as structural gains in gender equality are achieved. Hence, while a society may not be considered 'patriarchal' as measured by women's participation in the labor-force or politics, it may yet be rife with individual acts of violence. Consequently, Hunnicutt suggests that patriarchal systems should be envisioned as "terrains of power" in which both men and women yield varying types and amounts of power.[81] In fact, Hearn and Whitehead note that in many instances, men's dominance is not complete; women do resist and may dominate in *certain* situations, regardless or even because of men's structural and individual dominance.[82]

Conceptually, Hunnicutt's "terrains of power" concept is especially helpful in our understanding of space, place, and violence. Patriarchy is *relational*. It is composed not solely of relations between men and women, but also, for example, between men. Thus, studies indicate that within intimate heterosexual relations, men often use violence to maintain their dominance within the home. However, studies also reveal that the more disenfranchised men are from legitimate positions of dominance in the public sphere, the more likely they are to use violence to reinforce their perceived dominance in the home. In other words, when a husband beats his wife, it may actually stem from the man's perceived inferior position vis-à-vis his male co-workers. To this end, as Hunnicutt writes, "the victimization of women is [often] more a function of the status of males than of females."[83] Hunnicutt therefore concludes that understanding violence directed at women requires attention to terrains of power that include status distance *among* and *between* males, as well as between males and females.[84]

Hearn and Whitehead forward a similar position, emphasizing that "men and masculinities are formulated in differential relations not only to women but also to other men."[85] They elaborate that the "construction of masculinity through relations between men may be achieved by excluding women from space, emotionally or physically, in order to enact masculinity while avoiding challenges from women."[86] Hunnicutt also downplays the argument that men use violence against women to uphold patriarchy-as-an-abstract-ideal; indeed, she notes that this position not only simplifies male perpetrators as tyrannical, power-seeking abusers, but it also overlooks the fact that patriarchal systems can survive without violence. In fact, acts of violence are hardly necessary in a place where gender relations are so entrenched and self-perpetuating. Instead, violence is required when gender roles and relations are in flux. Furthermore, while male violence against women may be a manifestation of patriarchal systems and serve to reinforce those systems, such violence is rarely used consciously by men to maintain gender hierarchies.[87] Rather, acts of violence by men are not used to maintain patriarchal systems as a whole, but are used to maintain their own *personal* and *unique* understanding of gender roles and relations. As Hearn and Whitehead conclude, a man's:

> individual experience of his internalized sense of masculinity, what might be called his *ideal masculine self*, and the 'triggers' which precipitate his violence to his female partner, and the form that violence may take, seem as likely to be unique to him, as any other aspect of his identity.[88]

The net effect, of course, is to reproduce a system—and a 'place'—of patriarchy and male dominance, a place that is produced through the threat and actual use of violence.

Following Hunnicutt's argument, I suggest that patriarchy is more appropriately viewed as a performance, informed by particular 'scripts' that circulate within any given society. As Judith Butler explains, identities (or subjectivities) become *enacted fantasies*; coherence is desired, wished for, idealized, and this idealization is an effect of corporeal signification.[89] And paramount among the many scripted subjectivities in circulation are those of masculinity and femininity: ideologies of appropriate social and spatial gendered roles for men and women. The feminization of household labor, for example, confines women to a relatively isolated sphere where they are more subject to the power of their husbands and fathers and less able to form bonds with other women. It renders women dependent on the men who control family income and property and vulnerable to male dissipation of income, and it inculcates a powerful strain of nurturing that can disadvantage women in the competitive struggle with men in the larger world.[90] Gender, therefore, as an organizing concept, imparts an ordering of society based on perceived differences between men and women. Consequently, gendered norms construct 'appropriate' positions and responsibilities for women and men and allocate resources differentially based on these divisions.

Neither masculinity nor femininity is monolithic; rather, meanings of each are both historically and geographically grounded and intimately connected.[91] Indeed, quite different models of masculinity have prevailed at different times and in different locales; in other words, the social construction of masculinity has both a geography and a history.[92] However, as the preceding discussion of home and family revealed, constructs of masculinity and femininity are strongly associated with hetero-patriarchal assumptions of 'man' as provider and protector, and of 'woman' as nurturer and home-maker. Moreover, masculinity and femininity are mutually dependent: the production and performance of masculinity is correlated with ideas of femininity. Indeed, as Kristen Day explains, many men build masculine gender identities around ideas of femininity that emphasize women's fear and vulnerability. In effect, men's need to 'prove' their own masculinity may be advanced by regarding women as weak, vulnerable, and fearful—traits that are presumed antithetical to those of a 'real' man.[93]

With respect to the production of place, it should also be noted that notions of masculinity and femininity have been constructed and reconstructed around the home and, accordingly, so-called domestic virtues. As Valentine explains, the ideology of the nuclear family, based on a heterosexual married couple, has strongly conditioned societal expectations of appropriate roles and behaviors for men and women. These expectations, likewise, have been supported by state agencies and perpetuated in the media. Valentine concludes that "people face painful consequences both socially and materially if they fail to live up to [these expectations]."[94] In fact, according to Aitken,

> The perpetuation of [traditional family values] results in enormous harm and the oppression of men, women, and children. Part of this oppression derives from people trying to make their own family more like the images of the idealized family by striving to imitate a monolithic myth that comprises unworkable images of personal behavior, gender relations, and community embeddedness.[95]

The production of home as place, consequently, is important in our understanding of masculinity in that traditional gender roles coincide with traditional understandings of the home and family. As discussed earlier, the home is a crucial site for social reproduction. Gender identities are formed from birth as children are both socialized and taught socially approved patterns of masculinity and femininity; in other words, appropriate gendered roles for men, women, children, and the family as a whole.[96] Home, also, is a key link in the relationship between material culture and sociality; it is a concrete marker of social position and status.[97] However, and this is vitally important: *The use of violence as a means of resolving conflict between persons, groups, and nations is a strategy we learn first at home.*[98]

The home is a fluid place, marked both by challenges and by transgressions. Indeed, the home becomes a moral space, a site of intense surveillance and control. Consequently, within *hegemonic* patriarchal households, the father-husband figure may enact various disciplinary techniques to maintain *his* family fantasy. Through domineering actions, both subtle and demonstrative, the patriarchal figure attempts to ensure that members of the 'family' understand and keep to their proper places. Discipline, in other words, is required to maintain the fiction—the embodied fantasy—of appropriate gendered familial roles. Again, turning to Butler: gender ought not to be construed as a stable identity or locus of agency from which various acts follow; rather, gender is an identity tenuously constituted in time, instituted in an exterior space through a *stylized repetition of acts*.[99] Under patriarchy and capitalism, therefore, men and women 'do gender' based on rigid role expectations and scripts. Within patriarchal societies, women's lack of power vis-à-vis their male counter-parts is reflected in a particular form of social ideology: protective attitudes toward women, a reverence for the role of women as wives and mothers, and an idealization of women as romantic 'love' objects.[100]

So why do some men become violent toward the women they supposedly love and idolize? According to psychologists, violence is more likely among couples who deviate from the typically gendered configuration of the male as provider and of the woman as dependent. Studies indicate that violence often erupts when (mostly) men believe their female partners are not adequately playing the appropriate or expected/scripted roles of wife and mother.[101] Violence becomes a technique of role enforcement, a continuation of discipline 'required' to punish a woman's transgression from her normative roles in society and in the home.[102] In turn, violence also may reaffirm a masculine identity for men who lack other means of demonstrating control and authority.[103]

Intimate partner violence, therefore, is "a 'tool' used to keep (usually) women in their 'proper place' in the gender hierarchy."[104] But it is also a tool to uphold men's conception of their own place in the home and society. James Gilligan, among others, suggests that violence may be more prevalent for men who (in their minds) fail to measure up to societal expectations of being a man/husband/father and thus may experience doubts as to their masculine identity. Gilligan continues that to "understand physical violence we must understand male violence" and that "we can only understand male violence if we understand the ... gender roles ... into which males are socialized by the gender codes of their particular cultures."[105] However, as Gilligan continues, this understanding must be relational.

> [We] can only understand male gender roles if we understand how those are reciprocally related to the contrasting but complementary sex or gender roles into which females are socialized in that same culture, so that the male and female roles require and reinforce each other.[106]

In many societies, but especially those characterized as patriarchal, men are rewarded for their violent behavior. Seen in both education and popular media, men are praised and exalted for being tough and aggressive; conversely, men are dishonored and shamed for being passive or weak. Douglas Kellner, for example, identifies what he terms a "crisis of masculinity," in reference to the dominant societal connection between masculinity and being a 'tough' guy. Writing specifically about American culture—but many of his conclusions are easily exported to other societies—Kellner describes "an out-of-control gun culture, and media that project normative images of violent masculinity and make celebrities out of murderers." These representations, he maintains, are especially prevalent in the ongoing militarization of society, the promotion of both gun and sports culture, and the overall media spectacle that surrounds acts of violence.[107]

Women, of course, are typically represented as being passive, subservient, and dependent upon men. Women are thus shamed or physically abused if they are perceived by their male partners as being too aggressive or too domineering. However, according to Gilligan, the "female gender role also stimulates male violence at the same time that it inhibits female violence. It does this by restricting women to the role of highly unfree sex objects, and honoring them to the degree that they submit to those roles or shaming them when they rebel." Within the 'home', aspiration to these gender roles "encourages a man to become violent if the woman to whom he is related or married 'dishonors' him by acting in ways that transgress her prescribed sexual role."[108]

Indeed, some studies indicate that 'less masculine' men may be more aggressive and violent, simply because they perceive themselves as being not able to measure up to their own expectations. Also, the opposite side of the coin also holds true: as women gain in autonomy and empowerment, men may resort to greater levels of discipline and violence.

Angela Hattery, for example, relates the experiences of Darren, a man who "beat his wife when he felt his masculine identity vis-à-vis his economic power in the household was threatened." In Darren's words, "I was contributing a lot less to the household. ... I didn't feel like I was the man of the house."[109] During one argument, Darren attempted to rationalize his violent behavior:

> *"I went into the kitchen. I grabbed my wife around the neck. I layed [sic] her on the kitchen floor. She rose up. I slapped her. She rose up again; I slapped her again. And then I made some threats. ... And I told her, listen, let's go sit down in the living room and we're going to talk about this and you're going to listen to me. Ok? I'm taking control of the situation, is how I felt. I'm going to take over. You're going to listen to me, regardless of whether you want to or not. You're not going to turn your back on me, you're not going to give me a sneer, you're not going to make a snide remark, you're going to listen to what I have to say."*[110]

Another man, also interviewed by Hattery, provides a similar justification (from his perspective) for his violent behavior. In Eddie's words:

> *"She's always complaining about that I don't treat her like a wife, because I don't buy her what she wants, things like I can't afford, she always throw up in my face like what her friend's husband, what kind of car he bought her and what kind of gifts he bought her. Of course he can buy her a brand new car when he, the assistant chief executive at Wachovia. And uh, she a RN, got a master's degree at Wake Forest, you know, and she complain about, oh and he just bought this 160 thousand house and you know you married me and you supposed to do this for me and my children, well what you, what you gonna do for yourself, and she always just nick-nagging at me."*[111]

Men like those interviewed by Hattery typically adopt behavior patterns consistent with their expectation of what a 'man' should be like, ideas that may be heavily influenced by society's projection of the 'macho' image, a representation that often entails violence or the threat of violence.[112] Cross-cultural studies also bear this out. In the Philippines, for example, findings indicate that men resort to violence more frequently when their perceived and assumed dominance is challenged by their wives; women, in fact, are subjected to greater levels of intimate partner violence when their decision-making capabilities improve. In Vietnam, also, men often use violence when they feel unable to fulfill their own traditional responsibilities of caring for their family; likewise, some Vietnamese men use violence because their female partners do not live up to societal expectations and therefore the men cannot assume their 'rightful' social spaces.[113] And in Bangladesh, as women generate higher personal earnings through membership in credit and saving associations, studies find that they are also more at risk of abuse from their male partners.[114] As Manju Rani and colleagues conclude, "as women achieve education, employment and financial capability at par with men, a conflict is produced between reality and notion of male superiority." They note that while men *may* realize the falseness of the notion of male superiority and adopt more egalitarian attitudes, they may also resort to use of force to provide the ultimate support for male dominance.[115]

But to blame intimate partner violence solely or primarily on patriarchy, as discussed earlier, is incomplete. To this end, it is inappropriate to render all (male) violence as an attempt to conform to patriarchal and (hyper)-masculine ideals. Indeed, a major problem with theories that posit that men simply respond to patriarchy is that most men, in fact, are not aggressive toward women, even though all men ostensibly receive similar cultural messages. Thus, while all men are presumably exposed to the same messages about masculinity, not all become violent toward their partners. Cultures of patriarchy cannot in-and-of-themselves be used as blanket determinants of intimate partner violence.

Hunnicutt explains that it is more likely that men exhibit ambivalence toward violence—an idea that conforms with the idea that humans in general exhibit such ambivalence.[116] Humans have the capacity for both conflict and cooperation. Whether a man (or woman) is violent toward another person is thus predicated upon underlying representations and ideologies of moral boundaries. The question becomes: why are some men violent toward some women (including their intimate partners)?

This is an important question, because within systems of patriarchy, we find that the category 'woman' becomes differentiated among both abusers and those who supposedly work to prevent or punish such violence (i.e., court judges, police-officers). Here, the work of Peter Glick and Susan Fiske is especially helpful. They note that sexism is typically conceived as a manifestation of hostility toward woman. However, this conventional understanding neglects a significant aspect of sexism, namely that subjectively *positive* feelings toward women often go hand-in-hand with sexist antipathy.[117] In other words, the construction of masculinity is predicated on a distinction between different types of women, that is, some women are 'worth' protecting, while other women are not. Glick and Fiske refer to this as *ambivalent sexism.*

According to Glick and Fiske, "one of the complexities of domination is that many women are not victimized because they are women. A common patriarchal value is the protection of women. Patriarchal ideologies carve out havens of protection for some women but not for others."[118] To capture this seemingly paradoxical aspect of masculinity and patriarchy, Glick and Fiske differentiate between 'hostile' sexism and 'benevolent' sexism. The former includes the feelings and attitudes of hatred toward women, or a belief that women are naturally subservient or inferior to men. Hostile sexist beliefs characterize women as unfit to wield authority over economic, legal, and political institutions.[119] Conversely, benevolent sexism includes a set of interrelated attitudes toward women that are sexist in terms of viewing women stereotypically and in restricted roles, but that are subjectively positive in feeling (for the perceiver) and also tend to elicit behaviors typically characterized as prosocial (e.g., helping) or intimacy-seeking.[120] Even though benevolent sexism suggests a subjectively positive view of women, it shares common assumptions with hostile sexist beliefs, namely that women should be confined to restricted domestic roles and are the 'weaker' sex.[121]

Ambivalent sexism refers to a process whereby men (but also women) may divide women into a favored group—consisting of women (e.g., home-makers) who embrace traditional roles that fulfill the paternalistic, gender identity, and sexual motives of traditional men—as opposed to disliked out-groups—consisting of women (e.g., feminists and lesbians) who challenge or threaten patriarchy.[122] A man, therefore, may easily hold two seemingly contradictory views of women (i.e., the familiar whore/Madonna dichotomy), but views that nonetheless are entirely consistent in his mind. Ambivalent sexism, however, also has a spatial component. Thus, while men may hold particular views about the proper roles for women, it is important to remember that these roles are assigned to particular spaces. Consequently, when a woman is perceived as transgressing beyond her proper 'place' in society, at home, or at work, some men may feel justified in their attempt to reestablish control through disciplinary acts and, ultimately, violent acts. Thus, by differentiating women in this manner, men can maintain a sense of attitudinal consistency, even though they are quite ambivalent toward women as a whole. This differentiation, moreover, may legitimate (in their minds) their attitudes as being not prejudicial toward women as a whole, because it is only the 'bad' women whom they dislike: the women who are 'out-of-place'.[123]

The spatiality of ambivalent sexism is clearly associated with notions of appropriate behavior and the subsequent policing of learned ideals. When men no longer feel that they 'measure up' to societal norms and expectations, when they experience feelings of insecurity, shame, and humiliation, violence becomes (in their minds) an option to reassert their perceived hegemonic place in the world. For the women in question, however, violence becomes an all-too-familiar component of their daily lives. As Angela Hattery writes,

> elements of ideologies of masculinity and elements of ideologies of femininity are mutually reinforcing and together they work to maintain a system of gender oppression ... that leaves women vulnerable to IPV and lets men off the hook when it occurs.

She maintains that "both systems will have to be unseated before we can expect to see a dismantling of this serious form of gender oppression."[124]

Same-Sex Domestic Violence

Intimate partner violence is not restricted to heterosexual couples. Indeed, in recent years considerable research has emphasized the scale and scope of violence within same-sex partnerships. Furthermore, this research has identified a range of complex relations and representations that differentiate 'same-sex' violence from 'opposite-sex' violence.[125] The differences, crucially, are strongly associated with alternative conceptions of home and family.[126]

Until recently, however, the issue of intimate partner violence among same-sex couples remained "buried, ignored, or denied."[127] As previously discussed, from the 1970s onward, intimate partner violence was conventionally viewed as being male-on-female and both theoretical and empirical work, consequently, linked violence to male gender roles. And to a large extent, this research provided key insights into the existence of men's violence, vis-à-vis the man's perceived authority to enforce hetero-patriarchic scripted gender roles. However, same-sex violence, and especially violence within lesbian relationships, largely went unexamined.[128]

This should come as little surprise, especially given that violence within same-sex relations has likewise been downplayed. It is not uncommon, for example, for members of same-sex relationships to *not* identify their experiences as abusive or violent. According to Jude Irwin, this occurs because dominant hetero-normative discourses lead to an absence of talk about violence in same-sex relationships, including those personally involved. Irwin quotes Isabella, who explains:

> *"I never really framed my situation as being anything but just a lesbian relationship that was struggling. I knew it was struggling. She never admitted that. I knew I was starting to feel really unhappy. I didn't frame it as domestic violence. And I just thought, being a lesbian, it's really difficult. People aren't going to believe me."*[129]

In Irwin's study of 21 lesbians, many of the women remained silent about their abuse because they saw domestic violence as a heterosexual issue that did not affect them; indeed, some women struggled to identify the violence because they did not believe that this could happen in lesbian relationships.[130] Similar findings are presented by Claire Renzetti. In her study, many respondents reported confronting denial of the problem by some friends and professionals. Indeed, Renzetti reports that many sources of formal or official help frequently available to heterosexual victims of domestic violence are not perceived by lesbian victims to be sources of help available to them. And of those lesbians who did seek help from women's shelters, most found them to be of little help or no help. The reason why this is so remains unclear, although Renzetti suggests that it may be because shelter-staff, similar to their academic counterparts, are trained to think of domestic violence in terms of male/female relationships.[131]

An increased awareness, and documentation, of same-sex couple violence requires a reevaluation of our understanding of violence. As Nicola Brown concludes, "abuse in lesbian, gay, bisexual, and trans relationships represent[ed] a significant theoretical challenge to the 'grand narrative' of partner violence as an outgrowth of patriarchy and power imbalances."[132] Such a challenge was required, as an increasing number of surveys found that the rates and types of abuse experienced within same-sex relationships were comparable to, and as variable as, those reported by heterosexual couples.[133] Rates for physical violence ranged from approximately 10 percent to upwards of 73 percent, while rates for sexual violence ranged from 7 percent to nearly 60 percent. When emotional or psychological abuse was considered, rates exceeding 80 percent were identified.[134]

Documented cases of same-sex violence within the household required a theoretical reworking of gender and sexual relationships within the home, but one that also extends to our understanding of gay, lesbian, bisexual, and transsexual (GLBT) children living in heterosexual households. Indeed, for children and youth who identify as gay, lesbian, bisexual, or transsexual, the meanings and experiences of home are decidedly different. In the 'traditional' nuclear family, hetero-patriarchy is performed on a daily basis, wherein the husband/father and the wife/mother continually enact prescribed gender roles. However, Kirby and Hay note that the "family-based heteropatriarchal ideology of the home makes those places potential sites of alienation." They continue that "the parental gaze constrains freedoms to reveal gay identities."[135] Sue Kentlyn is more blunt in her assessment. She argues that "while the family may be a site of solidarity and value for groups struggling with various forms of oppression, current definitions of the family are abysmally oppressive for lesbians and gays."[136]

Home for GLBT youth can be especially alienating. Since the family home is a primary site of hetero-normative socialization, the experience of gay and lesbian youth residing in the home is often one of self-concealment and silence.[137] According to Andrew Gorman-Murray, "the family home, as a primary site of heterosexual reproduction and heteronormative socialization, often symbolizes precisely what young gay men and lesbians cannot be."[138]

According to Valentine, it is in the hetero-patriarchal home that many lesbians, while growing up, become particularly conscious that they do not fit in with the asymmetrical 'family' identity; that they do not conform to the expected heterosexual and gendered roles and relations. She explains that this perception of being out-of-place in the family home—made apparent through relatives' overtly heterosexual behavior and practices—contributes to a practice of self-discipline. The home becomes a place of concealment and suppression.[139] The implications are enormous; surveys indicate that gay and lesbian youth are more at risk than their heterosexual peers of experiencing depression, substance abuse, suicidal behavior, poor health, and practicing unsafe sex.[140]

Aside from becoming a place of alienation, the home for GLBT youth may also become a very dangerous place. Indeed, for gay and lesbian children residing in a 'hetero-patriarchal' home, disclosure of their sexual identity to relatives risks rejection, abuse, and even exclusion.[141] Two disturbing studies bear witness to the threat of violence. In a survey based in the United Kingdom, Joyce Hunter found that 61 percent of violent acts committed against lesbians and gay men were perpetrated by their family members; likewise, a study in the United States found that of those lesbians and gay men surveyed, 25 percent had been verbally abused by their parents and 10 percent had been physically threatened.[142]

Similar findings are reported by Valentine and her co-authors. They find that many of their interviewees were thrown out of parental homes or ran away as a result of negative parental responses to their sexuality. In addition, they note that fathers more commonly reacted to their gay sons with anger and disgust and responded to their lesbian daughters by reflecting on their own loss of an imagined future as father of the bride, grandfather, and so on.[143] In short, children and youth who identify as gay, lesbian, transsexual, or bisexual find themselves vulnerable to abuse from their own families, simply because they 'fail' to conform with traditional gendered and sexual expectations of a 'normal' family. So strongly felt are these perceived transgressions of prescribed societal norms, that family members may resort to violence in an attempt to discipline the home-place.

But what about members of the GLBT community who live in their 'own' homes? Home might function as a potentially important site of resistance to hetero-normative socialization; the home, in other words, may become a place in which queer identity may be fostered and sustained in the context of wider societal disapproval.[144] This is not to suggest, however, that the home for gays, lesbians, bisexuals, and transsexuals is a 'safe haven'. Indeed, both feminist and queer scholars have contested the monolithic portrayal of the home. For non-heterosexual individuals and couples, the concept of home carries with it many different meanings and experiences.

In contemporary Western society, as we have seen, 'home' has become connected with a range of normative meanings, most often centered on ideals of *the* hetero-patriarchal nuclear family. This idealization, which is found in house design, public policy, and social convention, often renders members of the GLBT community as being 'out-of-place' both in society and at 'home'.[145]

The idealized 'home' is a private place and (for many women) the primacy of familial privacy has hidden a legacy of domestic violence. As discussed earlier, the notion of 'home' as a private place often precluded authorities from intervening in incidences of male-on-female violence. Within the GLBT community, however, privacy assumes a different meaning.[146] Given that privacy is closely linked to enabling control over one's own home and the activities that take place therein, individuals and couples are able to produce a relatively safe and secure place. And for many gays and lesbians, the privacy of the home does assume a crucial importance—a potential safe space from societal exclusion. As Stewart Kirby and Iain Hay write, "heterosexuality is expressed powerfully in most everyday places," thereby rendering public space as intensely disciplined.[147]

To this end, Wayne Myslik details the pervasiveness of heterosexuality within public spaces. As a dominant space of representation for appropriate roles and behaviors, public spaces are replete with images of heterosexual couples participating in everyday acts that serve to promote and legitimate their intimate relations:

> engagement announcements, bridal showers, wedding ceremonies and rings, joint tax returns, booking a double bed at a hotel, shopping together for a new mattress, casual references in conversation to a husband or wife, a brief peck on the cheek when greeting or leaving a spouse, photos of spouses on desks at work, holding hands at the beach, and even divorces.

All of these "are public announcements and affirmations of one's heterosexuality." One should not forget, moreover, that "Sexual relations between gay lovers [and lesbians] are illegal in many areas, gay marriages are not recognized and the courts frequently deny the rights of gay men to be parents by taking their children from them."[148]

Not only is heterosexuality constantly represented in public space, it is frequently reinforced through the threat, if not actual use, of violence against non-heterosexual behaviors. As Karen Corteen writes, "When negotiating the heterosexual street, sexual dissidents can feel out of place … as they can be subject to violence ranging from the homophobic gaze to homophobic violence or hate crime."[149] Indeed, surveys indicate that gay men are four times more likely to be assaulted than other men, and lesbians six times more likely than other women, in public spaces.[150] For members of the GLBT community, therefore, the private spaces of the home appear to be the only environments where they can be themselves, forget the habit of self-concealment, and feel safe enough to express their sexual identity without fear of exposure or violence.[151] Consequently, gay and lesbian couples' homes are often the only places where they can be intimate and not feel inhibited when expressing their sexual identities.[152] Sarah Elwood, for example, finds that for some lesbians, the "home becomes a place where they make their sexual identity visible in a conscious attempt to challenge assumptions of heterosexuality and to contest societal pressures to confine and hide lesbian sexuality within private spaces."[153] Valentine likewise finds that for many lesbians, the private space of their own 'home' is the only place where they feel safe.[154] She explains that in certain public spaces, lesbians feel out-of-place and fearful of discrimination or violence not only because of homophobia directed at them because they have been identified as the homosexual 'Other', but also because of a patriarchal backlash, directed at them because they are women who are relatively independent of men and therefore a threat to the hegemony of patriarchy.[155]

However, forces outside the home, embodied in societal disapproval or homophobic neighbors, may still regulate the supposedly 'private' space of the gay man or lesbian's home.[156] Elwood elaborates that lesbian home-places are seen by some members of society as challenges to heterosexual culture, as places that contradict more traditional expectations of the proper constitution of 'family'.[157] As both feminist and queer theorists have identified, the interface between the home and the spaces beyond is a crucial boundary in social life. Saunders and Williams, for example, explain that this boundary often

> is marked out physically—with fences, front doors, net curtains, privet hedges, spyholes, burglar alarms, gates and signs—and socially—by rules governing 'dropping in', by rituals such as dinner parties, by reserved regions such as the 'front room' where 'guests' and 'visitors' are entertained, by legal statutes governing rights of entry and exclusion, and by norms regulating uninvited intrusion.[158]

This is an important point, and one that has tremendous implications for our understanding of same-sex intimate partner violence.

According to Mona Domosh, "When we move out of the house and on to the streets, our identities are constantly being monitored, judged, constituted, negotiated and represented."[159] Hence, Elwood finds that for many lesbians, home is not private, but rather a place of surveillance by a dominantly heterosexual and sometimes hostile world.[160] Indeed, houses occupied by adult gay men and lesbians, as Gorman-Murray explains, often undergo hetero-normative regulation from the surrounding community. Houses may be targeted for anti-gay harassment and vandalism.[161]

Home, for members of the GLBT community, becomes a contested site that blurs the public–private divide. It may constitute a space of identity affirmation; and it may be a place of resistance. However, home may also be a place of intimate partner violence. Diane Miller and her colleagues maintain that although lesbian relationships, for example, are often presumed to be free from the power dynamics fueled by sexism and misogyny that often plague heterosexual couples, research does not support this conclusion. In their review of the literature, they cite numerous studies that have found evidence of emotional harassment, verbal abuse, rape, and various forms of physical violence.[162]

Similar to violence within heterosexual couples, intimate partner violence within same-sex couples is related to discipline and control. However, additional factors, such as the impact of cultural oppression and moral exclusion need to be considered. In their discussion of lesbian relationships, for example, Kim Balsam and Dawn Szymanski write that these women's experiences "must be viewed through the additional lens of cultural homophobia and heterosexism." They note that while women in same-sex relationships must contend with the same stressors as women in heterosexual relationships, such as financial issues, decisions about parenting and child rearing, career stresses, and so forth, these women must also face stressors due to their sexual orientation.[163]

As Kentlyn writes, the queer home can be a site of oppression, exploitation, and abuse; it cannot always be assumed that it will be a safe place for individual lesbians and gay men. She elaborates that gender is still (re)produced, though not in the form of conventional understandings of masculinity and femininity.[164] Miller et al., for example, suggest that lesbians lack the culturally assigned power available to men, and that their oppression in society—particularly the effects of internalized misogyny and homophobia—may be more significant than 'power' in accounting for intimate partner violence within lesbian relationships.[165] In their study, they found that some women employ violence as a tactic for achieving 'interpersonal power' or control over their partner; Miller and her co-authors conclude that perhaps it is hardly surprising that some lesbians may feel a strong need to exercise authority in those areas where it remains within their power to do so.[166] There is a danger in forwarding this argument, however, in that it may be used by some abusive partners as a justification or excuse for their violent behavior. Indeed, it strongly echoes the argument forwarded by some men who perceive themselves as having little power in the work-place and thus excuse their violence toward their wives or girlfriends.

Lynda Johnston and Gill Valentine also find that the lesbian home, similarly to the heterosexual home, may become a place of conflict and disagreement. They explain that even lesbian identities come under surveillance from other lesbians.[167] It is not uncommon, for example, that notions of 'authentic' or 'appropriate' behavior of sexual identity are used to justify and perpetuate intimate partner violence within same-sex couples. Indeed, some studies find that partners questioned or challenged their lesbian or transsexual partners' queer identities as a tactic of control. In these relationships, normative assumptions of 'appropriate' non-heterosexual identities were used as means of coercion to establish dominance within the home. Other women reported that they were pressured into sex in order to prove that they were really lesbians.[168]

In other instances, partners may be accused of harboring heterosexual desires and be punished for these perceived transgressions. In her book on woman-to-woman violence, Lori Girshick introduces Maureen, a lesbian who was abused by her partner who was jealous of Maureen's friendship with a man. Maureen explains, "On several occasions her jealousy was out of control and she took it out on me sexually, by holding me down on the bed, grabbing my breasts, and trying to force something into my vagina, insisting that 'this is what you want from him' or words to that effect."[169]

Confronted with societal disapproval, some members of the GLBT community also may attempt to insulate themselves within their own home. Nicola Brown, for example, finds that some members of the GLBT community struggle with how to *place* themselves within gendered frameworks of 'normalcy'; this proved especially so for transsexual partners who were transitioning (i.e., female-to-male). The women who were involved with these transsexual men expressed particular uncertainty with respect to expectations of 'normal' behavior.[170] Behaviors of self-isolation are related to a broader question of 'outness'.

For example, as Balsam and Szymanski explain, "In the context of cultural oppression, lesbian and bisexual women are faced with decisions, as individuals and as couples, around how and when to disclose their identity and relationship to others." They note that while disclosure of sexual orientation can contribute to relationship quality by potentially increasing acknowledgment and validation, a lack of disclosure can lead to women becoming isolated within their relationship. According to Balsam and Szymanski, this secrecy and isolation can place additional pressures on the relationship and may in fact be used by one partner to control the other.[171] And in fact Carolyn West finds that homophobic control is used as a method of psychological abuse and discipline. An abuser might 'out' her partner without permission by revealing her sexual orientation to others.[172]

In short, intimate partner violence is not limited to heterosexual couples. Academics, activists, and counselors have increasingly recognized that violence occurs also within same-sex relationships. And though many similarities exist between hetero- and homosexual partner violence, significant differences are found. As Girshick reflects, "Sexism and male dominance neatly explained violence against heterosexual women." What is now required, she argues, is a framework that is more inclusive, one that considers how both men and women create and condone a culture of violence.[173] This is all the more urgent as we enter a decidedly more mobile world in the twenty-first century, a world replete with different and changing social and familial relations. Indeed, our increasingly globalized world means that our homes may also become more globalized. Transnational marriages, inter-country adoptions, the hiring of 'foreign' nannies to look after our children: these social *and* spatial practices all portend radically different forms of household relations and interactions. Consequently, our understanding of violence within the home will likewise require considerable rethinking. In the following section, I consider but one of these forms—the violence directed toward mail-order brides.

Home, Nation, and Violence

The 'world' is an increasingly mobile place. Well into the twenty-first century, upwards of 130 million people live and work outside the country of their birth. Current processes of globalization, coupled with the emergence of more pervasive migration institutions, have significantly impacted the everyday lives of individuals and their families. Consequently, it becomes increasingly untenable to consider the *meanings* of home, family, and intimate partner violence outside of a multi-cultural or trans-cultural context.

As people respond to the changing conditions of the international division of labor, and of changes in the global labor market, different 'transnational' family formations emerge. Researchers now speak of seasonal orphans, solo parents, flexible citizens, and shadow households.[174] And these migrations, as a process, significantly alter both the meanings and experiences of 'home' and of 'family'. According to sociologist Pierrette Hondagneu-Sotelo, gender relations are both reconstructed and selectively reproduced through migration and resettlement.[175] She explains that while people construct their lives out of cultural resources within a social structural context, the process of migration and resettlement transforms these ideals and guidelines for appropriate behavior.[176] In other words, home-as-place is reworked in the context of migration.

This has important implications for our understanding both of patriarchy as structure and of intimate partner violence as practice. In Hondagneu-Sotelo's study of Mexican immigrants to California, for example, she found that significant transformations in patterns of family authority occurred following immigration. In some households, for example, the decision-making processes became more egalitarian, especially as immigrant women became more autonomous and assertive through their employment and subsequent economic contributions to the family.[177] However, this is not always the case. Indeed, many studies indicate that women's new-found sense of autonomy and economic liberation precipitated violence.

As Eleonore Kofman explains, a crucial element to be considered is the role of marriage within the migratory process and how this affects family formation and notions of 'home'. However, the relationship of marriage and migration is not so straight-forward. Kofman notes that "There are those who marry in order to obtain a more secure status to escape from poor employment prospects or deskilling, or to acquire a long-term residence permit. ... There are those who bring in spouses as part of family reunion policies, whether it be from their own country or the wider diaspora (intracultural) or from another country (intercultural). There are also those who move for the sake of another member of the family, whether it be for their children's education ... or to look after an elderly relative."[178]

Transnational migration and family formation introduces other, critical aspects to the meanings and experiences of home—including violence.[179] In particular, studies have found that the vulnerability of one partner increases tremendously when that individual's immigration status is dependent upon his/her spouse. As Uma Narayan explains, women with dependent immigrant status are not only disempowered by all the factors that affect battered women who are citizens, but they also confront legal prohibitions against seeking employment and the threat of deportation if they leave abusive marriages.[180]

Social and spatial isolation may also be significant factors as many immigrants leave behind family and friends. This lack of extended social networks works to reinforce the dependency on the immediate partner. Language, likewise, is important, in that a lack of fluency in the destination language may impede women from learning about and gaining access to protective and legal services.[181] And even if immigrant victims of domestic abuse are able to contact the proper authorities, help may still be denied. Intimate partner violence within *intra-cultural* households has often been 'explained away' as simply being part of that group's culture. Kathleen Ferraro, for example, found that in the United States, police officers not infrequently viewed arrests in domestic violence situations among immigrants as a 'waste of time' because violence was thought to be a 'way of life' for those people.[182] Lastly, different culturally based gendered (and aged) roles and expectations may provide a source of tension. In this section I consider one particularly vulnerable social relationship, that of 'mail-order brides', and highlight how transnational understandings of gender and 'race' within the context of mail-order marriages inform our understanding of space, place, and violence within the home.[183]

Although definitive studies are lacking, many researchers acknowledge that 'mail-order brides' are exceptionally vulnerable to intimate partner abuse. In a remarkable study of Australian homicide data, for example, Chris Cunneen and Julie Stubbs document the increased risk of death for Filipina women married to Australian men. Between 1989 and 1992, for example, they found that the rate of homicide for women aged 20 to 39 and born in the Philippines (and married to non-Filipino men in Australia) was five times as great as the rate of homicide for all women aged 20 to 39 in Australia.[184]

What are 'mail-order brides' and how do these social arrangements expand our understandings of space, place, and violence? To be sure, arranged marriages have existed in many societies throughout humanity. The contemporary mail-order bride industry began in earnest during the mid-1970s when private 'correspondence agencies' were established to facilitate arranged marriages between (usually) women from the 'Third World' and men from Western, industrialized countries. Initially, these agencies relied on print catalogues, such as *Cherry Blossoms*; today, 'marriage brokers' rely on the Internet to conduct their business. Indeed, there are currently an estimated two hundred 'mail-order bride' websites in the United States alone, advertising between 100,000 and 150,000 prospective brides.[185]

Although the content of intermarriage websites varies considerably, there are some commonalities that relate to the pervasiveness of the hetero-patriarchal norms and expectations that underscore the business. Most commonly, thumbnail photographs of women are presented; these photos are usually in color and show either a 'head-shot' or a full 'body-shot'. Women are assigned code numbers and categorized by age. Information on age, height, weight, education, religion, and occupation is provided, as well as a brief description of the woman's hobbies and 'ideal' husband. Frequently, women are coached by the marriage agency in crafting these narratives; other times, the agency itself simply writes the description. Not surprisingly, these narratives are couched around patriarchal frames of female docility and subservience. For a fee, men are able to acquire the addresses of the women of their choice. Mail correspondence is subsequently established.

The majority of women who 'become' mail-order brides are young and originate from unstable and impoverished countries (e.g., the Philippines and, more recently, from Eastern European countries and regions that were formerly part of the Soviet Union). According to

Narayan, "many of these women come from backgrounds marked by grinding poverty, unemployment, and political turmoil." Conversely, the men "who seek these women as marriage partners have motivations in which sexist and racist stereotypes play significant roles." She elaborates that men "who marry 'mail-order brides' [frequently] want women who will be totally dependent on them; they are disenchanted with changing gender roles and often blame the women's movement for their inability to find locally the sort of woman they wish to marry."[186] And that 'type' of woman is the one represented in traditional understandings of the patriarchal home. It is that 'type' of wife who knows exactly where her 'place' is. Thus, it is possible to discern strong elements of ambivalent sexism within the promotion and practice of mail-order marriages. Marriage agencies encourage their male clients to perceive themselves as 'real' men, as husbands and providers who can protect and nurture their younger, naïve wives.

Representations of mail-order brides—and especially of those who originate from Asia—typically revolve around two specific 'fantasies'. On the one hand, representations promote a particular family fantasy of the perfect wife: loving, caring, and compliant. Women from the Philippines, for example, are often portrayed as exceptionally affectionate, supportive, and subservient; indeed, devotion to one's husband is represented as an essential cultural trait of Filipinas.[187] On the other hand, normative representations promote a fantasy of these women as being the perfect sexual partner: compliant and completely accommodating.[188] Indeed, some mail-order agencies have even promoted 'virginity' in their brochures.[189]

Consequently, we find a brochure distributed by the California-based *American Asian Worldwide Service* stating that "Asian ladies are faithful and devoted to their husbands. ... They love to do things to make their husbands happy."[190] Or in Belgium and the Netherlands, we read of the following advertisement:

> FIVE HUNDRED EXOTIC DOLLS FROM THE PHILIPPINES. There is a lot of poverty in the Philippines and Filipino girls want men five to 15 years their senior who can provide them economic security—and never mind if the

man is divorced five times and has 22 children. Filipino women are travel pigeons with no qualms about leaving their families. It makes no difference to them when they come to Europe. Normally, they are small you would say they are just like dolls.[191]

And not to be out-done, a Canadian publication, *Island Girls*, referred to Filipinas as making the best 'house pets'. In defending this imagery, the publisher explained that

> it was not used as a derogatory term, on par with animal pets. I used the term once to denote that much-liked characteristics of Filipina women who love to attend to home and family, instilling in them the traditional warmth and hospitality. As you know, many still call their children or loved ones as 'pet', this part of the world.[192]

Significantly, many of these racialized, gendered, and sexed representations of women from Asia have been a main-stay of the (American) film industry and thus have been widely incorporated into popular culture. For example, film-makers in the United States have long exhibited a 'romantic fascination' with the geisha. Thus, whether in literature or film, Western conceptions of the geisha revolve around naturalized and normative images of sexuality and docility—providing lessons into 'appropriate' behavior for men and women. As Gina Marchetti explains, geisha tales even served as post-war (1950s) moral fables for independently minded American women, that white American women should put aside their own interests to return to the pre-war male-dominated order that their geisha sisters gladly accept as the 'natural' way of the world.[193]

A key to unpacking the dynamics around the use of extreme violence is through a consideration of masculinity, and of the relationship between masculinity and fantasies of power, desire, and sexuality.[194] Significantly, these fantasies revolve around the appropriateness of gendered behaviors within the home. Cunneen and Stubbs explain that these *male* fantasies about (especially) Asian women incorporate exotic sex, the promise of a relationship with complete security and compliance, and a fantasy about love which transcends age difference. They note that the final aspect of this fantasy is that the relationship can be bought cheaply; that it is a completely commodified fantasy that requires nothing more than money.[195]

According to Cunneen and Stubbs, the representation of Filipina women on mail-order bride websites as 'servile', 'submissive', and 'traditional' yet 'hyper-sexualized' contributes to the disproportionately high rate of Filipina women in domestic violence and spousal homicide in Australia; violence, they argue, is the result of the discordance between men's imagination and fantasy, and the husbands' attempts to maintain control and domination in the home.[196] Narayan concurs, noting that within 'mail-order' relationships, a 'good wife' is "not only a wife with the appropriately subservient attitudes toward her husband, but a wife who is materially and socially disempowered in ways that will prevent her from challenging their authority." In the end, the "dependency that makes these women 'attractive wives' ensures their relative powerlessness to confront violence within their marriages."[197]

Battered women are also often negatively portrayed in the media of their 'host' country. To this end, Cunneen and Stubbs detail how Filipina women who marry Western men become reinvented in the media as manipulative and self-seeking.

Consequently, women who are physically abused are seen as complicit in the violence against them while their abusive husbands are recast as victims. Consider, for example, the death of Rowena Sokol, a 17-year-old Filipina who was murdered by her 41-year-old Australian husband.[198] In 1985 Rowena was just 15 when she met and married Joseph Sokol in the Philippines. After moving to Joseph's home in Australia, Rowena soon gave birth. During their brief two-year marriage, Rowena was repeatedly beaten and abused. On February 23, 1987 Rowena was beaten in the head with a rifle butt before being shot and killed by her husband.

Throughout their marriage, Joseph became increasingly violent toward Rowena. And as the violence escalated, Rowena attempted to leave her husband. Remarkably, just one week before her murder, Rowena contacted the local police for assistance. While being escorted to her home to retrieve some belongings, Joseph declared "So much for

Filipino women being faithful and looking after you." Similar representations surrounded the trial, as Rowena was portrayed as being at fault in her own death.

In Rowena's case, as well as many others, Filipina mail-order brides are represented as being 'corrupt', 'manipulative', and only interested in securing money for their families in the Philippines.[199] Consequently, patriarchal attitudes that legitimate intimate partner violence are excused, tolerated, or condoned in both the popular media and even the judicial process. As Cunneen and Stubbs conclude, "violence against women becomes a way of enforcing compliance with what is, in the end, a masculine construction about appropriate female behavior." Specific to the context of Filipinas married to non-Filipinos in Australia, the "image of women is overladen with racialised and sexualized fantasies about Filipino women as perfect partners. The women who are murdered are recast as being complicit in their own demise when they fail to fulfill the requirements of male fantasy."[200]

The migrant-status of mail-order brides augments their vulnerability. Many of these women are alone in a foreign land; they may not be fluent in the host-country language and are most likely unfamiliar with the legal system. These factors alone contribute to an increased dependency upon their husbands. For example, in a study of Russian-speaking women married to American citizens, Crandall et al. found that women frequently did not know their rights and were often coerced by their partners, who said that they had complete control over the women's ability to stay in the United States.[201] Furthermore, several women in their study indicated that they experienced extreme social and spatial isolation; many were prohibited from meeting other people or of even leaving the house. For these women, the 'home' literally became a prison.

Empirical evidence suggests that women whose immigrant status depends on their husbands are more at risk of battery than women in general. Indeed, whereas between 12 and 50 percent of all married women might experience abuse, one study indicated that upwards of 77 percent of women with dependent immigrant status were abused.[202] Numerous studies have also documented techniques whereby men have used the woman's immigrant status to reinforce their own control and abusive strategies.[203] Marie Crandall and her colleagues, for example, found in their study of Russian immigrant women that threats of deportation were common; alternatively, husbands kept their wives uninformed about the immigration process and even failed to do the necessary paperwork that would allow the women to obtain permanent legal status.[204]

Conclusions

Far from a refuge from violence, the home reveals itself to be a site of potential, if not actual, violence. This stems from the observation that the home is a primary location of socialization, a space where children learn appropriate gender roles and expectations. The home, however, is also a dynamic place, a place composed of shifting social relations that both result from and contribute to larger societal transformations. Accordingly, norms and ideals are frequently challenged or transgressed. For some, the abrogation of gendered expectations requires constant vigilance and discipline—if not outright violence. As Wykes and Welsh conclude,

> non-compliance ... to a dominant masculine agenda is in practice *against* the norm, deviant and punishable whether in public (by the power of law) or in private (by power that is supported by law—lack of or failings in—should it become public).[205]

Any effort to confront violence must therefore begin in the home. We need to reconsider the plurality of identities within the home, and the interlocking systems of class, gender, sexuality, race, and so forth. In the first part of this chapter we have seen how the meanings and representations of 'home' and 'family' have transformed. These changes, moreover, are inseparable from broader political and economic changes of society. Indeed, we have witnessed how patriarchy, heteronormativity, and capitalism have evolved hand-in-hand. Combined, these structures have shaped, but also have been shaped by, social relations within the home: the meaning of the 'Father' or 'Mother', for example. Rather than as a place of refuge or security, we see the home as a place of multiple meanings: as a site of alienation; a site of control and domination; a site that does not end at the front door, but rather opens to the world outside.

Through an exploration of intimate partner violence, same-sex couples, and transnational (mail-order) marriages, we have gained some insight into the multiple and varied relationships that reside within the home; in so doing, we have more fully engaged in the ambiguities and fluidities of identities and the disciplining of identities.

In some respects, however, this chapter has merely scratched the surface in that there are many other types of 'hidden' violence within the home. Child abuse has been raised, albeit indirectly, and scant mention has been made of elder abuse. Well into the twenty-first century, how have the meanings and representations of 'home' and 'family' changed? How do beliefs of masculinity and femininity continue to shape our understanding of appropriate 'domestic' roles? What are the implications for these transformations on the enactment of discipline and violence? How have law enforcement agencies and social service providers responded to these changes? The home, as we have seen, is far from a simple place.

3
SCHOOL

> "Like most students [in high school], I lived in fear of the small slights and public humiliations used to enforce the rigid high school caste system. ... Students lived in fear of physical violence. There was a boy named Marty at my school ... who was beaten up daily for years. Jocks would rip his clothes, knowing that his parents could not afford to buy him a new uniform, and he would piss his pants rather than risk being caught alone in the bathroom. He couldn't walk the halls without being called a fag, and freshmen would beat him to impress older kids. ... While I didn't suffer the extreme abuse some of my friends did, I was fucked with enough to spend four years fantasizing about blowing up my high school and everyone in it."[1]

> "We are terrified by the prospect of innocent people being gunned down at random, without warning, and almost without motive, by youngsters who afterwards show us the blank, unremorseful face of a feral, pre-social being."[2]

For many observers, it began with the 1999 shooting spree at Columbine High School in Littleton, Colorado.[3] On a clear, sunny day in April, two teenagers—Eric Harris and Dylan Klebold—shot and killed 12 students and a teacher, wounding many others. In the aftermath of Columbine, and a spate of other 'school rampage' shootings, Stuart Aitken explains that "Much ranting and spouting off by religious leaders, journalists, politicians, and policymakers inevitably follow[ed]." Aitken elaborates that "Blame is apportioned to ineffective school security systems, the National Rifle Association, the existential angst of loners, the increasing use of gratuitous violence in movies, televisions and video games, and the penchant for spectacle in local and global media."[4] And there is some merit in any and all of these explanations. Certainly in the United States, there is relatively easy access to guns. Indeed, according to Joel Wallman, the United States has more federally licensed gun dealers than gas stations.[5] Studies likewise indicate that by age 18, "the average American adolescent has viewed about 200,000 acts of violence and 40,000 murders on television alone."[6]

What is too often overlooked in the hype surrounding school shootings is how very rare these events actually are. In fact, of all school-related homicides, 'school rampage' shootings account for less than a hundredth of a single percent.[7] Indeed, compared to the home, schools are among the safest places for children.[8] At school, most crimes are non-violent, and involve petty thievery of items from classrooms and lockers.[9] Furthermore, of all homicides that involve school-age youth, less than 2 percent occur at school.[10]

The juxtaposition of rampant school shootings and the apparently benign character of public schools set up a paradox. Violence in public schools is *both* more and less pervasive than politicians and pundits pronounce. On the one hand, the discourse of violence, although not necessarily the ubiquity of violence, does pervade public discussion of schools. As Glenn Muschert explains, while school shootings are not recent events—they have occurred throughout history, and in many different societies—the intense media coverage of Columbine and other shootings "created the public perception of school shootings as an emergent and increasing social problem."[11] School violence is thus more properly seen as a continuation and extension of an even larger moral panic, namely the demonization and criminalization of youth in society.

The specter of school rampage shootings (some would say 'hysteria') has led to the emergence of 'school violence' as a specialized field of study.[12] Indeed, the twenty-first century has witnessed the emergence of 'school violence' as an academic sub-field, punctuated by the introduction of specialized journals such as the *Journal of School Violence* and the *International Journal of Violence in School*. Likewise, a number of high profile international conferences on the subject have been convened and a handful of research centers, such as the European Observatory of Violence, have been established.[13]

On the other hand, schools are intensely violent places—but not because children are daily shooting one another. Rather, everyday violence at school is more banal. For many youth, taunting and bullying is a constant feature of their school day. And yet, similar to the silence surrounding intimate partner violence, there has been little public outcry over these 'mundane' forms of violence. This silence, when contrasted to the media blitz of rampaging youth armed with shotguns and pipe-bombs, becomes deafening.[14]

In this chapter I consider two aspects of school-related violence. In the first section I examine how the threat of violence has contributed to the emergence of the modern public school as a disciplined place. In so doing we will better understand how institutions, such as schools, are places in which social relations are rearticulated in ways that might account for their own violent practices. Moreover, the broader structural conditions—both political and economic—will be shown to significantly influence how discipline is represented and practiced within the school. Next, I explore the act of violence within schools—as practiced by children against other children.[15] Violence has been, and continues to be, foundational to the place-making of schools—but not because of the sensationalized and (fortunately) rare instances of shooting sprees. Rather, violence figures prominently in the discipline of school spaces because of its ordinariness—its mundane-ness that originates in the repetitive, day-to-day occurrences of social interactions. Consequently, the violence of the school is a microcosm of society at large—a place whereby structures of racism and sexism, for example, inform and are informed by our own daily actions.

Discipline In/Of Schools

As we move through our daily worlds, we develop strong connections (and emotional attachments) to *places*. The home, as discussed in Chapter Two, is one such place where identities and relationships are formed and transformed. And outside of the home, perhaps, no 'place' is as important in our social development as is the 'school'.[16] Equally important, however, is that our entry into the school will say much about societal attitudes toward children and youth.

Scholars, in recent years, have identified the 'school' as a significant place in the construction of 'self'.[17] As Prudence Carter writes, for most, if not all, of us, our socialization begins early in life, and much of this transformative socialization occurs during the compulsory years of schooling, from pre-school through high school.[18] Indeed, in most English and American schools children spend up to seven hours a day for four-fifths of the year in their primary school's buildings and playgrounds.[19] In other words, public-educated children spend upwards of one-quarter of their entire pre-adult lives in school. And while at school, students develop a sense of self, take stock of their feelings, and come to understand their ability (or inability) to relate to their peers and to adults.[20]

The school, though, is an intensely disciplined space as well as a (potentially) violent place. As Paul Hirschfield notes, "Order and discipline have always been an animus of American public schools."[21] And, in fact, many historians and cultural studies scholars emphasize that public education *began* as a means of social control.[22] According to Anne-Marie Cusac, for example, powerful ideas about punishment and even torture were part of British North America's pedagogic ideology almost from the beginning. She finds, for example, that American public education arose out of a concern with saving depraved children from the Devil. Indeed, obligatory schooling was established in Massachusetts in 1647 following the 'Old Deluder Satan Act'. It was believed that if children inherited Adam's sin and thus belonged to Satan, then it was imperative for adults to destroy that part of the child's personality that was afflicted from birth by the Devil.[23]

Some might argue that public schooling in the United States (as well as many other Western countries) has not changed much since the 1600s. The place of religion in school, for example, continues to be debated. However, the modern public school is a decidedly different institution. In both Chapters One and Two, we have encountered Henri Lefebvre's concept of *spatial practice* and have learned that every mode of production (e.g., feudalism, mercantilism, or industrial capitalism) will inscribe itself on the landscape. In other words, every economic system will reflect, both materially and discursively, a particular spatial practice. This includes architectural styles, urban morphology, business practices, and so on. Significantly, the modern public school in North America emerged within a specific period of economic transformation—from a predominantly rural agrarian society to an urbanized, industrial society.

The first thing to note is that this was a period of tremendous population growth and social change. Between 1860 and 1910, the population of the United States increased from just over 31 million inhabitants to nearly 92 million. The American population, moreover, was becoming more urbanized. During this 50-year period, the number of people living in incorporated municipalities of 2,500 or more increased from just over 6 million to more than 44 million—a percentage change in urban population from 19.8 percent to 45.7 percent. In fact, between 1860 and 1910 American cities experienced a seven-fold increase in population. And many of these new urbanites were in fact recent immigrants to the United States. Indeed, of the nearly 12 million *new* city dwellers in 1910, approximately 42 percent were immigrants.[24]

The urbanization of American society was part-and-parcel of the industrialization of the American economy. During this period, the United States underwent a transition from a trading economy, to a mature agricultural economy and, later, to an embryonic industrial economy. These structural changes were impelled in part by the arrival of industrial technology and newer, innovative methods of industrial and commercial organization. Concurrently, technological improvements in agricultural productivity and utilization of formerly marginal land resulted in less demand for labor on the larger farms. These changes, also, contributed to massive rural-to-urban migrations.[25]

The most important aspect of the late eighteenth and early nineteenth centuries, however, was not industrialization or urbanization per se, but rather the expansion and intensification of capitalism into all facets of social life.[26] Reformers, for example, identified the public school as a means of preparing future generations for the economic demands of a capitalist society. To this end, owners and managers of businesses and factories came to believe that the populace was ill-prepared for the demands of most commercial and industrial enterprises. In precapitalist, agrarian societies, by and large, economic activities were determined by the rising and setting of the sun, and by seasonal change. Industrial efficiency, however, required regimentation, regularity, punctuality, and docility. Embedded within the capitalist practices of the mid- to late nineteenth century was the promotion of order, rationality, discipline, and specialization.[27] Proponents of public education maintained that compulsory schooling would instill these values.[28]

Public education was to be organized along the lines of the corporation and the factory; schools were to be more efficient institutions for the training of good workers.[29] It is significant, therefore, that early proponents of public education were far less concerned with the pedagogic potential of mandatory schooling. The cultivation of skills and intellectual abilities as ends in themselves did not have nearly as much importance in the view of early school promoters as the problems which public education might resolve.[30]

The public school of late nineteenth-century America was designed along the factory model and was thus consonant with other institutional changes of the era. These were the decades that saw the introduction of large-scale custodial institutions, such as prisons, reformatories, and insane asylums.[31] Previously, state-supported or federal institutions played only a minimal role in North American society; the 'mentally ill', for example, lived with other members of the community, though often in local poor-houses; criminals, likewise, were confined to local jails for relatively brief periods of time, awaiting trial and punishment.[32] Increasingly, shapers of social policy embodied in concrete form the belief that rehabilitation, therapy, medical treatment, and education should take place within large, formal institutions.[33]

The modern public school was itself reflective of the broader concern for social uplift through rational management and is thus part-and-parcel of the same social reforms that led to the creation of insane asylums, prisons, and other 'correctional' institutions. In the writings of educational theorists, there was a consistent theme that the school could train children to live in a society of cities and factories.[34] Consider, for example, William T. Harris. Harris served as superintendent of schools in St. Louis from 1867 to 1880 and later as U.S. Commissioner of Education. A conservative educational philosopher, Harris emphasized the necessity of inculcating a set of traditional values that would provide the discipline necessary for youngsters to face the complexities of urban life. As such, he emphasized that the "school should teach a respect for authority" as well as "habits of punctuality, silence, and industry." These qualities, coupled with perseverance, earnestness, and truthfulness were, for Harris, essential to getting along in the city.[35] In short, educational reformers, such as Harris, proposed that education should conform to new patterns of economic organization—meaning the factory—and stressed the need for regularity in school administration and pupil discipline.[36]

The necessity of juvenile training was seen as being particularly acute. As North American society became more industrialized and urbanized, there occurred a concomitant decline in the use of youth apprentices and child-servants. Furthermore, subsequent labor laws would limit (if not prohibit) children from working if they were below a certain age. With growing fear of masses of aimless and vagrant youths roaming wild in the streets, the establishment of public schools, with compulsory attendance regulations, was hoped to reduce the proportion of idle youths.[37]

These sentiments were manifest in the physical infrastructure of the modern public school. The spatial organization of both the school building and the classroom were designed to ensure efficiency *and social control*. Schools, as sites of labor-force reproduction, visually reflected the ideologies of capitalist rationality and management. The emphasis has always been on the orderly movement of students and their obedience to strict codes of conduct.[38] Classrooms, for example, were arranged for optimum surveillance and discipline. Simon Catling describes the arrangement of the classroom as a 'power geography'. He explains that how the classroom is arranged and how it is allowed to be 'used' signifies much to the children who inhabit it; in effect, the physical organization of the classroom is both an actual and symbolic exercise of power by the teacher.[39] Hallways likewise were designed to maximize student movement from room to room. Even the school playground was initially designed to instill dominant ideologies regarding moral behavior.[40]

Capitalist imperatives also contributed to the feminization of the modern public school. Both compulsory education and mass immigration led to increased enrollments. Simultaneously, as men left the classroom—historically, a male occupation—for better paying commercial and industrial occupations, heavy pressure was placed on local school districts to meet the demands for public education. The employment of women seemed to provide a *rational* solution. Thus, while more and more productive and reproductive tasks were transferred away from the home, women were increasingly (but selectively) viewed as a ready supply of cheap labor. Indeed, female teachers were routinely paid half as much as male educators.[41]

The feminization of education also was associated with changing attitudes toward both women and the family. As discussed in Chapter Two, the late nineteenth century witnessed a separation of work and home, with women increasingly responsible for the moral and spiritual upbringing of children. On the one hand, this 'ideal' of domesticity justified a not-so-subtle attempt to keep women within the home and subservient to their husbands. On the other hand, the notion of domesticity also elevated the 'importance' of women as the moral guardians and spiritual saviors of an increasingly corrupt and irreligious society.[42] As Katz explains, it was through the embodiment of a familial environment that the new institutions—but especially the mental institution and the school—would perform their rehabilitative, therapeutic, or educational work.[43] Women's incorporation into the educational system thus complemented and indeed augmented more pervasive patriarchal attitudes.

The moral and spiritual role assigned to women not only justified but made imperative their entrance into classrooms as 'surrogate mothers'. Katz elaborates that if the school, like other mid-nineteenth-century institutions, was to resemble a home, it should be presided over by a 'wise' and 'loving' mother-figure. Thus, the shift from teaching as a primarily male occupation to a mostly female occupation paralleled the shift in primary moral responsibility from husbands to wives in the ideal middle-class home.[44]

That a nurturing environment was deemed important is not happenstance. In the face of increasing immigration and urbanization, reformers raised fear of serious problems afflicting society, including poverty, public health, crime, insanity, disease, and conditions of the work-place. At the beginning of the nineteenth century, many of these 'problems' remained largely untended.[45] However, by the end of the century, each had become subject to public debate, legislative activity, and supervision of newly created state administrative bodies with full-time expert staffs.[46] Indeed, the social and civic reformers were increasingly composed of men and women who were becoming specialists in the expanding fields of law, medicine, social work, criminology, education, and other professions. These reformers, in turn, began to apply their expertise toward the alleviation, if not elimination, of perceived societal problems.[47]

It is important to remember that whether crime and poverty actually increased during this period is largely irrelevant. What is significant is that there emerged a widespread belief (or fear) among the 'respectable' classes that there existed an epidemic of crime and poverty and that these social ills threatened the moral fabric of society.[48] Further, this perception was fueled by belief that these ills were perpetuated primarily, if not exclusively, by both the 'lower' classes and immigrants. Throughout the mid- to late nineteenth century, Social Darwinists in the United States (and elsewhere) evinced a consternation bordering on hysteria that society was tampering with nature. Many social programs, including charity, were seen as interfering with the natural laws of evolution. Moreover, fueled by Darwinian concepts of sexual selection and evolution, the (re)discovery of genetics, Malthusian ideas of overpopulation, and an incipient environmental determinism, widespread fears of societal degeneration appeared in both popular and academic venues. These fears were augmented by a growing documentation and scientific analysis of demographic changes: the massive numbers of immigrants from Asia and also from eastern and southern Europe, and the relocation of southern African-Americans into northern cities. Citing these changes, John Commons would decry in his popular book *Races and Immigrants in America*, "The change is one that should challenge the attention of every citizen."[49] Studies of the time, conducted by 'specialists' in the fields of sociology, anthropology, and demography, revealed that immigrants exhibited higher fertility rates, thus contributing to a proportional decline in the 'original' Nordic stock of the American population.[50] Contemporary fears were reflected in both popular and purportedly scientific texts: Madison Grant's *The Passing of the Great Race* (1916), Lothrop Stoddard's *The Rising Tide of Color Against White World Supremacy* (1920), and James Herbert Curle's *Our Testing Time: Will the White Race Win Through?* (1926).[51]

Although it was generally believed that adult immigrants were too old to be 'corrected' of their cultural defects, it was still possible, in the minds of social reformers, to acculturate and assimilate child-immigrants and the North American-born children of immigrants. It was this belief that led to the widespread establishment of kindergartens in North America. Modeled after the German educational system, kindergarten programs were used to extend the reach of schools into the expanding immigrant neighborhoods. Pedagogically, kindergartens stressed the importance of pleasant surroundings, self-activity, and physical training—all as a means of developing learning capacities and providing a foundation to becoming productive *American* citizens.[52] Indeed, as the editor of *Century Magazine* wrote, this age marked "the earliest opportunity to catch the little Russian, the little Italian, the little German, Pole, Syrian and the rest and begin to make good American citizens of them."[53]

In short, the public school was viewed as a key instrument to stave off societal degeneration. Thus, while dominant attitudes continued to believe that crime and pauperism were largely the result of individual failure, there was also a growing hope that schools could provide the means to enable people to adjust to new societal demands.[54] The modern public school was predicated on belief that education could *rehabilitate* deviant youth. Indeed, public officials and other experts were exceptionally optimistic in their promotion of public schools as agents of social reform.[55] At the very least, it was assumed that public educational systems would provide a cheap and possibly better substitute for prisons and poorhouses.[56]

At the beginning of the twentieth century, the modern public school was a place of capitalist conformity. It was a space where students learned their proper place in society, and how to become productive citizens of the state. Discipline and punishment were ever-present, but these practices stressed reform and rehabilitation. In time, however, they gave way to a more punitive, indeed, vengeful, school. When students do not conform to school regulations, it is understood that a level of punishment will follow. How this punishment is administered, however, is a political decision—one that often says more about societal attitudes toward children and youth than it does about educational goals.

Throughout the second half of the twentieth century, disciplinary practices of public schools were transformed from basically 'productive' goals (i.e., the training of capitalist workers and the promotion of assimilated citizens) to a warehousing function of 'unruly youth' and 'problem children'.[57] In the 1960s and early 1970s, for example, school-related punishments often assumed the form of suspensions and expulsions. These disciplinary approaches appeared to offer a practical solution to youthful transgressions. 'Problem students' were immediately removed from proximity to other, 'well-behaved' students.[58] However, educational reformers began to rethink their approach of spatial exclusion. It was found that students who were routinely disciplined through suspension or expulsion were more likely to drop out of school altogether. Furthermore, these practices sent the 'wrong' message. Thus, to suspend students who regularly went truant was counter-productive; the objective was to keep students *in* school—and, by implication, off the streets. Disciplinary techniques, it was determined, should be enforced while students remain on school grounds.[59] By the 1980s, therefore, students were no longer exiled from school grounds but instead were spatially segregated in detention halls.

The transformation of school punishment in the 1980s heralded an even more dramatic shift toward punitive practices. Indeed, the years ahead were marked by what Hirschfield terms a 'criminalization' of school discipline. According to Hirschfield, 'criminalization' refers to a shift toward a *crime control paradigm* in the definition and management of the problem of student deviance. This shift, consequently, was part of a larger shift in the public's reception of criminal activities. As Beckett and Sasson document, in the United States criminal activities—and especially violent criminal activities—did not increase appreciatively during the 1980s.[60] And based on nation-wide surveys, neither did the public's awareness (or fear) of violence and crime noticeably increase during the period. What did change, however, was a use by both the political community and the mass media of the language of *public violence* as a resource.

In his book *Political Language*, Murray Edelman explains how certain events come to be labeled as a 'national crisis'. According to Edelman, the word 'crisis' connotes a development that is unique and threatening; he elaborates that crises are portrayed as being different from the political and social issues we routinely confront and come about for reasons outside the control of political leaders.[61] In the 1970s, a series of 'national crises' erupted throughout the United States and other Western societies: sex rings, death drugs, serial killers and psycho killers, Satanic cults.[62] Social conservatives, in particular, blamed the current societal ills on 1960s liberalism, including the Civil Rights movement, anti-war protests, and both the feminist and gay liberation movements.

The ascension of Ronald Reagan as United States president in 1981 solidified 'crime' as a central component of the national political agenda. Significantly, Reagan's approach was to reject the idea that crime and social ills have socioeconomic causes, preferring instead to 'find' criminal causality within the body of the criminal. According to Reagan, the social welfare programs of the 1960s, exemplified by the 'war on poverty', simply created a cycle of dependency in which not only did the poor get poorer, the poor also became more violent. That studies indicated the opposite, namely that increased welfare spending did in fact reduce criminal activity, was of little consequence.[63]

Throughout the 1980s conservative political leaders continued to emphasize the problem of *street crime* in their efforts to steer state policy toward social control and away from social welfare.[64] Portraying their democratic opponents as 'soft on crime', the Republican Party critiqued rehabilitation measures and instead promoted increasingly more draconian punitive practices. Underlying these efforts was a continual theme that criminal behavior was essentialized within 'evil' people who were therefore beyond the hope of rehabilitation.[65]

The criminalization of youth and a purported connection between childhood and criminalization paralleled the conservative political agenda.[66] Throughout the late 1980s and 1990s the criminalization of public education escalated, as 'zero tolerance' policies became the norm rather than the exception. Ironically, throughout this period most schools reported no serious crimes; most urban schools did not experience any 'rampages'; and overall rates of school violence steadily decreased. Statistics, for example, indicated that 57 percent of violent crime was carried out by adults over the age of 25 and 80 percent of violent crime was committed by people over 18 years of age.[67] But moral panics do not require empirical evidence, but rather a simple political push.

"Most legislative responses to school deviance," according to Hirschfield, "do not codify new crimes or escalate penalties. Rather, legal reforms mandate that certain behaviors—already illegal—such as drug and weapons possession are referred to the police when they occur on school property."[68] In effect, the modern public school became criminalized and thus may be seen as a microcosm of broader societal fears of violent crime. As I discuss in detail in Chapter Four, both the United States and much of Europe adopted 'tough-on-crime' policies designed to rid the streets of unwanted criminal elements. New York City, for example, promoted a 'zero tolerance' program that was ostensibly enacted to take hardened and career criminals off the streets. These policies, subsequently, were 'transferred' throughout Japan, Britain, France, and other countries throughout Europe.[69]

At this point, suffice it to say that these crime control policies were extended to the public school. Schools, for example, implemented their own versions of zero-tolerance policies. In practice, this neither afforded room for compromise nor provided any consideration of mitigating circumstances. Students were found either guilty or not guilty of school violations; and if found guilty, punishment would be swift though not necessarily 'just'. Disciplinary discretion, moreover, has been reduced for teachers and school authorities. Students are 'judged' by *disciplinary codes* which resemble the 'mandatory' sentencing laws implemented throughout North America and Europe. Increasingly, punishments are harsher and less forgiving. Indeed, many public schools have reverted to the earlier practice of suspensions and expulsions, as the overall attitude among many education agencies is one of 'deterrence' and 'incapacitation'. To this end, masked behind the rhetoric of 'security', many schools now resemble prisons. A suite of disciplinary and security practices have been introduced, including the use of book-bag searches, locker searches, and even body searches. These practices have been facilitated and augmented through the introduction of metal detectors, drug sniffing dogs, video cameras, and armed police officers. The school itself has become a fortress, protected also by high-tech security gates, barricades, and surveillance cameras.[70] One unfortunate consequence is that students are increasingly being treated like actual or suspected criminals while simply entering and attending school.[71] Indeed, the daily presence of real police officers (also termed 'School Resource Officers') in schools indicates that these public institutions now interpret all young people as potential criminals.[72]

And the criminalization has not occurred without its own share of violence *toward* students. Anne-Marie Cusac writes of a 'punishment creep' wherein new technologies used to 'combat' crime have been incorporated into school disciplinary programs. Such technology includes the use of stun guns and tasers. One study, in fact, indicates that 32 percent of the police departments surveyed used tasers in local school systems.[73] And these *weapons* have been used with some regularity. During the writing of this book, for example, in January 2010, a police officer in Kankakee, Illinois tasered three junior high school children who were engaged in 'demonstrations'.[74] School-based police officers, likewise, are not required to obtain permission from anyone to make an arrest of a student. Not only does this practice further erode the traditional disciplinary role of teachers and other school authorities, it provides a direct link between the school and the juvenile detention system and, ultimately, prison.[75]

A fear of violent behavior pervades the modern public school. This fear itself is part-and-parcel of a broader cultural shift that, beginning in the 1970s, began to posit evilness and criminal intention in the bodies of children. As a result, crime control programs, designed to 'clean up' society, were implemented within the public school system. Ironically, these disciplinary and punitive practices were claimed to provide a higher level of security to children. Such practices were given added weight following the highly sensationalized coverage of school rampage shootings. What these policing measures did not address, though, was the prevalence of a more pervasive, yet mundane form of violence—a violence that in many ways resembles the pervasiveness of intimate partner violence within a heterosexual and patriarchal society.

School Subjects and Violence

The modern public school is among the most important of all socializing institutions of youth.[76] Indeed, the production of good and responsible citizens has long been the central tenet of public education.[77] The modern public school was first modeled as a capitalist-induced 'factory'. Currently, many public schools throughout North America and Western Europe appear prison-like, as politicians and school boards both generate and respond to fears of youth-led violence. Thus, while citizenship may still be an important component of school socialization, greater emphasis is placed on the 'normalization' of students. Consequently, through regulatory practices, schools attempt to produce 'normal' students and, by extension, 'normal' boys and girls. Children are expected to conform to a set of administratively defined normative standards.

Teachers play a crucial role in the construction of children as 'normal' or 'deviant'. Indeed, in his study of primary and secondary schools in the United Kingdom, Stephen Waterhouse finds that teachers frequently used such constructs as 'normal' or 'average' when referring to some pupils. Likewise, other students were seen by teachers to be 'outsiders'. Students were labeled as 'different', 'odd', 'marginal', or 'behaviorally unusual' or even 'extreme'.[78] Now, rule-breaking and trouble-making students are more likely to be defined as criminals—symbolically, if not legally—and treated as such in policy and practice.[79] What we are witnessing is the simultaneous social construction of deviancy, and the essentialization of youth-as-criminals.[80] As Waterhouse writes, "when teachers make inferences about the core identity of a pupil as apparently either 'normal' or 'deviant', this may have implications for their own future interactions and dealings with such children."[81] Teachers pre-judge students' subsequent behaviors based on this initial construction. Consequently, once the dominant category of 'normal' or 'deviant' has been adopted by a teacher, it then becomes a pivotal identity for future social interactions and interpretations.[82] Students who are initially constructed as 'normal' are more often excused for 'bad' behavior. Likewise, those students who are labeled as 'problem-students' or 'deviant' are routinely disciplined as such; even future 'good' behavior is seen merely as an aberration to that student's 'normal' behavior.

The origins of deviance, therefore, are to be found "not in the characteristics and dispositions of 'deviants', but in the interpersonal processes occurring in situated incidents."[83] The social construction of deviancy, in fact, is highly spatial. Recall from Chapter One that neither space nor identity are *inherently* fixed; both are open to interpretation and intervention.[84] Edward Soja refers to this process as a socio-spatial dialect: social and spatial relations are dialectically interactive and interpretative.[85] Hence, when students are labeled as 'deviant' or 'normal', they may internalize or adopt these constructs. These students, of course, also associate with other children. This has important implications for student–student interactions. For example, when a teacher 'identifies' one student as 'deviant', other students will likewise 'identify' that child as 'deviant' and treat him or her accordingly.

There is a double-process in the individualization of students. On the one hand, students attempt to individuate themselves within a context of homogeneity; they seek to stand apart, to develop their own 'identity' within parameters of externally defined norms. On the other hand, students are collectively inscribed by others. Students attempt to discipline other students—to homogenize other students while at the same time developing their own individualization.

Although discipline is practiced by adult-teachers toward children-students, this does not imply passivity or a lack of agency on behalf of the students. The public school is also a *place* in which students relate, both to adults (i.e., teachers) and to other children. How do students interact within the contemporary punitive school? What do these interactions say about our understanding of place, space, and violence? It is important to consider how school-as-place promotes and facilitates social affiliation and belonging, creative self-development, and positive identities.[86] But too often, we must recognize also that schools reproduce dominant societal norms of heterosexuality and patriarchy—as well as the promotion of violence.

Place-making in school, in short, is a relational process; places are produced and reproduced through social relations and interactions. Teachers and administrators are primarily responsible for most rules, routines, activities that constrain the everyday lives of students.[87] However, within the classroom, or on the school yard, children may attempt to modify, or even subvert, these spaces to their own interests.[88] Students are active agents in the production of school spaces. It is important therefore to locate the individual, or 'subject', not as a passive recipient that is imprinted upon or 'socialized' by society, but as a subject imbued with agency and self-knowledge; children actively construct and negotiate through social and spatial interaction.[89] Indeed, the dominance of a controlled and orderly space as conceived by school administrators is far from complete, as these authorial representations rarely go unchallenged. Consequently, the spaces of a school are in a state of flux, as competing representations of appropriate and inappropriate uses are challenged, contested, and negotiated. The seemingly mundane spaces of rooms and hallways, playgrounds and dining halls, are instead highly regulated and disciplined spaces.

Within any given school, students construct and regulate numerous 'spaces': public spaces, private spaces, welcoming spaces, spaces where you feel safe, spaces where you feel valued or devalued, forbidden spaces, unhappy spaces, comfortable or uncomfortable spaces; spaces where you learn, spaces where you are intimate, and so on and so on.[90] These spaces may be those of the classroom, hallway, or school yard; likewise, they may be demarcated, for example, by the placement of school bags, lunch boxes, jackets, sticks, stones, or branches. And students often 'protect' spaces that they claim as their own in both overt and subtle ways. Indeed, students frequently retaliate against perceived transgressions into their territory.[91] Consider, for example, the hallway. For many administrators and teachers, hallways are simply conduits—corridors to funnel students from one 'place' to another. Students, conversely, reappropriate these spaces for their own uses. Indeed, according to Jennifer Tupper and her co-authors, students often negotiate their emerging identities, peer group affiliations, and sense of citizenship within school hallways. These scholars contend that by examining how students inhabit, move through, and interpret the geography of hallways, researchers can achieve some understanding of how identities are formed.[92] The playground is another highly contested space and thus an integral part of the "labyrinthine geography" of the school.[93] Designed by architects and other 'experts', the playground is a visually demarcated space with pre-determined 'places' of activities. Marked by painted lines or signs, areas are set aside for, say, soccer or baseball. Spaces may also be restricted by both formal and informal rules and regulations. It is not uncommon, for example, for playgrounds to be segregated by class level. Some spaces may also be set aside for socio-spatial exclusion, that is, time-out areas.[94] Students, however, either challenge or transgress these spaces. For some children, these efforts constitute their own power-play. For others students, they seek sanctuary from taunting and bullying, and thus form 'safe spaces' away from other children.[95]

How might a conceptual engagement with violence inform our understanding of school places and spaces? To answer this question we must move beyond the headline grabbing stories of school rampage shootings and consider, instead, the more 'mundane' or banal forms of violence, commonly termed 'bullying'. Bullying (also known as 'punking') includes myriad practices, including teasing, ostracism, humiliation, and name-calling. I argue that it is exactly the everydayness of bullying-as-violence that assumes importance. Indeed, these banal acts of violence may be understood as public spatial performances that constitute and reproduce particular ideals of gender and sexuality.[96] We find therefore that violence-in-school says much about our understanding of space and identity.

It is well established that the school is an important place for the production and maintenance of identities. It is within schools that children learn to establish (and challenge) in-group and out-group boundaries; these, in turn, may correspond with how welcomed or included students feel at school.[97] Students position themselves (and others) in groups with self-identifying labels (e.g., *jocks*, *geeks*, and *nerds*). To be 'popular', one must wear the right (name-branded) clothes and shoes; excel at athletics, and not appear as being too smart—lest one be labeled as a wimp.[98] Of course, both 'individual' and 'group' identities are not singularly possessed but instead are continually created through a series of performances and repetitive acts that constitute the illusion of 'proper' or 'natural' categories.[99]

'Identity' "can be conceived of as a set of psychological characteristics, or as a social role, as recognition of the appropriateness to oneself of a classification, or as membership of a group."[100] Bodies, in other words, become *identified*. In Chapter One I argued that the body has a material existence; however, this physicality does not necessarily pre-determine 'identity'. Rather, bodies are conditioned and classified and, through social interactions, become, for example, *raced*, *sexed*, and *gendered*. In other words, bodies are subjected—both internally and externally—to competing discourses of 'race', sex, gender, and so forth. Moreover, it is important to acknowledge that the term 'subject' reflects its own ambiguities, its own double-meaning. Catherine Belsey writes, for example, that

> As a free subject, I plan my life (within certain obvious constraints), affirm my values, choose my friends ... and give an account of myself: 'I am ... this or that'. But I do so on condition that I invoke (*subject* myself to) the terms, meanings, categories that I and others recognize, the signifiers we have learned.[101]

Identities (or subjectivities) are not therefore entirely of our own choosing. 'Identity' formation is both relational and contextual, and is informed by pre-existing structures and institutions. As Gill Valentine reminds us, children's geographies are not just woven into the temporal fabric of everyday life, but are also bound up with much wider geographies and structures.[102] Indeed, according to Chris Weedon, the social institutions which we enter as individuals—such as the school—pre-exist us. She explains:

> We learn their modes of operation and the values which they seek to maintain as true, natural or good. As children we learn what girls and boys should be and, later, what women and men should be. These subject positions—ways of being an individual—and the values inherent in them may not all be compatible and we will learn that we can choose between them.[103]

Free will, however, does not reign free. Thus, while I agree with Weedon and Belsey that we are free to identify ourselves however we like, we may only do so to the degree that we accept a certain subjection to cultural norms.[104] In other words, there will be others who seek to limit—to discipline—our own subject formation. For some, including those who bully and those who abuse their spouses, "coherence is desired, wished for, idealized."[105] And violent practices may be used to maintain this coherence.

Discipline is not random, but rather used for specific purposes by specific individuals, groups, or institutions. Mary Thomas, for example, explains that youths "become invested in social differentiations like gender, class, age, and race-ethnicity through identification" and that these youths "reproduce social meanings by incorporating them as aspects" of their own self.[106] Such a process, however, is heavily conditioned by the actions and attitudes of other youth. Thomas finds that many of the girls in her study experienced feelings of discomfort when they entered the 'wrong' racial-ethnic territory of their school; consequently, when a girl entered into a racial-ethnic territory that she is not seen to properly 'embody', she is met with stares, verbal assaults, and ultimately she is encouraged to leave.[107] Thomas writes of a policing of space and a construction of racialized places. She elaborates that while the girls may not have personally identified with their own 'ethnicity', they were routinely subjected to externally imposed identities. Filipina girls, for example, were called 'Asian' or 'Chinese'. Thomas's work is important in that it highlights the gap opened up between the girls' racialized bodies and how they subjectively embody difference.[108]

Through observation and experience, children learn 'appropriate' behaviors. But they also learn to enforce those behaviors: to *discipline* other children who deviate too widely from societal norms and expectations. In other words, school violence is a mirror of societal norms and expectations; children are socialized into particular beliefs and attitudes regarding proper behavior and those children who deviate too far from the expected and accepted societal parameters risk verbal harassment, emotional and psychological abuse, and even physical violence. The public school, consequently, reflects broader societal ideas and ideals, including what it means to be a boy (man) or a girl (woman).

That the modern public school as an institution reproduces societal norms and expectations regarding 'proper' gender and sexual identities is also not in doubt.[109] In classrooms, hallways, and playgrounds, gender and sexuality are routinely performed; these performances, subsequently, are 'naturalized' through repetition and regulation; they are shaped also by other dimensions of identity, such as age, 'race', and disability.[110] In many societies, and not just those in North America and Western Europe, there exist strong cultural taboos against certain gender and sexual transgressions. From an early age, we are socialized into particular roles and we learn appropriate behaviors. For example, in most Western societies, girls are culturally defined as in need of more direct supervision and protection; boys are taught to be strong and independent.[111] As C. J. Pascoe elaborates, "people are supposed to act in ways that align with their presumed sex; *people hold other people accountable for 'doing gender' correctly.*"[112] Sandra Lee Bartky, for example, finds that a woman who is unable or unwilling to submit, or subject, herself to the appropriate body discipline may face severe sanctions in a patriarchal society.[113] Indeed, as discussed in the previous chapter, many women who 'fail' to conform to societal expectations of a 'proper' wife are subject to verbal and emotional abuse, marital rape, and death. Similarly, children who fail to conform to, or refuse to comply with, cultural norms are subject to discipline and violence. So too are children punished who unwittingly transgress or deliberately contest established practices regarding proper gender and sexual behavior. In short, we expect those classed as women to act like women and those classed as men to act like men.

The imposition of hegemonic identities may be overt; notions of proper gender and sexual behaviors and expectations may literally be codified in rules and regulations. This is perhaps most clearly seen in the imposition of school dress codes, designed in part to impress upon children ideals of 'acceptable' or 'normal' gendered and sexual identities. It is not uncommon, therefore, that the public school will replicate both heterosexuality and patriarchy as normative behavior and expectations. C. J. Pascoe details the myriad ways in which heterosexuality is institutionalized within schools. She argues that "beginning in elementary school, students participate in a 'heterosexualizing process' in which children present themselves as 'normal' girls or boys through discourses of heterosexuality." Consequently, through disciplinary practices, student–teacher relationships, school events, and the curriculum itself, schools "convey and regulate sexual meanings ... in ways that are heteronormative and homophobic."[114] As discussed below, this institutionalized heteronormativity is crucial for our understanding of school violence. As Pascoe notes, the "ordering of sexuality from elementary school through high school is inseparable from the institutional ordering of gendered identities."[115] *It is the enforcement of these gendered and sexed identities that underlies much school violence.*

Consider the promotion of both masculine and feminine ideals throughout the school. Pascoe finds that adolescent masculinity is best conceived as a "form of dominance usually expressed through sexualized discourses." She explains that for boys, achieving a masculine identity entails the repeated repudiation of the specter of failed masculinity. Boys lay claim to masculine identities by "lobbing homophobic epithets at one another. They also assert masculine selves by engaging in heterosexist discussions of girls' bodies and their own sexual experiences."[116]

In many respects, Pascoe's study confirms the arguments forwarded by Doug Kellner. According to Kellner, Western societies (but especially the United States) today are distinguished by a *hegemonic masculinity*, whereby dominant models of an aggressive—and sometimes violent—masculinity are constructed that reinforce gendered hierarchies and reinforce men's power over women. He elaborates that hegemonic masculinities

> in the contemporary era in the United States are associated with military heroism, corporate power, sports achievement, action-adventure movie stars, and being tough, aggressive, and macho, ideals reproduced in corporate, political, military, sports, and gun culture as well as Hollywood films, video games, men's magazines, and other forms of media culture, and sites like the frat house, locker room, boardroom, male-dominated workplaces, bars, and hangouts where men aggregate.[117]

To this we can easily add 'the school'.

In fact, the cultivation of a hegemonic (or hyper-) masculinity within the school setting is part-and-parcel of the on-going militarism of many societies. Throughout the late twentieth and early twenty-first centuries, public schools, particularly in the United States, have been the site of an overt militarism. In the United States, for example, the military spends billions of dollars each year on a wide variety of recruitment activities. In 2006, according to Aimee Allison and David Solnit, approximately $3.9 billion was spent across American schools for the promotion of military ideals and of the military as a life-style choice. As explained by Allison and Solnit, the most blatant indication of military recruiting on campus is the regular presence of uniformed recruiters. In addition, school counselors often work hand-in-hand with recruiters, encouraging (if not requiring) students to take the Armed Services Vocational Aptitude Battery Test, or to join military clubs such as the 'Young Marines'.[118]

Of immediate concern here is not so much the pervasive practices that permeate the everyday lives of school children; rather, it is the attendant *militarist* values that are promoted. As explained by Andrew Bacevich, "Americans in our time have fallen prey to militarism, manifesting itself in a romanticized view of soldiers, a tendency to see military power as the truest measure of national greatness, and out-sized expectations regarding the efficacy of force." He continues that "Americans have come to define the nation's strength and well-being in terms of military preparedness, military action, and the fostering of (or nostalgia for) military ideals."[119]

Although many Western (and a sizeable number of non-Western) countries are becoming increasingly militarized, the United States has in recent years upped the ante when it comes to militarizing its school children. However, taking a page from Billig, the promotion of militarism is often exceptionally banal. The Pentagon, for example, hires companies like Teenage Research Unlimited to help in recruitment efforts, while the Department of Defense—through its Joint Advertising Market Research and Studies (JAMRS) program and Mullen Advertising—has created a vast repository of 16–25-year-old youth data. Containing approximately 30 million records, this data set includes information—names, birth dates, addresses, Social Security numbers, students' grade-point averages, field of academic study—for about 90 percent of the United States' high school population.[120] Branches of the United States military (e.g., the Army, Navy, Airforce, Marines, and Coast Guard) likewise utilize films, sporting events, websites, and cartoons to promote themselves.

The effects of an overt militarism on school-aged children are profound—but rarely acknowledged. To become militarized, Cynthia Enloe explains, is to "adopt militaristic values (e.g., a belief in hierarchy, obedience, and the use of force) and priorities as one's own, to see military solutions as particularly effective, to see the world as a dangerous place best approached with militaristic attitudes."[121] Schools within a militarized society, accordingly, become intensely disciplined places that promote the acceptance of violence as a means of resolving problems.

Boys are expected to stand up for themselves as dominant playground masculinities are conceptualized as being constructed through discourses of power, control, and aggression. Those boys who 'fail' to live up to societal expectations of male aggression, or are considered too effeminate in their attitudes, are partially blamed—by both adults and other children—for being bullied. It is not uncommon, for example, for teachers and administrators to counsel teased and bullied boys to 'toughen up' and to become and behave like 'proper' boys. Likewise, boys who are unable or unwilling to 'fight back' may be further taunted and harassed. They may be called 'sissy', 'pussy', or some other derogatory term. In terms of discipline, conversely, those "boys who adopted the more traditional macho role received a far greater level of tolerance than those who transgressed."[122]

A pervasive attitude of 'boys-will-be-boys' sets in motion a process whereby some male students are rewarded for their aggressive, violent behavior. Violence throughout the public school, consequently, mirrors that of domestic violence within the home. According to Debby Phillips, practices of violence are strategies that work to affirm the 'norm' when other strategies to achieve or maintain the 'norm' fail or are unattainable.[123] However, the problem is deeper. Within patriarchal societies, violent strategies *are* the norm. In other words, in many societies a 'normal' man is defined by his *strategic* and *selective* use of violence. As Elizabeth Stanko writes, "boys' physical confrontations are typically considered normal by those who believe that participating in fights toughens boys and shows them how to be men."[124] This is a lesson that is all too often learned at school.

Girls, however, are constructed through different codes. Girls are expected to be passive.[125] But of course, girls are also limited in their day-to-day interactions by the familiar double-standards of a patriarchal society. Girls, for example, are not always able to respond to verbal taunts. As Phillips explains, boys often resort to the use of feminizing language produced by misogynist discourses to objectify and humiliate other boys, such as calling another boy a 'girl', 'sissy', or 'pussy'. Reciprocally, this practice serves to simultaneously objectify and degrade women. Girls, however, do not have access to 'comparable' discourses; a girl most likely would not call another boy a 'girl' as a derogatory epithet. Indeed, a girl cannot attack a boy's masculinity by equating them with 'femaleness' because so doing would simultaneously degrade the girl.[126] Becky Francis likewise finds that girls are severely restricted in their ability to chastise boys by the lack of vocabulary of insults relating to masculinity. The majority of insults denote femininity; male derision of things female is often portrayed in the verbal insults girls reported experiencing from boys.[127]

Schools may also be exceptionally violent places for gay, lesbian, and bisexual youth. According to recent surveys, queer youth are often the victims of attacks ranging from verbal harassment to physical assault.[128] As noted in the previous chapter, queer youths are often marginalized at home. They are subjected to various forms of violence, including name-calling, psychological abuse and humiliation, and even physical violence. It is not uncommon, in fact, for parents to literally expel their gay sons or lesbian daughters from their home. Consequently, queer youths live their home-lives in silence. According to Joyce Hunter, queer youths are often an invisible population in that many do not share their sexual orientation with their family, friends, or peers because they fear rejection and violence.[129] School, much like the home, may be a place of isolation and alienation.

Andi O'Conor explains that for gay, lesbian, bisexual, and transgender youths, the school may become a hostile and dangerous environment. She notes that gay and lesbian youth are often the most frequent victims of hate crimes, and that the school is the primary setting for this type of violence.[130] Anthony D'Augelli and his colleagues, for example, in their study of 350 lesbian, gay, and bisexual high school students, found that more than half of the respondents were verbally abused, nearly one-quarter were threatened, and over 10 percent were physically attacked.[131] Similarly, in her study of 500 self-identified queer youths, Hunter found that 40 percent (201 teenagers) reported that they had experienced violent physical assaults. Many of the youths in Hunter's study were either African-American or Latino; consequently, these individuals also reported being the recipient of racist attacks.[132]

Discrimination and violence toward gay, lesbian, bisexual, and transgendered students can be augmented through the informal and even formal promotion of heteronormativity. Studies routinely identify that public educational systems promote heterosexuality as the norm. Administrators, for example, may look the other way when homophobic terms are used (but punish those making ethnic slurs). Indeed, O'Conor finds that while teachers often punish students who make racist remarks, homophobic comments are typically unchallenged—and sometimes even perpetrated—by teachers.[133] Stanko likewise finds that teachers often condone, or look away, when in the presence of homophobic attitudes. She relates the story of one young man who was beaten in a school restroom. After the attack, one of the teachers told the man, "For a faggot, you're not that bad of a person."[134] This double-standard reinforces prejudicial practices and helps produce an environment ripe for social and spatial exclusion.

The consequences of homophobic teasing and violence are significant. According to Dorothy Espelage and her colleagues, queer youths who are subjected to such violence are at a significantly greater risk for suicidal ideation, depression, and isolation.[135] Consequently, according to O'Conor, in order to survive at school, many queer youth construct a 'false heterosexual self'. They may engage in sex with members of the opposite sex to 'prove' that they are straight; they may participate in homophobic name-calling and indeed, some queer youth might actually engage in anti-gay violence in an attempt to hide their own sexual orientation.[136]

Conclusions

School violence is a legitimate source of concern, but not primarily because of media-hyped school rampage shootings. As tragic as these events are, such myopia risks neglect of the more pervasive sexism, racism, and homophobia that continue to shape the space and place of school. It is significant that while conservative politicians beginning in the 1970s identified violent crime as a serious issue, they specifically excluded domestic violence on the grounds that it was "not the kind of street violence about which it was most concerned."[137] It is likewise significant that on-going discussions of school violence too often overlook the more mundane forms of violence that *daily* affect our children.

In this chapter we first considered how the threat, or fear, of violence produced the modern public school as a place of discipline. We have seen how fears of violent behavior on the part of unruly youth have permeated discussions of the public school and, in turn, have helped shape particular educational policies and practices. Most recently, for example, these fears are manifest in the perception that some children embody 'evil' and are 'natural' criminals. Consequently, many public schools have instituted harsh policies that mirror broader crime control programs that have been designed to 'clean up' society. Ironically, these draconian policies have been implemented with the stated purpose of providing greater security to schools—a security discourse founded on the continued (and highly publicized) coverage of school rampage shootings. Of course, these policing measures did not address the more prevalent form of violence that pervades modern public schools.

In the second half of this chapter, therefore, we explored more closely how 'race', sex, and gender play out in the many and varied spaces of the modern public school. We discussed, for example, how schools are important places in the formation of youth identities, but that 'identity formation' is both relational and contextual. What it means to be a 'boy' or a 'girl' for example is a contested process. Discipline—and violence—emerge as specific and purposeful behaviors enacted by children against children in an attempt to enforce normative meanings of 'race', sex, and gender. In short, we have seen more clearly how schools are places for rearticulating social and spatial relations and why violence often figures so prominently.

As Nancy Brener and her colleagues write, "Aggressive behaviors such as fighting and weapon carrying are extremely common in the daily lives of many adolescents."[138] Often, the violence that surrounds these behaviors is related to cultural practices and attitudes of masculinity, femininity, and sexuality. According to Stanko, "Keeping men heterosexual ensures that men retain their position of dominance vis-à-vis women, and this dominance is considered a natural extension of how women and men relate to each other." She continues that "By demanding that men be heterosexual, other boys and men carve out a proper place amongst men."[139] Significantly, many boys and girls learn these 'places' within school.

4
THE STREETS

> *Despite the fact that the majority of interpersonal violence is perpetrated by non-strangers, stranger crime is what most of us dread. It is the stranger lurking in the alley or the bushes who captures our imagination and stirs our fears. Strangers are anonymous and dangerous, while our friends and acquaintances are known to us and therefore nonthreatening.*[1]

In previous chapters we have seen how two 'sites', the home and the school, are routinely portrayed as 'safe' spaces and yet are often very violent places. Our understanding of the 'public street', conversely, should be relatively straight-forward. As children, we are taught to be wary of the street, and especially of strangers. We read daily of senseless and anonymous muggings and thefts, rapes and murders, that occur on public streets. Through film, television, and now video games, we routinely witness random acts of violence. The lesson is clear: streets are to be avoided. Women, we are taught also, are especially vulnerable. And whether this is true or not is largely immaterial. In practice, fears of stranger-danger have supported patriarchal assumptions and attitudes that serve to restrict women's mobility. In other words, there is a politics of fear underlying our representation of the street—a politics that should negate any simple cause-and-effect relationships between street danger, women's use of space, and social control.[2]

That said, it is worthwhile to consider more thoroughly the representations of stranger-danger and what these representations say about space, place, and violence. Why do we continue to view the 'street' as a dangerous place, while viewing the 'home' as a place of security and safety? Who, or what, is present in the street to warrant such fears? Even a cursory engagement with true-crime novels, television detective shows, or thriller-films offers a range of candidates: drug dealers, gang members, disgruntled postal workers. However, no figure personifies the fear of stranger-danger more than the serial killer.

In her book *Mapping the Trail of a Serial Killer*, for example, Brenda Ralph Lewis writes "A serial killer is much more than a killer who murders a minimum of two—or by most definitions three—people within a certain length of time. For what statistics can never take into account is the *extreme fear serial killing generates*."[3] Lewis continues that serial killings'

> premeditated, predatory nature is horrifying, and spreads a particular type of terror among the community in which it occurs. Where will the killer strike again? Who will be the next victim? Are we safe and secure in our homes, on the streets, at night, when we are alone?[4]

Curiously, serial killing, by any of the available definitions or statistics available, is a rare crime. And yet it achieves a disproportionate level of coverage in both fictional and scholarly accounts.[5] This holds especially true when compared with the prevalence of, say, domestic violence. Why should this be? Is there *something* else underlying the public's fascination with the serial murderer? Asked differently, how might serial killing help us reconceptualize our understanding of public space? In addressing these questions, I hope to provide further insight into our overall project of understanding the interactions and interrelations of space, place, and violence. To do so, I begin with a brief discussion of *the serial killer* as concept. Next, I forward the argument that, within the North American context, our current understanding and portrayal of the serial killer is a product of the modern urban landscape. Subsequently, I indicate how our 'embrace' of the serial killer reveals much about our attitudes toward women and sexuality. Finally,

I draw comparisons between serial murder in North America and the on-going 'femicide' in Ciudad Juárez, Mexico. Throughout, I question how the representations of both the modern serial killer and the victims of serial murder work to discipline space and to reinforce dominant social relations.

Modernity and the Serial Killer

Is the 'serial killer' a product of contemporary, that is, modern, society? Or, conversely, has the serial killer always existed? To address these questions, we must first consider homicide within the context of humanity. Violence, aggression, and even murder are part of our human history. As both archaeological and anthropological work has made clear, "whenever modern humans appear on the scene, definitive evidence of homicidal violence becomes more common."[6]

But what allows (or impels) humans to kill one another? There are many existent models and theories, ranging from psychological to sociological accounts.[7] As Daly and Wilson write,

> A hundred answers spring to mind. ... Because violent people were themselves abused in childhood. Because of envy engendered by social inequities. Because the penalties are not severe enough. Because of brain tumors, hormone imbalances, and alcohol-induced psychoses. Because modern weapons bypass our natural face-to-face inhibitions and empathies. Because of the violence on TV.[8]

Daly and Wilson conclude, however, that humans conduct violence because we have evolved the *capacity* to kill each other. This is not to suggest that humans are *programmed* to kill. Rather, humans are ambivalent toward killing; we *are* capable of violence, but we are also exceptionally sociable and cooperative.[9] We are in fact also capable of preventing violence. In other words, humans are neither naturally violent nor inherently violent.

Our propensity to engage in violence, and specifically in the killing of other humans, is largely contextual. And given that violence, and particularly homicide, has been a part of human existence since the very beginning,[10] we are left with the question as to whether *serial homicide*—the repetitive killing of other humans—is a feature of the human story. Harold Schecter, on the one hand, contends that the "harsh truth is that we belong to a violent species; the kinds of outrages committed by serial killers have been an aspect of human society at all times in all places."[11] He thus discounts the argument that serial murder is a modern phenomenon. On the other hand, scholars such as Philip Jenkins and Kevin Haggerty argue that while there have always been people who serially kill, the phenomenon in today's society is qualitatively different. For example, Haggerty argues that the serial killer as a concept did not exist until the twentieth century and, therefore, it is not appropriate to consider those individuals who killed multiple victims prior to the twentieth century as serial killers. Although I am not entirely comfortable with this argument, I do acknowledge that our present-day attitudes and understandings of 'the serial killer' are heavily conditioned by current representations.[12] Consequently, it is not far-fetched to argue that although 'multiple murders' have long been a feature of human existence, there is something *different* about serial killings of the past century. To this end, some scholars, most notably Elliott Leyton, have identified a periodization of serial killings. Leyton, for example, proposes a three-part history, with both killers and victims selectively derived from dominant social classes of the time. Thus, in the pre-industrial period, according to Leyton, the multiple killer was most likely an aristocrat who targeted peasants. During the industrial era, by contrast, killers were drawn from the bourgeois and stalked and murdered prostitutes, runaways, vagrants, and other 'marginalized' groups. Now, in a post-industrial age, according to Leyton, serial killers are typified by the faded bourgeois who primarily targets college-aged women and other middle-class individuals.[13]

Even a cursory understanding of recent history makes clear the limitations and inaccuracies of Leyton's typology. However, the basic premise that 'serial killers' are a product of their time *and* space is worth considering. Haggerty, for example, presents six preconditions for contemporary serial killing which are distinctly *modern*. First, according to Haggerty, the mass media has both stoked the fear of serial killings and, in the process, contributed to the rise of a celebrity culture of killers. Haggerty explains that although serial killing is among the most statistically rare forms of crime, it receives a disproportionate amount of attention from the media. Indeed, Haggerty notes, "few other topics have been so persistently exploited over the past quarter century." The result has been that the media provides "the basic institutional framework and cultural context for the operation of modern forms of serial killing."

A second distinctive characteristic of modernity is the rise of urbanization. Haggerty explains that in pre-modern, rural settings, everyone knew everyone. This insular familiarity worked against the ability of a stranger to randomly and continuously target potential victims. With the advent of industrial capitalism, however, and the growth of cities, our everyday lives became more anonymous, more faceless. Our daily lives are composed of nothing more than mundane, superficial, and impersonal encounters. Haggerty suggests that dense urban environments represent ideal settings for the routinized impersonal encounters that typically define serial killings.[14] Related to this, Haggerty proposes that the dispassionate style of rational thought that characterizes modernity has contributed to the modern serial killer. According to this line of reasoning, serial killers "reproduce this rationalist framework and push its distinctive form of value-free means/ends and rationality to its most fantastic extreme."[15] Such an argument conforms also to the tendency of serial killers to meticulously plan out their murders; indeed, studies suggest that for many killers, it is this rational planning that is most integral and pleasurable to the crime. Fifth, our modern societies are replete with 'cast-offs', those groups of people perceived to be marginal to our way of life. These denigrated Others, such as prostitutes and vagrants, are also some of the most frequent targets of serial killers. This is a theme that will be explored at length in this chapter. Finally, one of the hallmarks of modernity has been the promotion of social engineering. This is seen, for example, in the efficiency of the factory and especially of the modern school (recall, for example, Chapter Three). Haggerty carries this idea further, suggesting that serial killers embody this quest for rationality and efficiency in their attempts to personally (and violently) create a better society.

In sum, Haggerty suggests that the twentieth century is characterized by an increased prevalence of depersonalized, bureaucratic language that serves to dehumanize victims, and serial killers reproduce society's rationalist framework through their killings. Modern serial killers, with few exceptions, systematically *plan* and *justify* their torturing, rape, and murder of other people.[16] The victims of the modern serial killer are reduced to a 'means' toward a particular end; such an 'end' may be personal satisfaction and self-aggrandizement. Conversely, the end may be a desire to *cleanse* society of a perceived threat. This overlaps with two of Haggerty's pre-conditions, specifically those of societal denigration and social engineering. In most, if not all societies, certain segments of the population have been marginalized. Such peoples may have been those exhibiting some physical deformity. Most prevalent, however, has been the marginalization of peoples based on occupation or lack thereof. Prostitutes, historically, have been placed on the fringes of society; so too have the homeless, vagabonds, migrant workers, and even homosexuals. Steven Egger refers to these individuals as being 'less dead'. He identifies an increased prevalence of societal encouragement to kill a type of person who, when murdered, is 'less dead' than other categories of homicide victims.[17] Thus prostitutes, gay men, homeless transients, runaway youths, senior citizens, and the inner-city poor have been perceived by society as 'less dead' than, say, a white college girl from a middle-class suburb.[18]

Haggerty concurs, noting that serial killers often embrace and reproduce the wider cultural codings that have devalued, stigmatized, and marginalized specific groups: prostitutes, runaways, homeless persons, racial and sexual minorities. Serial killers, in other words, reflect back and act upon society's distinctive valuations. Indeed, Haggerty writes, it is often easier to identify who modern serial killers *do not* kill. In North America and many other Western countries, for instance, serial killers rarely murder wealthy, white, heterosexual males—those individuals who are iconically positioned in the most esteemed cultural category.[19]

There is also a clear racial, gendered, and sexual bias in America's celebratory fascination with serial killers. From the standpoint of both publishers and film producers, African-American killers or victims are less likely to appeal to the mass audience. Peter Vronsky notes that the serial murder of five University of Florida students in Gainesville inspired breathless national coverage by *Time* magazine and network television; however, the concurrent systematic killing of 11 crack-addicted black prostitutes in Detroit hardly made the news.[20] The pantheon of (in)famous and celebrity serial killers is populated with Dahmer, Bundy, Gacy, Ridgway. One rarely hears of Alton Coleman, Milton Johnson, Calvin Jackson, Carlton Gary, or Coral Watts.[21]

The failure to draw attention to *non-white* serial killers might in itself arise from a form of racial bias within the media and law enforcement.[22] Law enforcement agencies, for example, are often less likely to seek or to find evidence of serial murder activity in areas that exhibit high concentrations of African-Americans. Such 'avoidance' may be an indicator of overt police racism and bias; it might also indicate that these are areas where police resources are simply not invested.[23] And serial killers are not unaware of these biases. The prolific serial killer Albert Fish, for example, specifically preyed on black children in Washington D.C. and New York City. It was not until he abducted and murdered a white girl that his crimes attracted sufficient attention to warrant an in-depth investigation.[24]

Moreover, hardly any 'thrillers', detective novels, or films focus on the investigation of crimes involving African-Americans as either murderers or victims.[25] One could argue that society holds these individuals in such contempt, that there is relatively little enjoyment in watching the 'less dead' be murdered. More entertaining is the spectacle of attractive young (white) middle-class women being abducted, tortured, and murdered.

The *selection* of victims thus parallels long-standing societal discourses of social engineering and planning and indeed 'societal worth': to remove the so-called detritus from society in an attempt to create a more utopian world. Indeed, serial killers are often quite forthcoming in their post-conviction justification of murder: they targeted victims that needed to be removed from society and/or because the victims would not be missed. Consider Gary Ridgway, the 'Green River Killer'. In November 2003 Ridgway pleaded guilty to the murder of 48 prostitutes in Washington State. While the killings were taking place, mostly between 1982 and 1984, the Green River Killer did not attract much attention, in part, because Ridgway's "victims, as street prostitutes, [were] held in such low esteem in society that even the remarkable number of deaths did not evoke more than mildly routine press coverage outside the Washington State area."[26] After his capture, Ridgway explained that he picked prostitutes as victims because he hated most prostitutes and did not want to pay for sex.[27]

In a perverse fashion, therefore, serial killers typically "articulate uniquely modern ambitions for social betterment," that is, their "killing is connected with utopian designs for social improvement."[28] In other words, a particular and normative geographical imagination underlies the justifications and motivations of individual killers: a specific geographic vision is sought for society and informs the serial killer's understanding of who is selected—and why. It is on this basis that I forward the idea that the contemporary serial killer is a product of modern urban space.

The Serial Killer as Urban Redeveloper

If we make the argument that the modern serial killer is a product of the urban landscape, we must first take a detour and consider those spaces that comprise that landscape. The urban landscapes of North America and much of Western Europe underwent profound changes in the 1970s. In part, these were the physical manifestation of a deeper systemic restructuring of capitalism—namely a shift from industrial capitalism to a phase known alternatively as 'post-industrial capitalism', 'corporate capitalism', or 'advanced capitalism'.[29] The causes of this economic shift are multiple, and, as Knox and Agnew explain, must be seen as the product of a conjunction of trends. These include a slowing down of economic growth and a steady fall in profits; a drastic rise in oil prices as a result of the Organization of Petroleum Exporting Countries (OPEC) cartel; rising levels of inflation; and increased international monetary instability, associated with both the transition from fixed exchange rates to floating exchange rates and problems of indebtedness among newly industrializing countries.[30]

The decline of North American and European cities must be situated within these broader, global economic changes. By the 1970s and early 1980s, for example, many corporations were relocating their manufacturing operations to overseas locations where lower labor costs and greater tax breaks promised higher profit margins and/or larger market shares. In American cities such as Pittsburgh, Buffalo, Akron, Cleveland, and Detroit, companies fired or relocated workers, closed factories, and moved out of the region or country. Overnight, the historical 'industrial' belt of America was transformed into the 'Rust' belt.[31] As Bluestone and Harrison find, the deindustrialization of America's economy was truly devastating. They estimate that somewhere between 32 and 38 million jobs were lost during the 1970s as the direct result of private disinvestment in American business.[32] And the effects of disinvestment and deindustrialization were not necessarily confined to the old manufacturing belt. Indeed, approximately half of the jobs lost to plant closings during the 1970s occurred in the Sunbelt states of the American southwest.[33] As David Harvey summarizes, there

> were problems with the rigidity of long-term and large-scale fixed capital investments in mass-production systems that precluded much flexibility of design and presumed stable growth in invariant consumer markets. There were problems of rigidities in labor markets, labor allocation, and in labor contracts.[34]

And, as Gordon MacLeod and Kevin Ward bluntly attest, "the eventual erosion of the Fordist 'boom' was to leave a particularly devastating impact on the urban landscapes of North America and Western Europe."[35]

Throughout the 1970s there occurred also a simultaneous decentralization, a hollowing-out, of American and European cities. Throughout the late 1960s and 1970s, U.S. suburbs, for example, gained over 18 million people and more than three million jobs.[36] Subsequently, as higher-income taxpayers continued their trek to the outer suburbs, the inner-cities were left bereft of much-needed sources of income. "What was most pronounced," according to Paul Knox and John Agnew, "was the 'shake-out' of routine and labour-intensive inner-city areas—some of it destined for relocation in the suburbs, but much more destined for relocation in rural areas, peripheral regions, peripheral countries, or the bankruptcy courts."[37]

As tax bases dwindled, Philip Jenkins explains, cities found it more difficult to survive. Indeed, from New York to Baltimore to Cleveland, America's cities seemed to be on the verge of collapse. In response, urban planners, mayors, and other public officials sought to revitalize cities in the face of widespread deindustrialization and the flight of high-income earners from the central city. Federal governments, however, steadfastly refused to provide support. Consequently, urban governments were increasingly forced to engage in a more 'entrepreneurial' approach to recentralize and accumulate corporate capital into the inner-city and, more broadly, to revive a competitive position of their local economies.[38] As Short and Kim summarize, beginning in the 1970s, the

> main goal of government policy has been the creation of wealth rather than its redistribution. The aims of full employment, eradicating poverty and inequality and the creation of a balanced space economy have been jettisoned or much reduced. Reaganomics and Thatcherism marked a watershed: a definite cutback in welfare spending and an emphasis on effectively responding to market forces.[39]

During the 1970s and 1980s, local governments turned to public–private partnerships and growth coalitions in an attempt to leverage a diminished base of federal funding to finance downtown commercial construction designed to improve the physical and aesthetic landscapes of their downtowns.[40] Attempts were made to both gentrify and revitalize *selected* derelict landscapes of the city. This required a symbolic re-presentation of the city in order to promote inner-city places as alluring and inviting. And, as Sharon Zukin explains, abandoned to market competition for an image-conscious public, urban infrastructure projects focused on specialty stores, art, and food.[41] Thus, the new consumer spaces of the city were typified by *nouvelle cuisine* restaurants, trendy boutiques, and art galleries, alongside instantly recognizable coffee bars—with the ubiquitous *Starbucks* being the most emblematic.[42] In short, the promotion of conspicuous consumption, leisure, and tourism in revitalized downtowns became a key strategy in the global battle for 'jobs and dollars' that pits city against city.[43]

Cities are not isolated, and one important consequence of the political and economic changes of the 1970s and 1980s has been the "intense competition between cities for investment, both public and private."[44] As Short and his colleagues write, the "increasing mobility of capital and the growing competition between cities to attract capital is the economic backdrop to new rounds of civic boosterism, public relations campaigns, and the 'renaissance' of the downtown." Ultimately, this "involves rewriting the very meaning of the city."[45]

In the 1970s and 1980s, American cities "seemed dirty, dangerous, and locked in a cycle of continuing decline."[46] And both conservative and liberal discourse hyped the fears of urban Armageddon. This is perhaps best illustrated through the moral panic surrounding 'black-on-black' violence. As David Wilson details, 'black-on-black violence' became widely discussed in Congress, public schools, mayoral forums, churches, and presidential speeches as fear spread of uncontrolled *black* youth roaming the public streets of American cities. In actuality, 'black-on-black' violence was a political signifier and offered simple solutions in times of uncertainty. Blacks in particular, and youths more broadly, were cast as villains, contributing to a moral decay of both city and state.[47] And as we saw in the context of school violence, politicians were quick to cast themselves as being 'tough on crime'. The 'serial killer' would emerge as a key component of the remaking of American cities—but he was not alone. Accompanying the specter of the 'serial killer' were other characters of the same moral panic: demonized black youth, but also demonized youth in general.

It is oft asserted that the term 'serial killer' was coined by Robert Ressler, a Federal Bureau of Investigation (FBI) profiler. Indeed, we have become so used to the idea that the FBI invented (and has practically exclusive ownership of) the concept 'serial murder' that we rarely question the story's veracity. However, the origin of the term is part of a calculated mythology promoted by the FBI. Consider, for instance, that the behavior of one person killing multiple people over a given period of time was hardly novel in the 1970s. In the late 1920s, for example, the terms 'multiple murder' and 'mass murderer' came into usage. The term 'thrill murder' also was used as early as 1924; and by the 1950s it was possible to speak of both 'pattern murder' and 'psycho murder'. In 1958 Grierson Dickson introduced the concept of 'series murder'; he also introduced the term 'multicide'. Lastly, in 1966 John Brophy published his *The Meaning of Murder* (first released in England and appearing in the United States in 1967) in which he used the term 'serial murder'.[48]

So why the mythology surrounding the term? What changed in the 1970s? In part, the explanation parallels the rise of the aforementioned 'entrepreneurial' city, namely the competition for federal funds. In short, the FBI capitalized on the specter of serial killing as a means of increasing its own bureaucratic power and prestige. Moreover, the construction of serial murder as an explicitly federal crime in the early 1980s was part of a larger effort by the Reagan administration to extend federal jurisdiction to a number of serious crimes that were previously viewed as the exclusive property of local law enforcement agencies.[49] The irony is that prior to the 1970s, the FBI was almost completely uninterested in murderers, rapists, and child molesters; these criminals were seen largely as the responsibility of local law enforcement agencies.[50] The FBI, instead, was concerned with 'bigger' fish, namely communists and labor agitators.

Since the 1970s, the specter of serial murder has been exploited, not surprisingly, by official agencies (including the FBI) and the media.[51] It was claimed, for example, by both the FBI and true-crime novelists that the serial murder problem was approaching staggering proportions. It was commonly asserted, for example, that roving serial killers were leaving four thousand to five thousand victims in their wake each year; that victims of serial murder accounted for nearly one-quarter of all homicide deaths—compared to just 1 or 2 percent of homicides in previous decades.[52] A more accurate assessment conducted by the U.S. Justice Department determined that 331 serial murders killed 1,964 victims between 1977 and 1991—a figure far below the exaggerated claims that were through the 1980s continuously pitched by the FBI, true-crime writers, and the media. Now, it is commonly agreed by academics, the FBI, and police agencies that the number of victims to serial homicide is on the order of 70 per year, and that serial killings constitute approximately 1 to 2 percent of all homicides—a figure far below that of intimate partner violence or hate crimes.[53]

Such 'corrections' to the public's awareness of violent activities often go unannounced and, indeed, many federal agencies and individuals continue to play up the fear of serial killings. In the world of consumerism and mass marketing, crime pays. During the 1980s a curious symbiotic relationship was cultivated between federal authorities, true-crime writers, and, later, film producers. This is perhaps best illustrated in the discussions of the geographic mobility of serial killers. The true-crime writer Ann Rule, for example, testified before the U.S. Senate Subcommittee on Juvenile Justice. In her testimony she claimed that serial murderers are 'trollers'; that these killers travel constantly in search of unsuspecting victims. Indeed, she remarked that many of the killers whom she had personally interviewed traveled more than 200,000 miles per year looking for victims.[54] Local law enforcement agencies, it was argued, were ill-equipped to adequately track down and capture the geographically elusive serial killer—thus requiring the efforts of the FBI. But no one questioned such egregious claims; instead, the purported geographic hyper-mobility of serial killers translated into increased funds and resources for federal agencies ... and book sales for true-crime writers.

Urban redevelopment schemes therefore went hand-in-hand with the fictionalized moral panics of public violence and the pervasive and disproportional fear of serial killers. Gated communities and gentrified inner-city enclaves were promoted (and sold) through a politics of fear. Indeed, urban redevelopment was predicated on the ability to promote the new capitalist spaces as "suitably excluded from the real and perceived threats of another fiercely hostile, dystopian environment 'out there.'"[55] Hence, the new urbanist architects and planners asserted a neo-traditional and *neoconservative* sense of place and community through the construction of new urban villages and small towns.[56] Such was the context for the emergence of the *revanchist* city.

In his work on gentrification, Neil Smith introduced the idea of the 'revanchist city'. He argued that, beginning in the 1960s and continuing through the 1990s, "Revenge against minorities, the working class, women, environmental legislation, gays and lesbians, immigrants became the increasingly common denominator of public discourse." Furthermore, he argued that "Attacks on affirmative action and immigration policy, street violence against gays and homeless people, feminist bashing and public campaigns against political correctness and multiculturalism were the most visible vehicles of this reaction."[57]

The revanchist city, I argue, is inseparable from the moral panic that is embodied in the serial killer.

For moral conservatives in the 1980s, events of the previous 15 years had had a catastrophic effect on the moral fiber of American society. People feared that an increasing tolerance of divorce, abortion, homosexuality, drugs, sexual promiscuity, and civil and women's rights would lead to a downfall of society. And urban decline was but the most visible 'evidence' of societal break-down. For neoconservatives, the contemporary anarchy of the urban streets was contrasted with an idealized family-oriented society.[58] As argued by Don Mitchell,

> In the punitive city, the post-modern city, the revanchist city, diversity is no longer maintained by protecting and struggling to expand the rights of the most disadvantaged, but by pushing the disadvantaged out, making it clear that as broken windows rather than people, they simply have no right to the city.[59]

Revanchism thus represented an "accumulated resentment and rage associated with middle-class frustration in the face of severe economic recession and governmental retraction."[60] As MacLeod and Ward conclude, the revanchist ethos encompassed a whole raft of state policies that were wedded to a neoliberal anti-welfare ideology and included far-ranging attempts to 'cleanse' the public spaces of society's urban landscape.[61]

New York City provides the classic example of the revanchist city. Under the guidance of mayor Rudolph Giuliani, New York City adopted a form of policing termed 'quality-of-life' or 'zero-tolerance'. Under this approach, the police and other authorized entities were given extreme leeway in their attempt to deal aggressively with those who supposedly cause fear in the citizenry—panhandlers, subway turnstile jumpers, the homeless—in short, those groups viewed to be a threat to the quality of urban life.[62] Specific practices included the imposition of curfews, 'three-strikes' legislation, mandatory sentencing laws, electronic monitoring, and the introduction of newer weapons (e.g., stun guns and tasers).

Zero-tolerance policing has diffused widely during the past two decades. As part of a wider trend of 'policy transfer', American crime control programs have been imported by a number of countries throughout Western Europe. Tim Newburn, for example, documents that various police departments throughout the United Kingdom have embraced the idea of 'zero tolerance'. The 1998 Crime and Disorder Act, as a case in point, initiated far-reaching changes to the youth justice system and introduced a number of new orders—all of which were informed by developments in the United States—including curfews, 'three-strikes' legislation, privatized prisons, electronic monitoring, and even the establishment of 'drug czars'.[63]

Supporters of 'zero-tolerance' practices throughout North America and Western Europe maintain that these represent attempts to restore a sense of community (a topic revisited in the next chapter); that these are necessary programs designed to 'take back the streets' from the undesirable elements of modern society.[64] What I find curious (but also highly significant) is that the 'targets' of zero-tolerance police strategies are often the very same 'targets' of both fictional and real serial killers. Furthermore, these 'targets' are associated with the very same *spaces* that revanchist policies are designed to 'clean up': the public spaces of prostitutes and teenage runaways, the homeless and jobless, the drug dealers and drug users, are the very same spaces that 'experts' on serial murder identify in geographic terms as 'zones of opportunity'. These zones of opportunity are spaces whereby victims are understood as 'facilitating' their own demise—in other words, a practice of blaming the victim for being in the wrong place at the wrong time.

As Vronsky explains, some pundits and scholars argue that *certain* victims facilitate their own murders by the lifestyles they lead, or because of the places they live and work. In their popular text book on serial murder, for example, Holmes and Holmes explain that "in some cases some victims 'contribute' to their own victimization." They quickly add that "This is not to excuse the actions of the offender, but it does explain in some fashion the activity and the interplay between the offender and the victim."[65] Harold Schecter likewise explains that a "crack-addicted streetwalker in an inner-city slum ... is far more likely to end up strangled, dismembered, and left in a dumpster than a white suburban soccer mom." He continues that

Prostitutes (especially when they come from the underclass)—along with street hustlers, teenage runaways, vagrants, junkies, and other social outcasts—are what criminologists call 'targets of opportunity': people who are especially vulnerable to serial homicide because they are easy to snare and overpower and are so marginalized that no one, including members of the police and the press, pays much attention when they go missing.[66]

For strict advocates of social conservatism, *all* prostitutes choose their vocation; it is simply not contemplated that some women (and men) may be forced to engage in prostitution because of a lack of public safety nets. Likewise, *all* runaway teenagers willingly choose to leave the confines of their homes, despite the fact that many of these youths may be fleeing parental violence and abuse; *all* vagrants are homeless by choice, despite the fact that many may have lost their jobs and homes because of corporate disinvestment strategies. Thus, we may convict Peter Sutcliffe, but we *blame* Patricia Atkinson, Jayne Macdonald, Jean Jordan, Yvonne Pearson, and Helen Rytka because they were prostitutes. We convict Jeffrey Dahmer but we *blame* Matt Turder, Jeremiah Weinberger, Oliver Lacy, and Joseph Brandehoft because they were homosexuals.

Many serial killers do target those whom society has marginalized specifically because of societal antipathy. In the 1980s, for example, Douglas Clark, the 'Sunset Strip Killer', targeted young women—mostly runaways and prostitutes. For Clark, his victims were selected because they were easier targets, in that both runaways (while hitchhiking) and street prostitutes were more likely to enter the vehicle of a stranger. Gary Ridgway, the 'Green River Killer' whom we met earlier, likewise explained that "Prostitutes were the easiest. I went from having sex with them to just plain killing them." He elaborated that

> I ... picked prostitutes as victims because they were easy to pick up without being noticed. I knew they would not be reported missing right away, and might never be reported missing. I picked prostitutes because I thought I could kill as many of them as I wanted without getting caught.[67]

What strikes me as especially problematic and troublesome is not so much that some people (killers) selectively prey on the most vulnerable. Rather, my concern lies in the fact that *the arguments used by serial killers to justify their murderous rage mirror the arguments used to redevelop urban spaces*.

(Eliminating) Sex on the Streets

"Why are they [the community] *so upset with me? I killed whores. They spread disease. Don't they realize that I did a public service by cutting down on the rate of venereal disease?"*[68]

"I thought I was doing you guys a favor, killing, killing the prostitutes. Here you guys can't control them, but I can."[69]

It is well-documented that prostitution (and particularly street prostitution) is concentrated in specific and spatially constrained areas; however, until recently, researchers have said very little of the processes by which these spaces are produced and transformed.[70] According to Phil Hubbard, for example, the spatiality and visibility of sex work in Western neoliberal cities is markedly different from that evident in the industrial era. Previously, street prostitution was typically located in 'notorious' red-light districts contiguous with areas of lower-class occupations in the inner-cities. Now, in an era of neoliberalism, the purification of the central city is having a profound impact on the spatiality of sex work.[71] Throughout the 1980s and 1990s, as a case in point, with the emergence of the revanchist city, prostitutes and other 'indigents' have routinely been displaced (often forcibly) from gentrifying inner-cities to other, more marginal locations.[72]

Equally salient, however, is that contemporary scholarship has failed to draw a connection between the *justifications* of both revanchist city managers and serial killers. Street prostitutes, as a case in point, have been targeted both by urban developers and corporate capital, as well as by serial killers. And society has responded in kind, consuming images of ravaged, mutilated, and murdered *female* prostitutes at an alarming rate. Accordingly, the public fascination with serial killers and the simultaneous reclamation of urban space says much about societal attitudes toward women and violence.

Prostitution has long been stigmatized by society as dirty and deviant. As such, sex-related businesses have routinely faced removal from spaces associated with more 'respectable' populations. Therefore, it comes as little surprise to find that these activities became prime targets of the revanchist city as both local and federal authorities sought to clean up society. Indeed, the policing of commercial sex has been connected to the rise of policies that regard prostitution and pornography as antithetical to the reinvention of city centers as safe, middle-class, family-oriented consumption spaces.[73] According to Papayanis, for example,

> for those who would reclaim the city in the name of 'traditional values', X-rated bookstores and movie theaters, video palaces, topless bars, and peep-show parlors rank alongside the homeless and working poor as 'quality-of-life' issues, a euphemism for class-motivated warfare on the visible effects of poverty, economic disenfranchisement, and difference perceived as deviance.[74]

Writing in agreement, Hubbard elaborates that against a backdrop of ambient fear, convincing investors and consumers that city center spaces were 'safe' became a key priority for those city governors and promoters looking to sponsor an 'urban renaissance'. Moreover, given that sex workers are frequently depicted and essentialized as part of a criminal class, reducing the visibility of sex work in the central city was an obvious way that policy-makers could entice corporate investment. The displacement of sex work, therefore was an important precursor to the promotion of a middle-class, family-oriented gentrification.[75]

Hubbard argues, therefore, that the response to the visibility of vice in public space can only be understood when viewed in the context of such revanchism: sex workers are symptomatic of violent activities.[76] He concludes that female sex workers, caught up in the pernicious processes of spatial cleansing and 'improvement' initiated by 'city fathers', found their occupation of public spaces increasingly limited.

Consequently, these women were displaced to some of the marginal interstices that existed outside revitalized downtowns.[77] The procurement of public sex was not eliminated; rather, revanchist programs led to a spatial redistribution of activities and businesses. Throughout North America and Western Europe, for example, zero-tolerance programs led to the formation of 'toleration zones'. Hubbard explains that in Paris and London, for example, police 'vice squads' used powers of arrest in effect to concentrate prostitution in red-light districts, where unwritten rules of engagement between police, punters, and prostitutes conspired to create *de facto* 'toleration zones'; this spatial concentration of vice ostensibly allowed the police to enact strategies of surveillance designed, in theory, to minimize incidents of violence against female sex workers.[78] In practice, though, these policies often led to the formation of *'spaces of opportunity'* in which the aforementioned 'targets of opportunity' lived and died.

Within the revanchist city, public fear over street violence was often projected onto the stigmatized figure of the street prostitute; female sex workers, in particular, were scapegoated as a cause, rather than a symptom, of the economic, social, and environmental problems of urban public space.[79] And the continued stigmatization of these women contributes to feelings of indifference toward the murder of prostitutes. Indeed, unless the number of victims is astronomical, or the prostitutes are killed in a particularly novel or horrific manner, their deaths rarely receive any media coverage, let alone serious and sustained discussion that might shed insight into the conditions that lead to either street prostitution or serial homicide. Consider the case of William Lester Suff. Between 1986 and 1992 Suff killed 13 prostitutes in the Lake Elsinore region of California. While disposing of his victims in garbage dumpsters behind strip malls, he posed their corpses in such a manner as to highlight their drug use. However, Suff received little attention, overshadowed by the glitz of the O. J. Simpson trial. As Vronsky sarcastically writes, "What are thirteen dead crack whores compared to two shiny-white Starbucks victims in Brentwood at the hands of an enraged celebrity?"[80]

The policing of prostitution operates in an explicitly spatial manner which reflects and reinforces the marginal status of female prostitutes.

However, it is not simply legal restrictions and police enforcement that work to spatially concentrate sex work. Rather, these concentrations emerge from (and are produced by) an on-going and recursive relationship between the 'everyday' spatial behavior of sex workers and the spatial strategies enacted by the state, law, and community 'protest' groups.[81] In fact, part-and-parcel of the revanchist city has been the emergence of grass-roots campaigns to 'cleanse' public space of street prostitutes. Throughout the United Kingdom, France, and the United States, residents have sought to 'take the law into their own hands' in an attempt to rid their communities of prostitutes and the 'secondary' crimes associated with prostitution.[82] Thus, the 1980s and 1990s witnessed numerous campaigns designed to disrupt public sex work; frequently, these civic-minded activists resorted to verbal harassment and confrontation.[83]

The language used to 'cleanse' the streets of urban vice echoed the explanations forwarded by serial killers. Consider Peter Sutcliffe, the 'Yorkshire Ripper'. Between 1975 and 1981, Sutcliffe stalked and murdered 13 women in northern England. Most of his victims were street prostitutes, on which Sutcliffe explained that these women were "filthy-bastard prostitutes who were littering the streets." In Sutcliffe's mind, he was "just cleaning up the place a bit."[84] Consider also Beoria Simmons, an African-American man who shot three white women to death in Kentucky in 1982 and 1983. Aside from being a serial murderer, Simmons was also a serial rapist. Having abducted a woman whom he *believed* to be a prostitute, Simmons would hold a gun to her head and demand that she 'permit' him to rape her. He said that more than a dozen women said that he would have to kill them because they would not consent to having sex with him. Simmons explained that he would spare the life of these women. Of the three Simmons killed, he explained that their 'permission' to be raped 'proved' to him that they were prostitutes and hence undeserving to live. In his mind, their actions "validated their position as prostitutes."[85] Simmons justified his actions, claiming that it was his responsibility—his purpose—to kill prostitutes.

In Simmons' case, it is important to note that none of his victims were in fact prostitutes; they were simply women who happened to be out late at night. This fact is significant not because the women's deaths are any more tragic. Rather, the importance is found in the conformity between his justification for murder and the prevalent societal attitude that *respectable* women do not belong on public streets past dark. Of his victims, Simmons simply stated that "they looked like whores." He asked rhetorically, "What were 'nice' girls doing out at that time of night?" Furthermore, he questioned why people were so angry with him, given that he was, in his words, reducing the rate of sexually transmitted diseases by 'getting rid' of these women.[86]

We are left with the unpalatable conclusion that many victims are often "marginalized members of our society about whom few are concerned and whose deaths some even celebrate."[87] Indeed, throughout the 1970s and 1980s both 'prostitutes' and 'serial killers' were identified and promoted as part of societal down-fall. And yet serial killers were elevated to a position of celebratory status. How do we come to grips with this development? I suggest that the modern serial killer is in fact a *consumable* product of the revanchist urban environment.

Ironically, while cities were removing vice and violence from the urban landscape, corporate capital was simultaneously commodifying these social ills—and turning a healthy profit to boot. Andy Merrifield explains that the "ugly, the dangerous, the garish in city life can in fact be astonishingly titillating, a pleasure itself, a source of attraction, that simultaneously thrills and appalls."[88] Merrifield's writings in fact relate to an attraction–repulsion dialectic that permeates patriarchal societies. Prostitutes, for example, are widely considered to be contaminated and impure. This disgust, however, is often tempered with a masculine desire. The prostitute is both repudiated and desired.[89] This dialectic is widely reported among serial killers; Ridgway, for example, asserted that he was merely cleansing the city of vile women, yet would do so *after having sex with them*. Significantly, though, this dialectic is also apparent in our modern consumer society and the rise of slasher films and other graphic representations of violence.

Multiple murder and violence have long been staples of the American film industry. Edwin Porter's (1903) *The Great Train Robbery*, for example, described as the first narrative film, depicted a beating victim thrown from a moving train; the film climaxed with a massacre of the train robbers.[90] The 'multiple' or 'serial' murderer also appeared in early films. One of the first representations appeared in Alfred Hitchcock's (1926) depiction of Jack the Ripper, in *The Lodger*. This was followed by Fritz Lang's (1931) release of *M*.[91] In 1930, however, the film industry, in a gesture of self-regulation, passed the Production Code which limited the depiction of on-screen violence.

The censorship of filmic violence was steadily relaxed throughout the 1960s and early 1970s—just as the American public was witness to a series of spectacular trials of serial killers: Charles Manson, Ted Bundy, Richard Ramirez, David Berkowitz, and Kenneth Bianci and Angelo Buono. And films quickly reflected these events. In 1972 for example Sean Cunningham released the film *Last House of the Left*; this thriller was based in part on the Charles Manson murders. Cunningham would follow this film with his *Friday the Thirteenth* series. Over the next few years, the prevalence of filmic serial killers increased astronomically. In the 1980s there were approximately 20 films based on serial killers; throughout the 1990s, over 150 films focused on serial killers. And in the first decade of the twenty-first century, nearly 300 films have involved serial killing as a theme.[92]

Cultural theorists, such as Mark Seltzer and Philip Jenkins, have questioned the popularity of serial killer films, and especially those classified as 'slasher films'. They argue that who is killed, and who is doing the killing, is of significance when considering more broadly the role of violence in society. I concur, and expand this significance to suggest that the filmic representation of serial killings also informs our understandings of public space and of who has a right to that space.

Philip Jenkins contends that early slasher films, such as *Nightmare on Elm Street*, *The Hills Have Eyes*, and *Texas Chainsaw Massacre*, established the basic parameters of the genre. This last film, for example, introduced the idea of the killer as being a deranged monster, depersonalized through the use of a mask, and wielding bizarre murder weapons. The 1975 film *Stranger in the House* provided other influential themes, such as the use of college sorority settings that would allow the killer to stalk attractive (and always partially nude) young women.[93]

This last point demands further attention. For Jenkins, it is noteworthy that slasher films rarely depict a killer who chooses children or elderly people as victims, never a homosexual killer attacking young men, or a skid row slasher targeting vagrants. These 'plot lines' are supposedly too unacceptable or sordid; but the rape, torture, and murder of teenage or college-aged girls? This narrative is seen as both exciting and profitable.[94]

It is worth considering that not *all* the scantily clad women are doomed. Rather, it is frequently the virginal and upstanding girl who emerges largely unharmed. Conversely, those girls who are promiscuous, or out late at night, are slated for a gory and graphic death. Such a narrative reinforces a deeper societal attitude that not all women are deserving of either respect or protection; instead, these women become complicit in their own brutal demise. Accordingly, slasher films reaffirm the conservative mantra of individual responsibility and of knowing one's place. These films by extension emphasize the responsibility of the individual and a denial of the effectiveness or validity of solutions that emphasize the state or the social dimension.[95] Real-life murderers such as Peter Sutcliffe, Beoria Simmons, and Gary Ridgway targeted prostitutes or women they equated with immoral behavior. In a disturbing parallel, the vast majority of female victims in fictional accounts of serial murder are also portrayed as being immoral and thus not worthy of life. And rarely, if ever, do we cultivate empathy for the victim. Their death, as in their life, is not worthy of our attention.

A similar theme is found in the life-stories of the filmic serial killer. When considered (and not all films explore the killer's childhood), the filmic serial killer most often mirrors a dominant narrative of true-crime fiction and so-called experts: serial killers are associated with familial dysfunction and are raised in non-traditional families, often the product of an unwanted pregnancy or illegitimate birth.[96] Once again, we see the dangers of women not fulfilling their proper nurturing role. Bad mothers produce killers. In short, therefore, the filmic serial killer is a visual manifestation of social conservative moral concerns and fears. In this manner, both killers and victims are held responsible for their own actions. And through film, these actions become consumable images of societal decay.

How then does the filmic serial killer square with the moral impulse of the revanchist city? I maintain that these filmic portrayals represent, first, a particular narrative of 'acceptable death'. Individuals who transgress the normative confines of a hegemonic culture are expendable; their brutal deaths confirm deep-seated and systemic attitudes of the proper place of women in a patriarchal society. Serial killers become the means to an end: the personification of revanchist policies designed to cleanse the public streets of societal vice.

Second, these films—and the pervasive fascination with serial killers, but not their victims—reassure the consuming public of their own proper place in society. Nestled safely within the confines of their gated communities or gentrified townhomes, viewers can titillate themselves in their consumption of brutal, horrific atrocities, secure in their knowledge that the horrific murders only happen *out there* beyond the narrow horizons of their own private utopias.

Some feminists argue that fictional accounts contribute to real-life crimes against women. Unfortunately, such explanations prove too simplistic. One need only consider the number of *female* serial killers—and their own high body-counts—to recognize that violence is not limited to men. Rather, I suggest that the selective representation of serial killers and their victims indicate the obverse. The problem with the literary and filmic representation of serial killers specifically, and of violence more broadly, is *not* that these media necessarily provoke acts of imitative violence or numb their audiences to the consequences of violence. Instead, the public's insatiable appetite for *male-on-female violence* is a consequence (not cause) of a pervasive patriarchy over the right to public space. Within the market-driven film and publishing industry—and here I refer specifically to both slasher films and true-crime writing—producers and publishers provide what the audience demands. And apparently, based on sales figures, the *American* public in particular mostly desires to see young, attractive white women being raped, tortured, and murdered.

The Streets of Ciudad Juárez

> Ciudad Juárez ... "the best city in the world to kill a woman."[97]

Outside of the United States, there are other streets where the killing of young women occurs frequently. The streets of Ciudad Juárez, in northern Mexico, for example, provide another grim example of space, place, and violence.[98] Here, there are many striking parallels with America's revanchist neoliberal city as well as some notable differences. Specifically, in both situations we see the interplay of capitalist imperatives and violence against females. However, unlike the consumable images of dead women in the United States, in Ciudad Juárez, we find an omission of female murders from the public narrative. In this instance, there is no desire among officials to 'capitalize' on the now-routine killing of women; indeed, Mexican authorities have by-and-large reflected the obverse—a disavowal of the killings. Consequently, a comparison between the public's fascination with the serial murder of women in the United States and the on-going femicide of women in Mexico provides important insights into the gendered spatiality of violence.

In Ciudad Juárez, the killings began in the early 1990s. Before 1993, there was an average of three women murdered *each year*; however, in 1993 an average of two women were murdered *each month*. And the killings continued to add up. By 2001 there was at least one woman found dead every week. By 2003, Amnesty International estimated that approximately 400 women had been murdered; other sources indicate that the number is probably considerably higher. Indeed, the number of 400 deaths does not include those women who have disappeared and have never been found.[99]

There has been a publicness to the killings of Ciudad Juárez. Most of the victims have been young women; many were apparently abducted while walking the streets on their commutes between home and work.[100] Of the victims who have been found, their corpses most often reveal signs of extreme violence and brutality.

Why have the streets of Ciudad Juárez been the sight of so much violence? Different authors have highlighted a variety of factors, including the prevalence of a deeply entrenched patriarchal culture, rampant drug trafficking and powerful cartels, illegal migration, and ineffective or corrupt law enforcement agencies.[101] However, another key component—and indeed, one of the prime economic drivers of the region—is the existence of hundreds of export processing zones (maquiladoras) along Mexico's northern border.

In 1965 Mexico initiated the Border Industrialization Program. As Justin Chacón and Mike Davis explain,

> In line with neoliberalism's emphasis on export-driven development and encouraged by the rapid growth of transnational corporations seeking to invest in overseas markets, the Border Industrialization Program ... redirected national efforts at industrialization away from the state and toward foreign capital.[102]

Indeed, the BIP should properly be seen as the complement to the deindustrialization of the United States.

Beset with a balance of payment deficit and a mounting debt, the Mexican government experienced increased intervention by external institutions, such as the International Monetary Fund and the World Bank. Citing both the 'South Korean miracle' and the 'Brazilian miracle', officials of these agencies concluded that rapid economic growth could only materialize through a strategy of export-oriented industrialization. Consequently, U.S. manufacturers were invited to move their factories south across the 2,000-mile-long border between the United States and Mexico to take advantage of lower wage rates, tax exemption, inexpensive electricity rates, and restrictions against unionization and strikes, while Mexican federal subsidies were used to provide needed infrastructure, including state-of-the-art industrial parks, roads, and sewage systems.[103]

Within a matter of years, the northern Mexico border, including Ciudad Juárez, emerged as a leading site for export-processing industrialization. Indeed, according to Chacón and Davis, the "profitability of moving assembly plants to Mexico proved irresistible to U.S. companies."[104] By the turn of the twenty-first century, there were approximately four thousand maquiladoras in Mexico, with a total employment of over one million; almost one-fourth of these workers were employed in maquiladoras located in Ciudad Juárez, and approximately 60 percent of these workers were women.[105]

The hiring practices of many multinational firms, and especially those that participated in Mexico's Border Industrialization Program, were (and remain) rooted in traditional gender-based division of labor that allocated men to the provider role and women to domestic responsibilities; hence, even though women were engaged in the waged labor market, their participation was considered peripheral and thus readily exploitable.[106] Multinational corporations thus benefitted (and continue to benefit) from a reduction in labor costs through the (selective) employment of women by capitalizing on patriarchal institutions, social relations, and gendered stereotypes.[107] Employers, for example, assert that a woman's income is supplemental to the maintenance of the household. Furthermore, these firms maintain that women's factory work is less skilled, given that it is presumed to be an extension of women's household activities. Female workers are coveted for their intrinsic 'feminine qualities' of dexterity, attention to detail, and patience; they are perceived to be perfectly suited for the repetitive minutiae that constitute much of the manufacturing tasks.[108] Indeed, the desire for these 'traits' is especially pronounced in the textile sector, where women are assumed to be 'naturally' adept at sewing. In short, by capitalizing on patriarchal structures which encouraged reduced labor costs, women's comparative disadvantage in the capitalist wage-labor market enhanced the comparative advantage of firms that employed women in the labor-intensive industries.

Another factor that contributed to the feminization of the work-force was the assumption that women workers were seeking only *temporary* employment. With respect to the spaces of violence of Ciudad Juárez this is a factor, that of temporariness, that merits more attention. Multinational firms benefit from the hiring of 'temporary' workers or, in other words, from the deliberate promotion of high labor turnover. According to Wright, turnover refers to "the coming and going of workers into and out of jobs." She explains that many industry analysts and administrators cite turnover as an impediment to the provision of more sophisticated procedures that could be staffed by highly skilled workers; according to these business leaders, workers who do not demonstrate job loyalty are not good prospects for the training necessary for creating a skilled base. Ironically, women who are hired as temporary workers are blamed for their high turnover rates; this, despite the fact that many multinational firms codify specific practices that guarantee high turnover rates. It is not uncommon, for example, for these firms to pay new employees less than the legal minimum wage while the employee undergoes a probationary training period. However, these workers are often dismissed prior to the completion of their training. This practice ensures higher profits through the payment of less-than-minimum wages and, in turn, provides 'evidence' of the temporary nature of women's employment. In the case of Mexican maquiladoras, Wright argues, women represent "workers of declining value since their intrinsic value never appreciates into skill but instead dissipates over time." She concludes that women workers of the maquiladoras personify "waste in the making."[109] In short, their lives are of little or no consequence. The young women workers, in other words, are literally disposable. Such a portrayal of 'cheap female' labor would prove decisive in the response to serial murder.

Initially, the murder of dozens of young women was met with silence. Unlike the moral panic that swept the United States with respect to serial killers lurking behind every lamp-post, in Ciudad Juárez it was as if nothing had happened. Indeed, when it came to the women's murders, the business and political elites abstained from publicly condemning the slayings. Diana Valdez explains that the business leaders benefitted from the labor of young women; the elite owned the industrial parks that leased the buildings to transnational firms; they produced the materials for housing the expanding work-force; and they produced and sold the consumer products purchased by the factory workers.[110] To call attention to widespread murders would significantly jeopardize business.

Only later, following widespread outcry among the residents of Ciudad Juárez, did the political and business elites find themselves needing to respond to growing violence and as Wright identifies, to counter arguments that economic and political programs contributed to the increasing violence. Rather than call attention to the deleterious working conditions and the hyper-exploitation of (especially) female workers along the border, the official response was to shift the blame onto the victims. Remarkably, public officials framed the deaths as a matter of access to public spaces.

When confronted with the mounting deaths, officials were concerned less with the acts of violence, but rather whether the deaths even mattered. Melissa Wright explains that in Mexico the discourse of the 'public woman' is pervasive. According to this discourse, "the public woman has her most famous representative in the figure of 'the prostitute', the consummately public woman who makes her living by selling her body on the street."[111] Wright relates, for example, that when asked why the violence was occurring, a spokesperson for the Ciudad Juárez Maquiladora Association countered with his own question: "Where were these young ladies when they were last seen? Were they drinking? Were they partying? Were they on a dark street?" Wright suggests that in blaming the victims for provoking the violence, and thereby, for not being 'innocent' victims, these leaders reproduced the subject of the public woman as the source of the problem.[112] Likewise, Francisco Barrio Terrazas, governor of the state of Chihuahua, concluded in 1998 that "They are women of doubtful conduct. They are responsible for what happens to them because of the life they lead. They lead a double life and therefore they are exposing themselves to be killed."[113]

The message was clear: respectable women would not be out late at night, unattached and without male protection. Consequently, the death of hundreds of young women says much about public attitudes toward space. Through reference to the 'public woman', officials establish a narrative that "any woman who is a prostitute or *who resembles one* does not represent a legitimate victim of violence because she, through her immoral activities, caused her own problems."[114] And hence, we see a parallel with the attitudes of those activists cleaning the streets of vice in North America and Western Europe; and we see a parallel with the justifications of serial killers themselves. Crucial to our understanding of serial killers, the policing of sex work, and the presence of female maquiladora workers is one of geography: who has a legitimate right to the street? Subsequent acts of violence therefore speak to both the literal and metaphoric 'place' of women within society. As discussed in Chapter Two, respectable women (regardless of whether they are actually selling 'sex' or not) are not to be found on public streets—especially after dark, or engaging in such activities as drinking or partying.

The discourse of the public woman has not gone unchallenged. Wright details how the binary of the public/private woman has been countered, and especially how victims' families and activists have had to respond to charges that the murdered women were somehow culpable for their own demise.[115] For example, Ni Una Mas, a social justice movement, emerged in 2002 to protest and to bring awareness to the on-going femicide. However, this group, and many others, has been charged by the political and business elites as not being legitimate. Indeed, members of Ni Una Mas are likewise portrayed as 'public women' and thus denied legitimacy in public forums. And in a further irony, the political and corporate elites have flipped the neoliberal argument on its head, charging that social justice movements, such as Ni Una Mas, are themselves profiting from the murders.[116]

Moreover, recent years have also indicated that the discourse of the public woman continues to be employed not only in the denial of serial murders, but in the corporate promotion of the city. Here, unlike the moral panic of serial killings in the United States, which served in part to justify gentrification policies and the policing of urban streets, we see a move to deny violence. Stated differently, in the United States, the serial murder of (white) women was promoted, and actually exaggerated, to serve capitalist ends in the neoliberal making of the city; in Ciudad Juárez, conversely, murders are downplayed to serve capitalist ends. As the murders continued into the twenty-first century, public officials redirected their attention to the public streets. This move, however, was not in an effort to resolve the serial murders but rather to remake the image of the city.

Similar to actions undertaken with the revanchist American city, Mexican political and business leaders used the deaths in an effort to 'clean' the city of unwanted vices. This had little to do with eliminating future murders, or even solving the murders, and more to do with the promotion of market imperatives. Thus, by the late 1990s officials in Ciudad Juárez recognized that their city's reputation had "shifted from one of a booming industrial city to that of a violent center of the drug trade, random crime, and outdated manufacturing facilities." Consequently, as Wright details, "In the face of declining corporate investment and the evisceration of tourist revenues, the political and corporate elites of the city ... devised numerous strategies to illustrate new and potential prosperity."[117] Urban boosters, corporate executives, and political elites worked to promote a more 'modern' city, a city safe from crime and vice, a city safe for *foreign* investment and tourism. The end result was a massive campaign to remove the 'public woman' from the street, for these women, whether appearing as maquiladora workers or as prostitutes, signified urban decay and decline. Their removal, their absence, would in turn signify the opposite: urban growth and prosperity.[118]

Wright further notes that "private business leaders have repeatedly criticized activists for drawing attention to the killings, which, they argue, scare away investors." Murder, in other words, is bad for both tourism and private investment. As such, Wright concludes:

> for the urban elites who are invested in portraying Ciudad Juárez as "normal," the attention to the murders, including the finding of corpses and the identification of victims in the public sphere, proves quite costly. ... If the crimes indicate trouble, then the political incumbents are not doing their job. If the victims are innocent, then the police officers are failing to provide protection. If the disappearance of women from public spaces exposes a social and economic system organized around poor, migrant workers who live in violence-stricken and impoverished communities, then the maquiladora industry and the backers of free trade have not delivered on their promise of progress.[119]

Consequently, it makes 'business sense' to consider the victims as less-than-worthy, to blame the women for their own abductions, rape, torture, and murder.

And so we circle back to the revanchist efforts to 'clean up the streets' of North America and Western Europe. In public discourse, female employees of maquiladoras are widely perceived as *disposable*. Hence, even if these women were not prostitutes or runaways, they personify a transgression of proper female behavior; they are essentialized as 'public women' simply by dint of their occupation. Wright concludes that "Such a vision of the Mexican woman as inevitably disposable is common to both the murder and turnover narratives." She explains that at the

> heart of these seemingly disparate story lines is the crafting of the Mexican woman as a figure whose value can be extracted from her, whether it be in the form of her virtue, her organs,

or her efficiency on the production floor. And once 'they', her murderers or her supervisors, 'get what they want from' her, she is discarded.[120]

The arguments of Melissa Wright readily conform with those of Verónica Zebadúa-Yañez. Describing Ciudad Juárez as both a "paradise of impunity" and a *"polis* of death," Zebadúa-Yañez writes that the killings should properly be seen as a political performance. She explains that the ritualized repetition of the killings—the sequence of abduction, torture, rape, strangling, disposal of the body in a public place—conveys a political message, but one that remains too often unspoken. For Zebadúa-Yañez, the killings-as-political performance say:

> You women are nothing! See, no one cares about you! You are not really a part of our society; at most you belong to its fringes; you live in a threshold area in which everything is possible. ... You may be killed, but your death is not punishable.[121]

Conclusions

The street can be a scary place. Deep within the dark recesses of the urban jungle hide strangers and danger. And no figure embodies these fears more than the 'serial killer'. Hiding in the shadows, he stalks his prey with deadly efficiency. No one is safe.

Or so we think. Statistically, serial killings are very rare. But they do populate our television shows, films, and novels with a remarkable regularity. What morbid fascination draws us to the serial killer? How does *his* presence help us think through space, place, and violence? I began this chapter by considering the historical emergence of the serial killer and how this figure has been culturally appropriated as a product of the modern urban landscape. I have suggested that our understanding of the serial killer says more about 'us' than it does about 'him'; that our fascination with serial killers speaks to deeper concerns of a modernizing and urbanizing society. Indeed, we find that the production of the serial killer actually speaks volumes to the *place* and *value* of women in society. In an ironic twist, we see that serial killers *and* urban redevelopers actually speak the same language. Both perceive their duties, their responsibilities—their missions—as one of cleaning up society. This implies a valuation of human life—of lives worth saving and lives worth removing. We have seen that the 'benefits' of urban redevelopment, of the moral claims of societal improvement, echo loudly with the statements of serial killers. Both killer and developer play upon fears of the street, and promote exaggerated claims of disease and danger to justify their actions. In the modern 'post-industrial' city, both urban redevelopers and serial killers claim to be 'cleansing' the city by 'removing' prostitutes. Capitalism, whether in ticket prices for slasher-films or the development of gated communities, profits from the literal and symbolic dismemberment of women.

We have seen how these fears play out cross-culturally. Shifting our geographic focus from the deindustrialized, post-industrial U.S. city to the newly industrialized Mexican city of Ciudad Juárez, we gain a better appreciation of how gendered violence interacts with the demands of capital. Here, amid the rising body count of female factory workers, we counter essentialist claims about street violence and give pause to the place of women in the city. This section, in particular, demonstrates the geographic specificity of who is deemed 'disposable' and who is presumed to have a 'right to the city'.

The 'sex worker/street walker' in the neoliberal city and the 'temporary' worker in the maquiladora: both are perceived as disposable; neither are considered as 'lives worth living'. Our exploration of the spaces and places of the street reveals an all-too-familiar story, one where racist, sexist, and gendered attitudes underlie both the act and the representation of violence. Who is granted the right to participate in public space—and indeed, who is granted the right to live—is thus a component of broader geographical imaginations. Our public streets are political spaces, subject to disciplinary surveillance, control, and violence. For some people, such as prostitutes, their exclusion is perceived as crucial to the betterment of society; for others, such as the maquiladora workers, their inclusion is partial and fleeting, but no less violent. In neither case are the (predominantly) women perceived as anything more than their ascriptive identities as 'immoral' Others. Indeed, their deaths *in place* become crucial signifiers of advanced capitalism.

5

COMMUNITY

The United States of America is a nation of immigration. Such a banal statement, however, oversimplifies the oft-contested nature of population movements both to and within the historical evolution and geographical expansion of the United States. This is particularly salient in the early years of the twenty-first century, as the demographic composition of the country is changing with a rapidity not seen since the early twentieth century. William Clark effectively captures the tension. "The debates about the future of American society," Clark explains, "are encapsulated in the struggle with the change from a white/Anglo-dominated society to a more inclusive mix of peoples." He elaborates that the

> underlying tension pertains to the role of assimilation and the role of the new immigrants in 21st-century America. Will the societal fabric stretch to accommodate the new arrivals, will the new arrivals help to reform the social fabric, or will the fabric tear under the impact?[1]

The concerns of Clark relate directly to those of space, place, and violence, for the simple reason that the *social fabric* is at its core a *spatial fabric*. This analogy is particularly apt, because like textiles, the fabric is composed, or patterned, of many different threads. Conceptually, this metaphor relates to another spatial concept, namely that of *community*. Until recently, geographers and other social scientists have skirted around the concept of 'community'. Too often the concept has been either romanticized and celebrated or dismissed entirely.[2]

The modern theoretical and empirical study of communities is often traced to the German sociologist Ferdinand Tönnies and his 1887 publication *Gemeinschaft und Gesellschaft*.[3] Writing at the end of the nineteenth century, Tönnies identified a *fin-de-siècle* shift. He argued that traditional communities, built around ideas and ideals of kinship, cooperative action, and attachment to *place*, were being replaced, or supplanted, by societies characterized by impersonal relations and *placelessness*.[4] This shift, as David Smith explains, was associated with industrialization and modernity and thus entailed a move from a communitarian identity to an autonomous identity. In the modern age, Tönnies argued, the community had disappeared and people became isolated from each other; *Gesellschaft*, for Tönnies, is artificial and mechanical. Unlike the tradition-bound *Gemeinschaft*, the new society existed merely by convention.[5]

Tönnies' observed shift from *Gemeinschaft* to *Gesellschaft* encompassed a moral transformation. Specifically, a 'partial' and localized morality was replaced by an ever-increasing 'universal' morality. This, according to David Smith, had important relational consequences, one of which was the rise of public welfare services in the cities.[6] Indeed, this is apparent in our earlier discussion of the rise of the modern public school, in that public institutions were viewed as the provider of universal democratic and capitalistic ideals. More immediately, however, this shift—in Western societies, at least—changed how people viewed themselves and their 'place' in the world. According to Smith, "The celebration of individual autonomy and liberty was closely associated with release from a socially assigned place in a spatial and structural moral order, and with freedom to find one's place rather than to know one's place." In other words, people were no longer confined to a rigid, caste-like existence in modern society; people were free (within some key constraints) to explore difference.[7]

Arguably, the apex of *Gesellschaft* occurred, in both North America and Western Europe, during the liberalism of the 1960s. Indeed, the "idea of diversity," as Philip Jenkins explains, became social orthodoxy. Writing specifically of the United States, Jenkins notes that the whole concept of Americanism and American identity was transformed; consequently, different social groups—whether defined by ethnicity, gender, or sexual orientation—proudly maintained their distinctive identities rather than seeking homogenized assimilation.[8] Accordingly, this 'celebration of diversity and difference' entailed a radical *geographical* reimagining of American spaces. From the southern-based lunch counter sit-ins of the Civil Rights movement, to the Stonewall 'riots' of the gay rights movement, ideals of community membership, engagement, and participation were redefined.

Ironically, both socially progressive and conservative debates throughout the 1970s and 1980s challenged the ideal of universal human rights and the promotion of international distributive justice. On the one hand, social conservatives and a broader neoliberal agenda began to critique, attack, and even dismantle the public welfare state in favor of a more parochial worldview. Neoliberalism, as we have seen, is not about the weakening of the state; rather, it is a rearticulation of the roles and goals of the state; a withdrawal from social service provision mixed with a reassertion of the state's role in repression and social control.[9] The criminalization of youth and public schools, for instance, may be viewed as exemplary of this return to *Gemeinschaft*. So too are the zero-tolerance policies and practices designed to 'take back the streets'. Consequently, a 'normative' vision of community was promoted, a vision that relied on particular understandings of community to "solve problems and to integrate marginalized groups"[10] while disinvesting the state from a traditional focus on "well-being and social justice."[11] Group plurality was threatening; it ran counter to the conservative ideals that were represented as the hallmarks of American communal life. Assimilation of these disparate groups into 'mainstream' society was again promoted as the ideal. According to Josh Inwood, these trends have "had a particularly deleterious effect on marginalized communities which have been forced to cope with a system of offering reduced social services and government regulation."[12]

On the other hand, the continued promotion of diversity (as exemplified by some strains of post-modernism and moral relativism) actually undermined the very practices it sought to correct. Indeed, as Iris Young notes, the "exclusionary consequences of valuing community ... are not restricted to bigots and conservatives."[13] Smith, for example, explains that "the rise of post-modern thinking, with its disdain for universalism and encouragement of ethical relativism (or nihilism), undermines the scope for critique of an increasingly unequal world, very much to the disadvantage of those marginalized peoples whom some versions of post-modernism claim to empower." He explains that the return of virulent nationalism, for example, may be one response to a pre-modern and myopic concern with the local and particular.[14]

Given these trends, Young adopts a highly critical view of community. She explains that "the ideal of community denies the difference between subjects and the social differentiation of temporal and spatial distancing." She continues that the "most serious political consequence of the desire for community ... is that it often operates to exclude or oppress those experienced as different." In short, "Commitment to an ideal of community tends to value and enforce homogeneity."[15]

However, as James DeFilippis and his colleagues write, such critiques of community as Young's "bring us dangerously close to political disempowerment by de-legitimizing collective action based on common experiences of oppression and injustice."[16] We need to take caution to not throw the baby out with the bathwater. Following McDowell, therefore, the term 'community' should neither be rejected out of hand, nor automatically seen as either a good or a bad thing. Rather, the complexity of its construction, its purpose, and its policing should be the subject for analysis.[17]

Echoing our understanding of place, DeFilippis et al. assert that "communities need to be understood as simultaneously products of both their larger, and largely external, contexts, and the practices, organizations and relations that take place within them."[18] In Chapter One I provided a working definition of 'places' as *lived and embodied spaces*. Places, in other words, come into being through social relations and social interactions. However, these relations and interactions are morally informed. Who, or which group, for example, is granted or denied access to a particular place? What activities are deemed appropriate or not?

Thus far, we have considered the discipline of home-, school-, and street-spaces in an attempt to disentangle broader questions of the construction of inclusionary and exclusionary spaces. We have seen, for example, that domestic spaces—homes—are often considered private places, and thus not under the purview of the state. Consequently, the 'home' as a private place for personal relations contributed to the perpetuation and often violent enforcement of a heterosexual patriarchy. Likewise, we have seen the promotion of zero-tolerance programs as a means of ridding the school and the public street of 'unwanted' individuals: those deemed criminal, deviant, or abnormal. In all cases, moreover, capitalist ideals have figured prominently in adjudicating the 'worth' of those bodies to be included or excluded. In this penultimate chapter, I consider more closely the discipline of space and the production of place through communal enforcement. Specifically, I consider the geographies of popular sovereignty as reflected in the practices of vigilante groups. I maintain that the rise of modern militias and vigilante groups constitute a *communal* counter-part to the neoliberal and revanchist tendencies of the late twentieth and early twenty-first centuries in North America, Western Europe, and beyond.

Communities and Sovereign Geographies

'Home', as we saw in Chapter Two, constitutes a 'mythic' place, replete with ideals of proper social relations and interactions. Linda McDowell, for example, describes 'community' as a relational, rather than categorical, concept; community is defined both by material social relations and by symbolic meanings; community, in short, parallels the concept of 'home': a fluid network of social relations, context dependent, contingent, infused with power relations and created by mechanisms of inclusion and exclusion.[19] 'Community' likewise retains a mythic, and fundamentally geographic, element. In ordinary speech in the United States, for example, Iris Young notes that the term community refers to the people with whom one identifies in a specific locale.[20] It is thus a concept that evokes *commonality*; an inclusive social group that shares particular values, beliefs, and morals. Community likewise implies a sense of security and solidarity; a togetherness often infused with a sense of purpose. For many observers, there is an implicit assumption that a 'lack' of community is a bad thing.[21]

Significantly, communities must be both defined and defended. As Stuart Aitken writes, if we assume that 'community', with its vague and generally nurturing meanings, is usually something that people desire, then it must be something people do not yet have (or fear losing) in the way that they want.[22] 'Community' entails a particular—and vulnerable—representation of space. In the United States, this is seen most clearly in the promotion of the 'American Dream', of the ideal to own a single-family, detached house, complete with white picket fence. To this end, Aitken notes that

> some families are attracted to media-perpetuated images of communities where children can be nurtured in safe environments replete with walls, security gates, and speed bumps, while their fear of urban violence is refracted onto the communities portrayed on reality television shows.[23]

Ideals of community thus underscore our discussion of the public street (Chapter Four). There, we saw how neighborhood—*community*—groups often band together in an attempt to rid the streets of unwanted and undesirable bodies: the homeless, the indigent, the prostitutes. Operating hand-in-hand with state and local law enforcement agencies, corporate real estate developers, and financial offices, numerous community 'protest' groups engage in grass-roots efforts to 'cleanse' the public streets of their community.

The promotion of 'community' is thus inseparable from both a discussion of discipline and a concern with socio-spatial exclusion. As David Sibley writes, "Who is felt to belong and not to belong contributes in an important way to the shaping of social space."[24] Amartya Sen captures this dualistic nature of 'community'. He notes, on the one hand, that a

> sense of identity can make an important contribution to the strength and warmth of our relations with others, such as

neighbors, or members of the same community, or fellow citizens, or followers of the same religion. Our focus on particular identities can enrich our bonds and make us do many things for each other and can help to take us beyond our self-centered lives.

However, on the other hand, Sen concedes that:

> a sense of identity can firmly exclude many people even as it warmly embraces others. The well-integrated community in which residents instinctively do absolutely wonderful things for each other with great immediacy and solidarity can be the very same community in which bricks are thrown through the windows of immigrants who move into the region from elsewhere.[25]

When we ask, therefore, who has the authority to include or exclude, we are properly talking about sovereignty and the right to public space. And very often, specific collectivities, or social groups, assume the right to decide (and police) matters of communal, or civic, participation. Remarkably diverse in both organization and ideology, these community-based organizations may be considered as 'vigilantes'.[26]

While the term 'vigilante' is controversial and difficult to define, it is, as Roxanne Doty explains, particularly useful in our discussion of communal violence.[27] Etymologically, the term 'vigilante' was originally a Spanish word, derived from the same Latin roots as the English words 'vigil', 'vigilant', and 'vigilance'.[28] Thus, the word connotes the act of 'watching' or 'guarding'. There is, furthermore, an inherent geographic component to the term, in that it is generally assumed that what one watches over is in fact a *place*. And indeed, the emergence of vigilante groups is most often associated with frontier areas: spaces at the periphery of state oversight.

Numerous historical accounts, from the United States to the United Kingdom, from southern America to southern Africa, have documented the activities of vigilantes. And despite the diversity of these groups, historians have identified some key commonalities. Perhaps most significant, these disparate groups tend to share the belief of the public's inherent right to monitor and regulate their own spaces—with or without governmental support or intervention. As Doty explains, vigilantism is intimately connected with sovereignty and it entails at least an implicit relationship to the law, and by extension, to the state.[29]

Vigilante groups typically have very clear (and geographically based) ideas and understandings about the place and the role of the state in communal life. Community groups, for example, are often contrasted with the state wherein the personalized, caring nature of social relations within small communities contrasts sharply with the impersonal and uncaring attitudes of the state.[30] Communities however are also frequently concerned about their own common (and largely self-defined) interests—and how best to protect those interests. In some respects, the return of a revanchist *Gemeinschaft* highlights the tension between individual and community rights. To the extent that the state is required to protect the rights of *all* individuals, regardless of, say, legal status, the aspirations and demands of some communities may be perceived to be in jeopardy. The ideal of universal human rights and the protection of undocumented migrants, for example, may be seen by some vigilante groups to trump individual rights. The state is perceived as reneging on its obligation to the community (*Gemeinschaft*) in favor of extending its commitment to the support of 'foreign' individuals (*Gesellschaft*). In fact, vigilantism (as a form of popular sovereignty) finds fertile soil in the revanchist practices of the current neoliberal order. And perhaps this accounts also for the fascination with the 'outlaw' serial killer who single-handedly cleans up the mean streets of society.

When vigilantes perceive a threat to their security, a sense of emergency is generated and with it a willingness to take extraordinary measures, including violence. And while legal channels may be used to impel the state into action, communal members may also use direct action—vigilante justice—against the threat itself. Community groups are therefore *not* revolutionary in the sense that they seek to abolish or overthrow the state. Indeed, many vigilante groups are formed to prevent *other* groups from disrupting or overthrowing the state. Far from being revolutionary, vigilante groups are best understood, politically, as being reactionary in their attempts to promote and protect their own values and ways of life that are viewed to be under attack.[31] Therefore, in defense of their extra-legal, and often violent, actions, community members claim that the state has failed 'the people'; they are demanding that the state be *more* sovereign, that it forcefully exercises its sovereignty.[32]

In earlier chapters we saw that violence is 'purposive behavior'; that most perpetrators of violence—whether they be abusive partners in intimate relationships, or bullies picking on smaller children on the school-yard—understand their behavior as being both rational and justified. Vigilante violence is no different, in that vigilantes typically lay claim to the moral high ground as the guardians of society.[33] This is a crucial point, and one that separates vigilante violence from mob violence. Whereas mob violence is associated with spontaneous, unorganized, and uncoordinated acts of violence (i.e., looting and rampaging), vigilantism is viewed as a form of 'establishment violence', wherein violence, or the threat of violence, is both planned and purposive toward *a particular end or goal.*[34] Indeed, vigilantism as planned, pre-meditated, and organized violence constitutes the first of five key characteristics of vigilante violence. As Les Johnston explains, for vigilantism to occur, the participating agent must engage in some form of preparatory activity—such as the surveillance of an intended victim or the observation of a particular location.[35] In other words, there is a disciplining both of individuals and of space; vigilante activities thus emerge as crucial components in the production of place.

Second, vigilantism is engaged by *private* (i.e., non-state) agents; these agents, moreover, may or may not be recognized by the state. In the case of neighborhood watch organizations, these collectivities are clearly sanctioned and sponsored by the state. Conversely, other organizations (such as the Black Panther Party) are themselves repressed by state agencies. A third and related characteristic, therefore, is that vigilantism is a voluntary activity engaged in by 'active citizens' without the state's sanctioned authority or support.[36] Keep in mind that the state may *tolerate* and even *encourage* these activities, but ultimately vigilantism is seen as a private initiative. Indeed, as alluded to above, vigilantism most frequently arises because the concerned action group believes that the state has failed in its responsibilities.

A fourth component of vigilante violence is that it is directed toward specific individuals or groups. Vigilante violence is far from random but instead purposeful in intent. Frequently, the targets of vigilante justice are those individuals who belong to morally excluded groups, such as gang members, drug users and dealers, prostitutes, or the homeless. Targeted individuals may also belong to marginalized or 'foreign' groups or people that are perceived as threatening the homogeneity of society (e.g., gays, lesbians, bisexuals, transgendered, immigrants, feminists, communists, labor union organizers, and so on). To this end, vigilante justice entails a fifth (and related) characteristic, namely that this form of violence carries a normative dimension. Vigilantism arises when some established social (or spatial) order is perceived to be under threat from the transgression (or potential transgression) of communal norms. Vigilantism is thus "a reaction to real or perceived deviance."[37]

Vigilante violence, in sum, is an extreme form of socio-spatial discipline. It is a collective practice that emerges in response to perceived social threats and transgressions; its purpose is to promote and to maintain a particular *place*. At this point, as illustration, we turn our attention to the place-making of the U.S.–Mexico border.

Shifting Borders, Shaping Communities

> The same people were suddenly different.[38]

The interesting thing about borders is that they become an enduring feature of one's nationalized geographical imagination. Those who decry the movement of Mexican migrants across the U.S.–Mexico border, for example, often question why they (the Mexicans) don't just stay in their own country. What these outspoken proponents of strict immigration control fail to acknowledge is that many of the places that comprise the southern tier of the United States once *belonged* to Mexico. Indeed, these territories only became part of the United States following the Mexican–American War of 1846–1848.[39]

As stipulated by the Treaty of Guadalupe Hildalgo, the Mexican government ceded California, Arizona, New Mexico, Nevada, Utah, Colorado, and parts of Wyoming and Oklahoma to the United States; additionally, the Mexican government dropped all claims to Texas. In return, the United States' government paid a token U.S.$15 million for what amounted to nearly half of Mexico's territory and three-fourths of its natural resources.[40] Overnight, approximately 125,000 Mexican citizens found themselves living as outsiders in a foreign state.

Despite the presence of an 'international border', throughout much of its existence, the U.S.–Mexico border has *not* been regulated. Indeed, as Nevins explains, the continued economic transactions and social networks that daily served to bind the United States and Mexico throughout the many border towns meant that residents had to be 'taught' how to accept and embrace the line.[41] In other words, border enforcement meant that existent communities were gradually but inexorably sundered—but only to the extent that federal authorities deemed appropriate.

According to Peter Andreas, the United States and Mexico not only quietly tolerated but actively facilitated and encouraged the influx of workers across the border.[42] This is not to say that there was no oversight of the border. Throughout the 1880s, for example, U.S. border officials, known as 'Chinese inspectors', were created to stop the influx of illegal Chinese immigrants. Beginning in 1875 with the Page Law, followed by the more restrictive 1882 Chinese Exclusion Act, laborers from China were prohibited from entering the United States. In response, however, Mexico became a conduit for smuggling Chinese laborers into the United States. Having crossed the Pacific Ocean into Mexico, prospective Chinese migrants would gather south of the California–Mexico border, at cities such as Ensenada, Guaymas, or Mazatlán. From there they would pay five dollars to be transported to the border, and another 40 dollars to be smuggled into California.[43]

Ironically, border enforcement was directed also against European immigrants. In 1921 Congress passed a temporary immigration act that represented the first quantitative immigration law based on national origin. The system was made permanent in 1924 with the passage of the Johnson-Reed Act. According to the Immigration Act of 1924, immigrants of any nationality were limited to 2 percent of the 1890 population of that nationality, as counted by the U.S. census. In intent, the 1921 and 1924 acts were designed to limit, if not eliminate, immigration from southern and eastern Europe. Consequently, a clandestine system to smuggle illegal Europeans from Mexico into the United States was established.

As border control agents worked to stop the inflow of Asians and southern and eastern Europeans from entering the country, Mexican workers not only could enter relatively easily, they were also actively recruited. Indeed, strict controls against Mexicans crossing the border were widely perceived as neither viable nor desirable.[44] As other supplies of migrant workers were barred, an ever-greater need for Mexican workers grew. In the United States, for example, the rapid expansion of agriculture throughout the southwest (but especially in California) necessitated larger numbers of workers; these shortages, of course, were compounded by the restrictions imposed on Asian immigration. Likewise, America's entry into the First World War in 1917 led to significant labor shortages in many sectors of the U.S. economy. Mexican workers in particular were recruited to meet these demands. Between 1901 and 1920, there were 268,646 Mexicans admitted legally into the United States.[45]

Economic transformations within Mexico likewise contributed to the growing movement of people. For one thing, American corporations began to entrench themselves into the Mexican economy. By 1920, for example, U.S. corporations controlled 80 percent of Mexico's railroads, 81 percent of its mining industry, and 61 percent of total investment in Mexico's oil fields.[46] To satisfy huge labor demands, American companies actively sought Mexican laborers to build and maintain railroad lines and to work in the mines and oil fields. And Mexican labor was increasingly easy to obtain. Throughout the late nineteenth and early twentieth centuries, the consolidation of the hacienda system displaced a growing peasant population from its traditional, and communal, system of land tenure. These changes generated a massive surplus of landless workers who lacked both access to land and reliable sources of employment.[47] By 1910, approximately 96 percent of all Mexican farming families were landless. These conditions continued throughout the twentieth century. Between 1940 and 1980, for example, 20 percent of Mexico's arable land was controlled by just 2 percent of the population; the remaining lands were distributed among medium, small, and subsistence farmers.[48] The majority of Mexican citizens, however, had no access to land.

Denied access to land and livelihood, many Mexicans looked northward for employment opportunities. And in the United States, a plethora of American business interests welcomed these landless workers. Mexican workers served as a reserve army of labor. They could be paid less than 'American' workers and, strategically, could be leveraged against unionized workers.[49] And they were (and remain) largely expendable. Historically, American corporate and government authorities have preferred to recruit and hire Mexican laborers via temporary migration agreements; this practice, according to Patricia Zamudio, has the advantage of being flexible enough to be used in times of need and discarded when no longer needed.[50] During the Great Depression, for example, upwards of half a million Mexicans—including permanent residents and U.S. citizens of Mexican descent—were deported.[51]

America's entry into the Second World War precipitated a major change in U.S.–Mexico border policies. In face of incipient labor shortages in agriculture, the U.S. government in 1942 launched a contract labor program, known as the 'Bracero Program', which allowed Mexican laborers to engage in farm work legally in the United States on a temporary basis. Throughout the existence of the Bracero Program (1942–1964), approximately five million temporary labor contracts were issued to Mexican citizens.[52] However, the demand for braceros surpassed the number allowed by the program and American employers engaged in the large-scale hiring of undocumented workers. In turn, the U.S. government initiated numerous programs that would 'legalize' the undocumented workers.[53]

Ironically, the Bracero Program epitomized the often Janus-faced approach of the American government toward Mexican immigration. Thus, while permitting both legal and undocumented workers into the United States, the U.S. government simultaneously launched a massive deportation campaign known as 'Operation Wetback'. Vocal segments of American society, most notably labor unions, charged Mexican workers with depressing wages and displacing 'American' workers. In response, U.S. authorities apprehended and deported over one million undocumented Mexican workers.[54] Such is the quixotic nature of U.S.–Mexico border enforcement where one hand encourages immigration from Mexico while the other hand discourages the movement. Rather than a barrier, the border was a revolving door.

In 1964 the Bracero Program was officially terminated.[55] However, as Zamudio explains, the legacy of the Bracero Program remains especially salient. During the life of the program, for example, Mexican migrants acquired significant knowledge about how to cross the border and how to acquire jobs; key social networks and organizations were established to facilitate cross-border movement; and consequently, a significant movement of 'undocumented' workers developed.[56] According to Peter Andreas, the illegal nature of the post-Bracero migration benefitted both U.S. employers and the federal government. For employers, on the one hand, the undocumented status of the workers assured compliance and low wages. Lacking legal protection, undocumented laborers were less likely to organize or to complain about poor working conditions. For the federal government, on the other hand, it was no longer seen as being complicit in a work-program that supposedly 'stole' American jobs, nor was it seen as supporting a guest-worker program that was rife with inhumane working conditions.[57] In short, the elimination of the Bracero Program was an occasion from which both sides of the political spectrum could benefit.

Since the cessation of the Bracero Program, Mexican immigration—but especially undocumented immigration—continues to be one of the main sources of cheap labor for U.S. employers.[58] Consequently, the U.S.–Mexican border emerges as a key site from which to understand the intersection of space, place, and violence. To begin, we should recognize, as Andreas does, that the U.S. and Mexican governments' approach to border enforcement is starkly different. In short, how the space of the border is represented is extremely important. On the Mexican side, for example, border administration is seen primarily as a social and economic matter; on the U.S. side, conversely, border control is largely seen as a law enforcement matter.[59] However, as Chacón and Davis explain, the underlying idea of the border on the American side as a means to prevent movement has been neither the intention nor the reality.[60] It is significant to note (as discussed later) that vigilante groups commonly articulate the notion that the U.S. government is unable or unwilling to secure its southern border with Mexico. Historically, this is an accurate statement. It has been to the benefit of U.S. manufacturing and agricultural interests, among others, to maintain a porous border and, in fact, to promote 'undocumented' migration.[61] This is perhaps best illustrated in the Immigration Reform and Control Act (IRCA), passed by the U.S. Congress and signed into law by President

Ronald Reagan in 1986. Among its provisions were opportunities for undocumented immigrants to legalize their status. However, IRCA also introduced for the first time sanctions against employers who knowingly hired undocumented migrants. Specifically, IRCA required that employers verify that potential employees are able to work legally in the United States. In practice, though, IRCA was only minimally enforced and contained numerous loopholes that actually benefitted employers who hired undocumented workers. IRCA, for example, applied only to employees who were hired for more than three days. Consequently, contractors (especially those in the construction and landscaping sectors) could regularly visit the same day-labor site and hire the same laborers, day-after-day. Employment was technically informal but, in reality, could become quasi-permanent. For the employer, such an arrangement was ideal. The employers had access to a steady supply of cheap workers; did not have to pay benefits; and did not have to worry about unions, strikes, or work conditions. If a worker became too 'unruly', he simply wasn't hired; likewise, if a worker complained about his pay or his work conditions, the employer could threaten to inform the authorities about the workers' illegal status.

Nevertheless, *communal* concerns of the negative consequences of undocumented migration have spawned a burgeoning 'border control industry'. Beginning in the 1970s, for example, U.S. administrations supported an increasingly militarized and defensive southern border. Under the presidential administrations of Gerald Ford and Jimmy Carter, for instance, new technologies were introduced to ostensibly stem the tide of undocumented immigration from Mexico. These efforts intensified under the administration of Ronald Reagan, as increased U.S. military involvement in Central America led to a surge in refugees from both Nicaragua and El Salvador. For his part, President Reagan played upon long-standing nativistic fears of thieves, murderers, and rapists flowing uncontrolled into the United States. In turn, funds for the U.S. Border Patrol increased by 130 percent. Border communities likewise witnessed an expansion of federal detention centers, immigration checkpoints, and border patrol agents.

Border security and immigration reform emerged as crucial national concerns and in many respects California was at the forefront of this scalar shift. Throughout the 1980s and early 1990s, an estimated

400,000 people were migrating—both 'legally' and 'extralegally'—to California; this was a time, however, when the state's economy was in turmoil.[62] This economic insecurity, coupled with a rapidly changing (and highly publicized) demographic profile, renewed nativist fears among California's disproportionately white, middle class electorate.[63] These fears were codified in Proposition 187, known as the 'Save Our State' initiative.[64]

Proponents of the bill were angry, in part, that existing federal immigration controls, including employer sanctions, largely failed to contain the flow of undocumented workers.[65] Furthermore, proponents argued that undocumented workers stole jobs, utilized scarce public resources, and generally led to a decline in California's overall quality of life. In light of these concerns, Proposition 187 contained five major sections. First, the bill barred undocumented migrants from the state's public education system—from kindergarten through university. Consequently, the bill required public educational institutions to verify the legal status of students and parents. Second, all providers of publicly paid, non-emergency health services were required to verify the legal status of persons seeking services. Third, all persons seeking cash assistance and other benefits were required to verify their legal status, while fourth, all providers of services were to report suspected undocumented migrants to both the Attorney General of California and the Immigration and Naturalization Service. Fifth, the making, distribution, and/or use of false documents to obtain public benefits or employment by concealing one's legal status were made state felonies.[66] Although many proponents understood that key provisions of the bill would most likely be declared unconstitutional, they justified the bill on the grounds that it was explicitly designed and promoted as a symbolic gesture to express local frustration and to 'send a message' to the federal government.

As Chacón and Davis explain, border control and immigration reform are largely acts of political theater.[67] The theatrics surrounding Proposition 187 were no exception. In the months leading to election day, California's embattled governor, Pete Wilson became a vocal supporter of the bill. Facing a floundering campaign, Wilson blamed California's economic misfortunes on the federal government's inability to control the border. And in fact, at one point, Wilson pledged, "For Californians who work hard, pay taxes and obey the laws, I am suing to force the federal government to control the border and I'm working to deny state services to illegal immigrants. Enough is enough."[68] Remarkably, as Andreas reminds us, in previous years Governor Wilson had asked for a relaxation of border controls so that Mexican workers could cross the border to apply for special agricultural workers' visas.[69] Equally remarkable is that in the aftermath of the passage of Proposition 187, California Attorney General Dan Lungren called for a new guest-worker program that would bring temporary agricultural workers into the state.[70]

California's anti-immigrant sentiment helped elevate border control and immigration reform to the national level. Although border control was initially a low priority for President Bill Clinton, it soon rose in importance. In part, Clinton's approach to immigration control was in response to a Republican-dominated Congress. Not wanting to be seen as 'soft' on border enforcement, Clinton facilitated one of the largest expansions of the INS. Throughout the mid- to late 1990s, for example, the budget of the INS tripled.[71] It was also under the Clinton administration that a series of military-styled border enforcement policies were initiated. The first was Operation Gatekeeper, launched in 1994 as a means of securing a 66-mile stretch along the California–Mexico border. Operation Gatekeeper, which would later be expanded into Yuma, Arizona, was followed by other border enforcement campaigns, including Operation Safeguard (in Nogales, Arizona), Operation Hold the Line (initially in Texas, later expanded into New Mexico), and Operation Rio Grande (also in Texas). Combined, these military-based operations constitute the centerpiece of a broader strategy to supposedly secure and regulate the U.S.–Mexico border. Apart from the deployment of ever-larger numbers of border patrol agents—by 2005 the Border Patrol had become the largest federal law enforcement body, with over twelve thousand agents in the field[72]—the Immigration and Naturalization Service (and later the Department of Homeland Security) has availed itself of the latest military hardware. Thus, throughout the border, all manner of high-tech surveillance equipment has been installed, including underground heat sensors, infrared night-scopes, encrypted radios, computerized finger-printing equipment, and Black Hawk helicopters. Moreover, hundreds upon hundreds of miles of steel and concrete fences have been erected.

Border enforcement, not unlike the militarization and securitization of public schools, has become big business. Increasingly, defense contractors compete with each other to gain control of the emergent market of border enforcement; likewise, private security firms have sought to capitalize on the (in)security of the border. In an ironic twist, many 'security' corporations benefit from a porous border; indeed, for many of these corporations, it is important for their own bottom line to have undocumented migration continue.

Despite (or because of?) the billions of dollars injected into border enforcement, this militarization of space has been largely ineffective in stemming the movement of 'undocumented' migrants. Indeed, some studies suggest border policing fails to address one of the largest avenues of 'undocumented' immigration, namely the over-staying of visas. In fact, some studies estimate that upwards of 50 percent of the unauthorized immigrants in the United States have not entered illegally, but have simply overstayed their visas.[73] In other words, policing the border in an attempt to stop 'illegal' migrants would at best address only half of the so-called problem.

But of course, as the history of U.S.–Mexican border relations demonstrates, the border program "is not intended to halt the flow of migration so much as to rechannel it through less visible routes."[74] Andreas concludes that by disrupting traditional routes and methods of clandestine entry, the intensified border control campaign transformed the relatively simple illegal act of crossing the border into a more complex system of illegal practices. He explains that previously, unauthorized entry primarily involved either self-smuggling or the limited use of a local 'coyote'. Now, however, with the escalation of border policing, migrants required the services of 'professional' smugglers.[75]

It should come as no surprise, therefore, that the increased militarization of the border, coupled with the deepening penetration by criminal organizations to facilitate undocumented migration, has led to the border becoming a more violent place. Trans-border smuggling is estimated to be an 8-billion dollar industry; the practice is rife with stories of extortion, robberies, beatings, rape, and murder. Most egregious, however, has been the fact that these disciplinary practices have rechanneled migrant routes not only into less visible but also more violent environments.

Consider Operation Gatekeeper. This program formed but one component of a larger national strategy of border enforcement which was, according to Maria Jimenez, a "strategy of 'prevention through deterrence' to thwart unauthorized border crossings in populated urban areas with a visible display of Border Patrol agents and resources to redirect migrants toward remote, inhospitable areas."[76] Jimenez elaborates that the "deployment of personnel, equipment, technology and border infrastructure to population centers with the intent of channeling migrant flows to remote, dangerous areas became the standard method of dealing with undocumented border crossers."[77] In certain respects, this was an act of political theater. A high profile strategy of border enforcement in populated areas ensured ample publicity, thereby providing 'evidence' that politicians were committed to securing the border. However, given that the strategic practices did not stem the flow of border crossings, but rather shifted the point of entry to less populated regions, the policy also worked to 'hide' unauthorized border crossings. In short, migrants continued to cross the border; they did so, however, out of sight of the general public, thereby giving the impression that the policy was in fact reducing the number of unauthorized border crossers. According to Jimenez, these enforcement measures had not had an impact on the numbers of unauthorized migrants; in fact, between 2000 and 2008 the population of 'undocumented' migrants in the United States *increased* by 40 percent, from an estimated 8.4 million to 11.9 million.[78]

Joseph Nevins writes of a "shifting geography of migrant fatalities."[79] Maria Jimenez speaks of "death by policy." Both acknowledge that the dramatic buildup of a militarized boundary enforcement infrastructure has led to an increasing number of border-crossing related fatalities. The exact number is unknown; various sources indicate that between 3,800 and 5,600 migrants have died attempting to cross the U.S.–Mexican border since 1994. Whichever number is 'correct', this translates to more than one migrant death *per day*.[80]

Most migrant deaths have resulted from exposure to extreme temperatures and a lack of water. Others have drowned in an attempt to cross the All American Canal and other bodies of water. As Jimenez writes, "Death accompanied migrants with every new path carved in isolated, inhospitable terrain in order to circumvent stepped up resources and fencing around population centers."[81]

There is another component of the 'strategy by deterrence' approach that has contributed to an escalation of violence along the border— a component that is intimately tied to our discussion of community. Since 1994, Operations Gatekeeper, Hold the Line and so forth have redirected unauthorized crossings into more and more desolate areas; these are spaces *lacking* an official government presence. Consequently, for the residents of these areas, it appears as if the federal government has abrogated its responsibility of securing the border. Such a perception has contributed to the growth of vigilante-styled groups and, in the process, has contributed to the scale and scope of violence throughout the border region.

(B)ordering Communities

The emergence of civilian groups patrolling America's border communities is not a recent phenomenon.[82] Vigilante groups have a long and complex history in the United States and include such diverse organizations as the Ku Klux Klan (KKK), the Black Panther Party, and the Guardian Angels. The recent growth and spread of vigilantes, however, provides insight into the shifting intersections of space and violence and, crucially, speaks to questions of community and of belonging. To label these disparate vigilante groups as simply or solely 'anti-immigrant' is somewhat deceptive and misleading. These groups are remarkably diverse, and approach immigration and border control from a variety of perspectives. And whereas many are indeed both socially and economically conservative, and in general argue that undocumented immigration dilutes American culture, burdens the social welfare system, and contributes to Americans' unemployment, these groups also operate with very different philosophies and strategies to effect change.

An early example of contemporary border vigilantism was the Klan Border Watch, centered on San Ysidro, California. Founded in 1977 by KKK Grand Dragon Tom Metzger and Imperial Wizard David Duke, the Klan Border Watch patrolled the U.S.–Mexico border in an attempt to halt the flow of Mexican migrants. Similarly, in 1989 a group of private citizens gathered in their cars along a road overlooking the San Diego–Tijuana border. At night, they would beam their headlights along the border in an attempt to deter would-be migrants from crossing. Known as the 'Light Up the Border' campaign, these forms of protest, surveillance, and deterrence continued into the early 1990s.[83] Other groups were (and are) decidedly more aggressive than the 'Light Up the Border' participants. One such group is Ranch Rescue, founded in 2000 in Arlington, Texas, ostensibly to protect the property rights of U.S. citizens. Ranch Rescue conducts 'operations' throughout the southwest, as patrols of armed civilians and hunting dogs track and capture undocumented migrants, to be held until Border Patrol officers arrive.[84]

Vigilante groups proliferated in parallel with the increased militarization of the border. In 2003 Chris Simcox formed the Civil Homeland Defense (CHD) in Tombstone, Arizona. Concerned over what he saw as a lack of security along the U.S.–Mexico border, combined with fears that terrorists might exploit the porous border, Simcox and some friends began to offer their 'services' to local ranchers as private security guards. Soon, they began to actively patrol the border region. For new recruits into the CHD, the only requirement for membership was a concealed gun permit issued by the state of Arizona.[85]

In 2004 Simcox teamed with retired California businessman James Gilchrist to form the 'Minuteman Project'—an endeavor designed both to provide security and surveillance along the border and to raise national awareness regarding the threat of an uncontrolled border. An early 'success' for the Minuteman Project was a month-long campaign launched in April 2005. Hundreds of volunteers—many of whom were from out of state—patrolled a 64-mile stretch of the Arizona–Mexico border. The operation became a major publicity event and did in fact spur the formation of other border patrol groups. Within a year, however, Simcox split from Gilchrist and the Minuteman Project to form the Minuteman Civil Defense Corps (MCDC). Whereas Gilchrist's Minuteman Project focused most of its efforts on targeting U.S. companies that hired undocumented migrants, Simcox's MCDC continued both to patrol the border and to picket sites where Mexican day-laborers were hired.[86] Indeed, until its disbandment in spring 2010, the MCDC achieved a national prominence, with chapters established throughout California, Minnesota, New York, and Oregon.[87]

According to the Southern Poverty Law Center, there are currently 173 groups that constitute the nativist extremist movement. Although many are 'chapters' of either the MCDC or the Minuteman Project, many others have no formal connections. Such groups include the Border Guardians, Mothers Against Illegal Aliens, Arizona Freedom Riders, and the Border Patriot Alliance.[88] And although the animus of these groups—a perceived uncontrolled border with Mexico and the 'invasion' of thousands of 'illegal' immigrants—has as its focal point the southwestern states of California, Arizona, New Mexico, and Texas, the diffusion of vigilantism has been more widespread. Currently, anti-immigrant groups have established themselves in nearly all states of the Union, regardless of the presence (or absence) of 'undocumented' migrants.

Whether labeled militias, vigilantes, or border patrol groups, these social collectives present themselves as 'citizen-victims', concerned community members who feel imperiled by loss of order and normalcy.[89] Indeed, according to Andreas, the loss-of-control theme provides a powerful narrative—not only for vigilante groups, but also for politicians and other authorities. For law enforcement advocates, for example, the "seductively simple justification for escalation can be used to provoke alarm and mobilize support for further escalation."[90] Reminiscent of the moral panic (and often inflated statistics) surrounding serial murders in the 1970s and 1980s, those institutions tasked with border enforcement have witnessed substantial budgetary increases.

Furthermore, as Andreas explains, the stress on a *loss* of control understates the degree to which the U.S. government has, on the one hand, structured conditions and facilitated clandestine border crossings. Apart from the aforementioned guest-worker and amnesty programs initiated by the United States, other policies have served to more fully integrate—albeit unequally—the economic ties between the United States and Mexico. Consider, for example, the establishment of the North American Free Trade Agreement (NAFTA) in 1994. Among its many provisions, NAFTA guaranteed that the Mexican government would not interfere with the activities of foreign corporations operating in Mexico; the agreement also contained no binding protection for unions, wages, or displaced workers.[91] The consequences of the trade agreement were predictably devastating. In the industrial sector, approximately 40 percent of Mexico's clothing manufacturers went out of business, unable to compete with foreign corporations that were able to import cheaper fabrics from Asia. Other industries, such as toy, leather, and foot-ware manufacturers, also were adversely affected. Overall, an estimated one million jobs were lost in Mexico as a result of NAFTA.[92] Mexico's agricultural sector was similarly hard-hit. Following the passage of NAFTA, American-grown corn and grains flooded the Mexican market. Consequently, by 2004 over 1.3 million small farmers in Mexico were forced into bankruptcy.[93] And in the devastating aftermath of this economic tsunami, employers in the United States continued to benefit from these massive surpluses of displaced labor.

On the other hand, the loss of control theme overstates the degree to which the government has been able to control its borders in the past. In fact, as Andreas concludes, "there actually never was a time when the border was effectively controlled."[94] If anything, the border has served to regulate labor in a way that has facilitated the accumulation of capital.[95] It is thus insightful to consider those corporations and industries *opposed* to immigration control: the American Farm Bureau, the American Health Care Association, and the American Nursery and Landscape Association. For many of these sectors, undocumented migrants have always provided a ready supply of cheap, exploitable workers.

It is not uncommon, however, for these deeper, structural conditions and relations to be lost amid the salvos of simplistic and reductionist sound-bites that are shot between and among the participants of the 'border wars'. More typical are emotional and heartfelt pleas that speak to loss.

But what, exactly, is being *lost*? At a certain level, it appears as if a mythical ideal of community is at risk. If 'community', as discussed earlier, is commonly associated with emotions and feelings of security and belonging, if community is something that is actively sought, then it is also something that people would act to defend if threatened. To be sure, one might question why not substitute 'nationalism' or 'patriotism' for 'community'. And one would be hard-pressed to challenge such an argument. However, community also speaks more to 'places' that are *lived* and *experienced* day-by-day. Community is thus felt as something that is particularly local, but also intensely *personal*. Community, in short, is about belonging.

To belong to a community is, on the one hand, a legal question. We might consider the issue of citizenship, for example, and therefore the access to certain resources. And indeed, the status of citizenship and legality figure prominently in the debates over immigration. 'Undocumented' migrants, vigilante groups assert, are *illegal* and thus engaged in criminal actions. For these self-proclaimed purveyors of justice, the issue is about sovereignty, and about addressing the inability or unwillingness of the U.S. government to provide security from 'dangerous' criminals. Anti-immigration efforts are thus as much about disciplining the U.S. government as they are about disciplining 'undocumented' migrants.

Aside from legal concerns, questions of belonging are also spatial: to belong is to be *some place*. This spatial dimension, however, cannot be reduced simply to a question of territorial integrity—although this is indeed a strong component, one that closely intertwines with distinctions between 'legal' and 'illegal'. Rather, to belong is to relate with others. In Chapter One I suggested that spaces are produced through social relations and interactions, and that we are socialized (disciplined) into an understanding of these spaces as normal and natural. However, these socially produced spaces, these disciplined places, must be actively constructed and maintained. Communities, similar to homes, schools, and streets, are constituted through social relations and questions of belonging come to be defined through these social relations.

Belonging always entails a process of inclusion as well as exclusion. Indeed, as Sen explains, a "strong—and exclusive—sense of belonging to one group can in many cases carry with it the perception of distance and divergence from other groups."⁹⁶ And within these strong sentiments of social *and* spatial distance and divergence, violence emerges as a crucial practice in the process of disciplining place.

Likewise, belonging, as a member of a particular group or community, is rarely a matter of choice. Identity formation, as explained elsewhere, is both relational and contextual; who we 'choose' to be, and of which communities we seek entrance, is informed by pre-existing structures, institutions, and norms. Furthermore, we live our lives not in the 'singular' but in the 'plural'. As Sen writes,

> In our normal lives, we see ourselves as members of a variety of groups—we belong to all of them. A person's citizenship, residence, geographic origin, gender, class, politics, profession, employment, food habits, sports interests, taste in music, social commitments, etc., make us members of a variety of groups. Each of these collectives, to all of which this person simultaneously belongs, gives her a particular identity. None of them can be taken to be the person's only identity or singular membership category.⁹⁷

That said, we are free to identify ourselves only to the degree that we accept a certain subjection to those same pre-existing structures, institutions, and cultural norms in which we live and act. There are always those who seek to restrict and constrain the promotion of both different *identities* and membership into particular *communities*. In Chapter Two, for example, we saw how some men (predominantly) employ violence as a means of restricting women's freedom of choice; likewise, in Chapter Three, we detailed how children's identities are sometimes brutally contested both in and out of the classroom. Here, I draw on the concept of 'singular affiliation' to further explore how vigilante groups promote an exclusionary concept of community.

Communal Belonging and Losings

We are simultaneously many 'things': we are gendered, raced, classed, and so forth. We have many tastes, in food, fashion, and so on. And yet we are constantly forced to suspend these simultaneities, these different facets of our existence. In *The Archaeology of Knowledge*, the French theorist Michel Foucault declared, "Do not ask who I am and do not ask me to remain the same: leave it to our bureaucrats and our police to see that our papers are in order."[98]

And the bureaucrats have been most happy to oblige.

On job applications or loan applications, college admission forms or drivers' licenses, we exist within the rigid confines of pre-determined boxes. We *become* 'male' or 'female', 'Caucasian' or 'Black' (or 'Hispanic' or 'Asian'). And these supposedly self-determined choices of identity render us into manageable bodies. We are partitioned into component parts that do not necessarily add up to our whole being. Nevertheless, we routinely (and largely unwittingly) participate in a process that Amartya Sen terms 'singular affiliation'.

Despite our plural affiliations, our involvement in "identities of different kinds in disparate contexts," we are continuously rendered to a singular 'affiliation'.[99] We are, in effect, disciplined into discrete identities. It is in this context that Sen writes of "the divisive power of classificatory priority" whereby plural identities are submerged by an allegedly primordial way of seeing differences between people.[100]

Migrants are not, however, just rendered down to a singular attribute or identity. Rather, these people become infused with what Sen defines as "charged attributions." According to Sen, *charged attributions* incorporate two distinct but interrelated distortions: first, a 'misdescription' of people belonging to a targeted category, and second, the forwarding of this misdescription as the only relevant feature of the targeted person's identity.[101] This is seen most clearly in the attribution of 'illegal' and/or 'undocumented' status.

Robert Castro writes of a "language of illegality." He argues that the ascription of legality onto migrants brands them as 'criminal' and thus subject to exclusion. Consequently, this linguistic move, this 'language of illegality', shifts the immigration discourse from that of a labor-management issue to a law enforcement problem.[102] Solutions more often than not are predicated on criminal enforcement rather than social and economic concerns. Attention is turned away from the unequal economic conditions (including transnational policies such as NAFTA) that contribute to the movement of people from Mexico and

Central America into the United States. Such a move likewise deflects attention away from the historical recruitment and hiring of workers, and the fact that American farms and businesses have long encouraged and prospered from both documented *and* undocumented migration.

The 'criminalization' of migrants has wide-reaching consequences. Combined with the on-going militarization, and the heightened surveillance and policing of the border, we see how the perceived divide between 'us' and 'them' is more clearly defined. The *spatial* distance between 'legal' and 'illegal', between citizen and non-citizen, is further widened.[103] Moreover, according to Hayden, this language of illegality obfuscates racially based effects and the racist underpinnings of nativism by reference to other values.[104] Thus, we witness continued references to 'invasions'; we hear of attempts to 'defend' and to 'protect' America and the American way of life.

The 'language of illegality' contributes to the ascription of charged attributes. Once labeled 'illegal', all other features of one's identity disappear, subsumed by a singular, hegemonic descriptor. The 'undocumented' no longer appears as father or mother, brother or sister, son or daughter; the 'undocumented' has neither past nor future, for he or she is removed from the everyday. The 'undocumented' becomes an aberration, an outsider, some*thing* not belonging to the community. Indeed, coupled with the militarization of the border and a broader militarized society, 'undocumented' migrants are transformed into *enemy combatants*; their deaths dismissed as 'collateral damage'.[105]

Once established, the misdescriptor serves a semiotic function, whereby the initial label (i.e., 'undocumented') itself signifies other (usually more degrading) attributes. The status of 'illegal' migrant thus becomes of sign for other forms of illegality and illicit activity; the danger, Hayden warns, is that such a linguistic move may begin to exclude the undocumented from the category of 'human being'. For the vigilantes, Hayden writes, the "fact that people are here without proper documentation proves that they are unworthy of being part of an orderly, and therefore legitimate, nation."[106] Ostensibly, 'illegal' migrants would be welcomed if they would go back to their respective countries, obtain proper documentation, and enter the United States via legal avenues. However, what critics of the various vigilante groups and immigration reform advocates contend is that it is not the *illegality* of movement that is at the heart of the controversy, but something deeper. This 'something else' hinges on notions of community. As Chacón and Davis conclude,

> as the offspring of the white, upwardly mobile generation of the post-war, pre-civil rights era, Minutemen formations have concluded that the growth of immigrant and non-white communities and their access to citizenship benefits directly undermine their own privileged social position.[107]

Within the border vigilante communities, the criminalized identity of the 'undocumented' is deepened further with charges of deviance and degeneracy. Significantly, much of the rhetoric employed by vigilante groups draws upon imagery used in the post-bellum period of the United States. Consider, for example, the comments of a border volunteer of the MMP. The following account, posted on this person's website, retold the story of a rancher's wife:

> "Recently, a drunken illegal alien wandered onto their ranch at night. She was home alone with her children. The illegal alien pounded on the front door. Robin said she and her terrified children crawled on their stomachs to the back of their house to get away from him. While retelling this event, her pretty eyes were filled with both terror and humiliation."[108]

Certainly the presence of a stranger pounding on one's door at night is cause for concern and fear. But would not the fear be present regardless of the illegality of the stranger? What if the stranger had been a drunken, but legal, white person? The story, at this level, implies that the threat exists because of the illegality of the stranger, not from his drunkenness. Indeed, no one is advocating for a prohibition of alcoholic drinks. But moreover, my concern lies in the imagery of the story, and its parallels with the 'black beast rapist' narrative that permeated American society throughout the late nineteenth and early twentieth centuries. Consider, for example, the 1901 writings of George T.

Winston, President of the College of Agriculture and Mechanic Arts in North Carolina. In a paper published in the *Annals of the American Academy of Political and Social Science,* Winston contrasted the 'place' of African-Americans before and after abolition. Winston wrote that before the American Civil War, the "Southern woman with her helpless children" would sleep securely, knowing that she was "safely guarded by black men [her slaves] whose lives would be freely given in her defense." Following emanicipation, however, this changed. Now, according to Winston,

> when a knock is heard at the door, [the white woman] shudders with nameless terror. The black brute is lurking in the dark, a monstrous beast, crazed with lust. His ferocity is almost demoniacal. A mad bull or a tiger could scarcely be more brutal. A whole community is now frenzied with horror, with blind and furious rage for vengeance.[109]

The 'black brute' has been replaced with the illegal (Mexican) alien.

Reminiscent of the moral panics surrounding youth violence and serial killers during the 1970s and 1980s, the specter of the 'illegal' immigrant has become a pervasive feature of American society. Consequently, throughout the latter part of the twentieth century, and well into the twenty-first, the United States has witnessed a proliferation of vigilante groups—self-appointed groups who feel compelled to discipline and police their own communities. However, the widespread practice and acceptance of vigilantism serves to produce a particular *moral space of inclusion and exclusion.* As noted in Chapter One, *moral inclusion* "in the scope of justice means applying considerations of fairness, allocating resources, and making sacrifices to foster another's well being," while *moral exclusion* "rationalizes and excuses harm inflicted on those outside the scope of justice. Excluding 'others' from the scope of justice means viewing them as unworthy of fairness, resources, or sacrifices, and seeing them as expendable, undeserving, exploitable, or irrelevant."[110]

An overreliance on a singular affiliation or representation (i.e., 'undocumented' or 'illegal') renders moot all other components; open (and open-minded) political debate is curtailed. But more egregious is the tendency to view the 'undocumented' as a non-person, a non-entity. This form of social degradation serves only to make easier the use (or the condoning) of violence as a form of discipline. This follows from the argument that the "implicit belief in the overarching power of a singular classification is not just crude as an approach to description and prediction, it is also grossly confrontational in form and implication."[111] As Sen concludes, "quite often ascription goes with denigration, which is used to incite violence against the vilified person."[112]

Conclusions

Through their usage, some terms acquire negative, or pejorative connotations. To say that someone is 'ideological', for example, is not usually meant as a compliment. Other words, conversely, are generally held in a positive light. Community is one such word. Most of us like to belong to a community; we feel that we are *part* of something. Perhaps our communal affiliation provides a sense of identity. Maybe we respond to a feeling of a greater calling in life through our belonging within a community. And it is through these social practices, often, that space becomes place: our community. Of equal importance is that *our* home is located in *our* community. *Our* children attend schools that are located in *our* community. And we may even feel an obligation to protect *our* streets within *our* community.

Of course, the promotion of *our* community comes at a price. By definition, 'my' community is not 'your' community—unless, of course, we belong to the same community. Social relations, as well as spatial relations, therefore figure prominently in the production of community. Communities, as it turns out, are both socially and spatially exclusive as much as they are inclusive. Not everyone can belong to a community. Prostitutes and deviant youth, for example, are often excluded from community participation. Of concern is who is deemed acceptable and wanted in any given community.

This chapter has considered the place-making of the U.S.–Mexico border. It has done so through the forwarding of community as a sociospatial concept that *demands* discipline. To understand communal violence, we must confront the on-going place-making practices, the bordering and regulation of space, that serve to exclude *people* from the scope of justice. Those people—for *they are people*—are more than 'illegal' or 'undocumented'. They are fathers and mothers, aunts and uncles, sons and daughters. And yet reduced to a singular attribute of legal status, they are excluded from our broader community of humanity.

Nevins concludes: "The very making of the U.S.–Mexico boundary and the larger border region has always involved the effective deployment of power to include and exclude, and of violence—both physical and structural; it has thus always had life-and-death implications."[113] More recently, however, we see that the making of the border is predicated on the violent enforcement of place. The border as space becomes emblematic of the stark differences that are presumed to exist between the United States and Mexico; the border, in short, serves as both a material and figurative place, demarcating the 'First' from the 'Third' world, 'affluence' from 'poverty', and, yes, even 'white' from 'non-white'.[114] In practice, we see how communities become disciplined places.

6
VIOLENCE AND THE PEDAGOGY OF IMPUNITY

In his book *The Elephant in the Room: Silence and Denial in Everyday Life*, Eviator Zerubavel contemplates situations where everyone refuses to acknowledge obvious truths—the elephant in the room.[1] He details how 'cultures of silence' and a 'politics of denial' often arise in the context of these elephants, and that such societal attitudes explain, in part, why so many people *do nothing*. He makes the further point that "what we ignore or avoid socially is often ignored or avoided academically."[2] Indeed, this relationship between society and academia might actually be the obverse, that is, what we avoid academically, meaning 'in the classroom', we often ignore in our daily lives.

Despite (or because of) its pervasiveness, violence is a very well-fed, if ignored, elephant. And Geography's basic avoidance of direct, interpersonal violence can thus be seen as a microcosm for society in general. Academics, journalists, and the general public are all too eager to jump on the moral panic bandwagon. Sensationalized, spectacular acts of violence, such as 'stranger-on-stranger' killings, or school-rampage killings, captivate our imaginations; we succumb to the titillations of slasher-type murders of virginal and not-so-virginal sorority girls; we retain a morbid fascination with the bizarre, the lurid, and the macabre.

But we fail to adequately question the *most common* forms of violence, the elephantine violence that occurs daily. We too often look away when confronted with intimate partner violence; we too often dismiss the 'routine' bullying in the classroom as 'child's play'; we conveniently dismiss the unmarked deaths of migrants seeking a better life in a foreign country. In a remarkable essay, Elizabeth Stanko documented the prevalence of domestic violence *for just one day*.[3] From midnight to midnight on September 28, 2000, a Thursday, Stanko audited every police service in the United Kingdom, all women's refuge and national helpline services, and any other relevant institution tasked with monitoring violence.[4] Overall, Stanko estimates that an incident of domestic violence occurs in the UK every 6 to 20 seconds. She reports that the police received over 1,300 calls on that day for domestic violence (and more than 570,000 calls each year); that approximately 2,100 women and children were housed in refuges on that night—while another 200 women had asked for safe shelter, but were turned away because of a lack of space; and that nearly one in five counseling sessions of the over 900 sessions held that day at *Relate*, a national registered charity, mentioned domestic violence. With respect to the gender of the victims, Stanko details that 81 percent of those reporting domestic violence were women attacked by men; and that injuries on that one day included rape, cuts, stabbing and slashing, bleeding due to being kicked during pregnancy, bruising, and intimidation.[5]

These herds of elephants trample through society and we fail to see and, by-and-large, we fail to act.

Eviatar Zerubavel's concerns resonate with those of Susan Opotow, whom we encountered in Chapter One. Combined, their writings highlight our engagement in processes of moral exclusion—our responsibility for, and response to, exclusionary (and violent) practices. Such engagement, or more properly, lack of engagement, may range from unawareness to ignorance, or to the allowance and facilitation of exclusion. Engagement, moreover, relates directly to the idea of impunity. This latter concept more commonly refers to the exemption from accountability, penalty, punishment, or legal sanctions for a crime. Opotow likewise writes of a 'culture of impunity', as when impunity is institutionalized and widespread, when unjust practices are overtly or tacitly condoned and unpunished as a result of amnesties, pardons, indifferences, or simply 'looking the other way'. It is a 'culture of impunity' that permits societal injustices, that allows governments, for example, to ignore and, consequently, to condone, the continuation of various forms of direct and structural violence. However, we might also speak of a *pedagogy of impunity*, whereupon we fail to engage critically with exclusionary or violent practices and behaviors in our own work. When, in the course of writing our text books, or developing our curricula, or presenting our lectures, we fail to address violence, we implicitly condone violence and thus perpetuate an academy of impunity. When our pedagogy is silent on the pervasive issues of intimate partner violence, rape (in all of its horrific forms), child and elder abuse, murder and vigilante justice, we tell our students that these topics are not important; indeed, the lesson becomes clear: violence is not relevant to our geographies.

And yet, who would dispute that 'everyday' forms of violence have an economic impact? In 2003 the Centers for Disease Control and Prevention and the U.S. Department of Justice estimated the health-related costs of intimate partner violence (i.e., rape, assault, stalking, and homicide) in the United States at more than $5.8 billion a year—such costs include, but are not limited to, shelter for women and children, social services, police response, and judicial, legal, and correctional services; that female victims of violence lose a total of nearly 8 million days of paid work and nearly 5.6 million days of household productivity; that the total annual cost of mental healthcare for victims of attempted or completed rape is $863 million. Other costs are near impossible to calculate, such as the cost to school systems when children who have witnessed (or experienced) violence cannot perform well and are forced to either repeat grades, to drop out entirely, or to use services to assist them.[6] Should our economic geography texts *at least mention* these costs of violence and consider their spatial implications?

Zerubavel writes that "Noticing and ignoring are not just personal acts, since they are always performed by members of particular social communities with particular social conventions of attention and communication."[7] The media (inclusively defined) is one such community and, as we have seen, significantly informs our awareness and understanding of violence. Other notable communities that shape our attitudes of violence include police departments, the judicial system, and marketing firms. Of course, other 'institutions', such as home and school, reflect and reflect back various conventions of attention and communication. And, as earlier chapters illustrate, these communities and institutions are infused with particular (and contested) ideas and ideals of gender, class, 'race', sexuality, and so on.

Academia is no exception; both teachers and researchers are vitally important in influencing what is 'relevant' or 'irrelevant'. Friedrich Nietzsche famously wrote "Whoever fights monsters should see to it that in the process he [sic] does not become a monster. And when you look long into an abyss, the abyss also looks into you."[8] Geographers have recently stared into that abyss; and the images have been troubling. Harald Bauder, for example, writes of (and against) the commodification of academia; of the parameters of academic practice within which pedagogic activities take place.[9] Bauder, but also Noel Castree, Ron Johnston, Sue Roberts, David Smith, Don Mitchell, Eric Sheppard (and many, many others) have critiqued the fact that geographers (and other academics) now operate within a 'corporate' university; that our efforts are structured by the quest for external funds, that our curricula are predicated on 'practical' knowledge that is in demand by the state and/or private sectors, that publication decisions—especially those in the text-book market—are based on 'commercial viability'.[10] However, Bauder also highlights the 'socialization' or 'reproduction' of geographers—and, by extension, of Geography as a discipline. Bauder explains that reproduction begins with the selection of suitable undergraduate students who, he suggests, are those who "show potential to conform and submit to academic practices."[11] Once 'accepted' into the hallowed halls of graduate studies, students are further expected (disciplined) to conform through a series of 'apprenticeships'. Indeed, according to Michael Solem and Ken Foote, both graduate students and junior faculty are inculcated into appropriate (and compliant) strategies of performance.[12] The end result is that graduate students and junior faculty "are reluctant to challenge the norms and conventions" of the academy.[13]

To the extent that certain topics are considered taboo, they are routinely (and unquestioningly) omitted from our teaching and research. Whenever an instructor deems that something is irrelevant to the class, he or she *actively* contributes to a pedagogy of impunity; whenever a graduate student eschews a topic because 'it won't lead to a job', he or she *actively* contributes to a pedagogy of impunity; whenever a professor declares that a course is extraneous to a student's career path, he or she *actively* contributes to a pedagogy of impunity. Zerubavel notes that "ignoring something is more than simply failing to notice it. Indeed, it is quite often the result of some pressure to actively disregard it."[14]

Geography has not ignored the study of violence; but neither has Geography adequately engaged in the study of violence. In an attempt to more fully understand the 'hidden violence' of deeper structures, such as structural adjustment policies, unfair trade relations, or industrial pollution, we have not always seen the elephant in the room. Despite the prevalence of murder, rape, and domestic abuse that dominate the popular media, we don't always see what is before our eyes.

Violence is global; and 'locally specific' forms of abuse are widely documented. We read of *suttee*, the practice of bride-burning; we read of genital mutilation; we read of women being stoned to death or of having acid thrown in their faces; and yet, by-and-large, these issues are not covered in our introduction to geography or world geography texts; nor, for that matter, are the practices of intimate partner violence, homophobic hate crimes, or rape and murder discussed at any great depth (if at all) in these texts.

Lest I be accused of providing too broad a paint stroke, let me hasten to add that many geographers have critically engaged in related and relevant topics. Ruth Wilson Gilmore has written extensively on prisons and prison populations; more recently, Matthew Mitchelson has likewise addressed the economic costs of prisons. Katherine Brickell and Lawrence Di Bartolo have studied domestic violence in Cambodia and Australia, respectively.[15] Joe Nevins has provided both depth and sensitivity to the topics of mass violence, both in East Timor and along the U.S.–Mexico border.[16] And the scholarly contributions to the studies of fear, crime, and violence by Gill Valentine, Rachel Pain, Melissa Wright, and Stuart Aitken (to name but a few) have been noted in earlier chapters.

That said, considerably more needs to be done to challenge a pedagogy of impunity. We need to recognize that violence not only *takes place*, but that violence is *part of place*, that violence and place are iterative. In other words, both that violence contributes to the production of place, and that place is foundational to the practice of violence. This book, therefore, marks a break with a general neglect of direct, interpersonal violence within the discipline of Geography. I have attempted to highlight, albeit selectively, the significance of spatial and place-based concepts to the practice of violence: to highlight how violence is foundational to the production of space and place.

Space, Place, and Violence is inquiry-based; students are encouraged to think critically about how violence works in place, but also how violence *produces* place. I am less concerned with individual explanations of violence and even less concerned with isolated causal factors that might 'predict' why any given person might commit a violent act. Rather, I want students to question how violence is part of our day-to-day lives. In effect, to consider how violence is foundational to Geography; and how Geography is inseparable from the everyday.

These questions require us to reconsider the concepts of space and place. David Harvey, for example, reminds us that a reworking of concepts and categories cannot be formulated in abstraction; instead, they must be forged realistically with respect to events and actions as they unfold. He elaborates that our

> immediate task is nothing more nor less than the self-conscious and aware construction of a new paradigm for social geographic thought through a deep and profound critique of our existing analytical constructs. This is what we are best equipped to do. We are academics, after all, working with the tools of the academic trade. Our task is therefore to mobilize our powers of thought to formulate concepts and categories, theories and arguments, which we can apply in the process of bringing about a humanizing social change.[17]

To this end, I have provided a collection of four spatial vignettes to illustrate the interactions of space, place, and violence. We have seen how the home is a site of potential, if not actual, violence; how violence is used to repress certain identities (e.g., gender, sex, and ethnicity) that are perceived as challenging or transgressing hegemonic (and usually both masculinist and heteronormative) norms and ideals. We have seen how school yard violence reflects similar cultural attitudes and expectations, where young boys are encouraged to 'stand up' for themselves while simultaneously bullying those children who fail to conform to dominant gendered expectations; where violent behavior is excused or overlooked. After all, boys are simply 'being boys'. We have seen how women, especially, have been targeted for violence for simply being on the streets; how misogynist attitudes of female respectability both contribute to, and excuse, the brutal murder of women. We have seen how certain groups of people are literally hunted down and allowed to die because their presence is seen to threaten the fabric of community. And we have seen how politics and economics infuse these processes—how discipline and violence serve the spatial interests of capital.

At this point, however, I ask readers to do more than simply question these episodes of violence. As a critical approach to the study of space, place, and violence, it is important to produce our own, non-violent places and to overcome our complicity to a pedagogy of impunity. Intimate partner violence is a problem; school yard violence is a problem; the targeting of marginalized populations, such as prostitutes or homeless persons or 'illegal' migrants, by both killers and neighborhood watch patrols is a problem. We *know* these to be problems; the point is to work toward solutions. But how?

As students and teachers, as practitioners of higher education, we can begin first with our text books and our curricula. Ron Johnston, for example, identifies that text books are often viewed as "authoritative 'factual' statements of what we know and how we seek new knowledge." He continues that "texts are defining statements, and their authors gain greater authoritative status through the books' wide use by professional colleagues in the inculcation of students and the production of new generations of paradigm members."[18] Embedded in these statements is an acknowledgment that authors have a *moral* responsibility of inclusion and exclusion. Thus, do we or do we not engage with the elephant in the room? Do we critically question the place of violence in society, or do we not? Students, likewise, have a moral responsibility. Don Mitchell explains that:

Learning, like political change, proceeds through struggle. Only by engaging with ideas, debates, and intellectual and political positions, does knowledge advance. Only by struggling over why arguments are made, and theories are developed as they are, can one come to understand one's own position on matters of crucial political and intellectual importance.[19]

Students, therefore, must be critical in and of their own educational experiences.

Through our learning, though, it is insufficient to simply engage in questions of violence. Rather, the point (again) is to change violence. However, before asking how can we change violence, we need to be in agreement that we want to change our violent world; this means confronting otherwise taboo subjects. As geographers, as academics, we *need* to weigh in on controversial topics, such as gun control, or bullying, or spousal rape, or ... (?) We need, in short, to confront our pedagogic complicity with violence; we need to address what I term 'safe privilege'.

Elsewhere, feminists and critical race scholars have forwarded the ideas of both 'male' and 'white' privilege. The former concept, for example, refers to the special 'privileges' that are often afforded men within society, while the latter concept is predicated on the idea that the simple 'fact' of being white carries with it certain privileges. As explained by Peggy McIntosh, privilege (whether by 'race', gender, class, or any other social integument) is "like an invisible weightless knapsack of special provisions, maps, passports, codebooks, visas, clothes, tools and blank checks." Thus, McIntosh began to count the ways in which she enjoyed unearned 'skin' privilege and was conditioned into oblivion about its existence.[20]

By extension, it is not farfetched to think of 'safe privilege'; of the ability to go about our daily lives free from the *direct* effects of violence. For some of us, violence may not outwardly appear to be a facet of our everyday life—that is, if we view (erroneously, I think) violence as something extraordinary. We may not worry (excessively) about being beaten and abused by a family member; we may not be hunted like an animal in the streets or along the border. Sure, we may worry about crime, but for many of us, we may have the luxury to avoid spaces we perceive as dangerous. To live without fear is a privilege that many people in the world do not share. And this privilege, often, mirrors the aforementioned privileges of 'race' and gender, but also class and sex.

For those who benefit from safe privilege, there is a tendency to lose sight of violence; for violence to recede into the dark recesses of their mundane world, only to appear as diversion or entertainment. The continuation of these unequal geographies—between the 'safe' and the 'unsafe'—is not acceptable. We can and must demand change in our pedagogy. And in our lives.

Notes

Chapter 1

1. Philip Wander, "Introduction to the Transaction Edition," in Henri Lefebvre, *Everyday Life in the Modern World*, translated by Sacha Rabinovith (London: Transaction Publishers, 2002), vii–xxiii; at viii.
2. Hille Koskela, "'Bold Walk and Breakings': Women's Spatial Confidence Versus Fear of Violence," *Gender, Place and Culture* 4 (1997): 301–319; at 315.
3. Elizabeth Stanko, *Everyday Violence: How Women and Men Experience Sexual and Physical Danger* (San Francisco, CA: Pandora, 1990), 5. It should be noted, also, that in some places, people do in fact experience violence on a daily basis.
4. Timothy F. Hartnagel, James J. Teevan, Jr., and Jennie J. McIntyre, "Television Violence and Violent Behavior," *Social Forces* 54 (1975): 341–351; at 341.
5. Daniel J. Flannery, *Violence and Mental Health in Everyday Life: Prevention and Intervention Strategies for Children and Adolescents* (Lanham, MD: AltaMira Press, 2006), 7.
6. Flannery, *Violence and Mental Health*, 82–84. It is important to note also that exposure does not have to be 'direct'. Through film, television, and other media we are also exposed to actual (or virtual) forms of violence.
7. Etienne G. Krug, James A. Mercy, Linda L. Dahlberg, and Anthony B. Zwi, "The World Report on Violence and Health," *The Lancet* 360 (2002): 1083–1088; at 1083 and 1085.
8. Linsey Davis, Michael Milberger, and Kate Santichen, "Good Samaritan Left for Dead on City Sidewalk," *ABCNews*, http://abcnews.go.com/print?id=10471047 (accessed May 2011).
9. See, for example, Neil A. Weiner, Margaret A. Zahn, and Rita J. Sagi, *Violence: Patterns, Causes, Public Policy* (San Diego, CA: Harcourt Brace Jovanovich, 1990); Albert J. Reiss and Jeffrey A. Roth (eds.), *Understanding and Preventing Violence* (Washington, DC: National Academy Press, 1993); Peter Iadicola and Anson Shupe, *Violence, Inequality, and Human Freedom* (Lanham, MD: Rowman & Littlefield, 2003); Alex Alvarez and Ronet Bachman, *Violence: The Enduring Problem* (Los

Angeles: Sage Publications, 2008); Randall Collins, *Violence: A Micro-Sociological Theory* (Princeton, NJ: Princeton University Press, 2008); and Maggie Wykes and Kirsty Welsh, *Violence, Gender and Justice* (Los Angeles: Sage Publications, 2009).
10. Flannery, *Violence and Mental Health*, 7.
11. Collins, *Violence*, 1–2.
12. Arild Holt-Jensen, *Geography: History and Concepts*, 4th edition (Los Angeles: Sage, 2009), 130.
13. Ron J. Johnston, *Philosophy and Human Geography: An Introduction to Contemporary Approaches*, 2nd edition (London: Edward Arnold, 1986), 67.
14. Richard Mizen, "A Contribution Towards an Analytic Theory of Violence," *Journal of Analytical Psychology* 48 (2003): 285–305; at 285.
15. Violence is not limited to physical acts. Indeed, many scholars utilize a tripartite understanding of violence, which includes *interpersonal, institutional*, and *structural* violence. Interpersonal, or direct, violence refers to those physical acts that we commonly associate as criminal, or malevolent, behaviors. Such actions include assault, rape, and murder; however, such acts might also include bullying, harassment, and name-calling. Institutional violence, conversely, may be considered a more 'situated' form of violence. Here we might consider workplace violence, violence within military settings, or even state-sanctioned violence. Lastly, structural violence refers to discriminatory social arrangements, such as policies that preclude certain individuals or collectivities' (groups') access to equal housing or education. See Peter Iadicola and Anson Shupe, *Violence, Inequality, and Human Freedom* (Lanham, MD: Rowman & Littlefield, 2003).
16. Krug et al., "World Report on Violence," 1083–1088; at 1084.
17. Krug et al., "World Report on Violence," 1085.
18. Martin Daly and Margo Wilson, *Homicide* (London: Transaction Publishers, 2008), 146.
19. Alvarez and Bachman, *Violence*, 34.
20. Daly and Wilson are more blunt in their assessment, noting that "American social scientists fear and despise biology, although few of them have troubled to learn any." See Daly and Wilson, *Homicide*, 154.
21. The following is based on Sherene H. Razack, "Gendered Racial Violence and Spatialized Justice: The Murder of Pamela George," *Canadian Journal of Law and Society* 15 (2000): 91–130. See also the website *Injustice Busters* (www.injustice-busters.com/2003/George_Pamela.htm).
22. Krug et al., "World Report on Violence," 1085.
23. Alvarez and Bachman, *Violence*, 45.
24. Alvarez and Bachman, *Violence*, 48; see also Cathy S. Widom, "Does Violence Beget Violence? A Critical Examination of the Literature," *Psychological Bulletin* 106 (1989): 3–28.
25. Collins, *Violence*, 2.
26. Alvarez and Bachman, *Violence*, 65–66.
27. Alvarez and Bachman, *Violence*, 32.
28. David M. Buss, *The Murderer Next Door: Why the Mind is Designed to Kill* (New York: Penguin, 2005), 25.
29. Iris Young, *Justice and the Politics of Difference* (Princeton, NJ: Princeton University Press, 1990), 43, 53.
30. Susan Opotow, "Reconciliation in Time of Impunity: Challenges for Social Justice," *Social Justice Research* 14 (2001): 149–170; at 156.
31. James Waller, *Becoming Evil: How Ordinary People Commit Genocide and Mass Killing* (New York: Oxford University Press, 2002), 239.
32. Waller, *Becoming Evil*, 239.
33. Stanko, *Everyday Violence*.

34. Stanko, *Everyday Violence*, 41 and 45.
35. Geographers, and especially feminist geographers, have made a number of significant contributions to the geographies of (women's) fear. See, for example, Gill Valentine, "The Geography of Women's Fear," *Area* 21 (1989): 385–390; Rachel Pain, "Space, Sexual Violence and Social Control: Integrating Geographical and Feminist Analyses of Women's Fear of Crime," *Progress in Human Geography* 15 (1991): 415–431; Gill Valentine, "Images of Danger: Women's Sources of Information about the Spatial Distribution of Male Violence," *Area* 24 (1992): 22–29; Rachel Pain, "Elderly Women and Fear of Violent Crime: the Last Likely Victims?" *British Journal of Criminology* 35 (1995): 584–598; Hille Koskela, "'Gendered Exclusions': Women's Fear of Violence and Changing Relations to Space," *Geografiska Annaler* 81B (1999): 111–124; and Alec Brownlow, "A Geography of Men's Fear," *Geoforum* 36 (2005): 581–592.
36. For a notable exception, see Molly Warrington, "'I Must Get Out': The Geographies of Domestic Violence," *Transactions, Institute of British Geographers* 26 (2001): 365–382.
37. Donald G. Janelle, Barney Warf, and Kathy Hansen (eds.), *WorldMinds: Geographical Perspectives on 100 Problems* (Boston: Kluwer Academic Publishers, 2004).
38. Barney Warf, Donald G. Janelle, and Kathy Hansen, "Introducing *WorldMinds*," in *WorldMinds: Geographical Perspectives on 100 Problems*, edited by Donald Janelle, Barney Warf, and Kathy Hansen (Boston: Kluwer Academic Publishers, 2004), xvii–xxii; at xvii.
39. Derek Gregory and Allan Pred (eds.), *Violent Geographies: Fear, Terror, and Political Violence* (New York: Routledge, 2007).
40. Susan L. Cutter, Douglas B. Richardson, and Thomas J. Wilbanks, "The Changing Landscape of Fear," in *The Geographical Dimensions of Terrorism*, edited by Susan L. Cutter, Douglas B. Richardson, and Thomas J. Wilbanks (New York: Routledge 2002), 1–5; at 1.
41. Tim Cresswell, *Place: A Short Introduction* (Malden, MA: Blackwell, 2004), 1.
42. Nigel Thrift, "Space: The Fundamental Stuff of Human Geography," in *Key Concepts in Geography*, edited by Sarah L. Holloway, Stephen P. Rice, and Gill Valentine (Los Angeles: Sage Publications, 2003), 95–107.
43. Roger Matthews, *Doing Time: An Introduction to the Sociology of Imprisonment*, 2nd edition (New York: Palgrave Macmillan, 2009), 26.
44. Mona Domosh, "Those 'Gorgeous Incongruities': Polite Politics and Public Space on the Streets of Nineteenth-Century New York City," *Annals of the Association of American Geographers* 88 (1998): 209–226; at 210.
45. Cresswell, *Place*, 1.
46. Thrift, "Space," 104.
47. Paul C. Adams, Steven Hoelscher, and Karen E. Till, "Place in Context: Rethinking Humanist Geographies," in *Textures of Place: Exploring Humanist Geographies*, edited by Paul C. Adams, Steven Hoelscher, and Karen E. Till (Minneapolis: University of Minnesota Press, 2001), xiii–xxxiii.
48. Cresswell, *Place*, 37.
49. Michel Foucault, *Discipline and Punish: The Birth of the Prison*, translated by Alan Sheridan (New York: Vintage Books, 1979), 215.
50. Tim Cresswell, *In Place/Out of Place: Geography, Ideology and Transgression* (Minneapolis: University of Minnesota Press, 1996).
51. Thrift, "Space," 104–105.
52. Even in the context of 'mob' violence, we need to recognize that groups are composed of individuals. And while psychologists have long studied 'group mentality' as an important component of mob violence, an individual participating within collective forms of violence should not be able to use this as an excuse.

53. Alvarez and Bachman, *Violence*, 29.
54. Collins, *Violence*, 3.
55. David Livingstone Smith, *The Most Dangerous Animal: Human Nature and the Origins of War* (New York: St. Martin's Griffin, 2007), 37.
56. I am fully aware that certain brain injuries lead to violent actions; likewise, I acknowledge that there exist some individuals who are labeled psychopaths or sociopaths. However, as Alvarez and Bachman, among others, note, the overwhelming majority of violent acts, including murder, are *not* committed by these individuals. See Alvarez and Bachman, *Violence*, 37–39; see also James Gilligan, *Violence: Reflections on a National Epidemic* (New York: Vintage Books, 1996), 214–218.
57. Gilligan, *Violence*, 9.
58. Alvarez and Bachman, *Violence*, 7.
59. Buss, *The Murderer Next Door*, 231.
60. Alvarez and Bachman, *Violence*, 7.
61. Rob M. Kitchin and Phil J. Hubbard, "Research, Action, and 'Critical' Geographies," *Area* 31 (1999): 195–198; at 195.
62. See, for example, Susan M. Roberts, "Realizing Critical Geographies of the University," *Antipode* 32 (2000): 230–244; Duncan Fuller and Rob Kitchin, "Radical Theory/Critical Praxis: Academic Geography Beyond the Academy," in *Radical Theory/Critical Praxis: Making a Difference Beyond the Academy*, edited by Duncan Fuller and Rob Kitchen (Praxis (e)Press, 2004), 1–20; Nicholas Blomley, "Uncritical Critical Geography," *Progress in Human Geography* 30 (2006): 87–94; David Harvey, "The Geographies of Critical Geography," *Transactions, Institute of British Geographers* 31 (2006): 409–412; Nicholas Blomley, "The Spaces of Critical Geography," *Progress in Human Geography* 32 (2008): 285–293; Elizabeth Olson and Andrew Sayer, "Radical Geography and its Critical Standpoints: Embracing the Normative," *Antipode* 41 (2009): 180–198.
63. Blomley, "Uncritical Critical Geography," 88.
64. Kitchin and Hubbard, "Research, Action," 195.
65. Olson and Sayer, "Radical Geography," 185.
66. Olson and Sayer, "Radical Geography," 185 and 187.

Chapter 2

1. Quoted in Elizabeth Stanko, *Everyday Violence: How Women and Men Experience Sexual and Physical Danger* (San Francisco, CA: Pandora, 1990), 31.
2. Linda McDowell, *Gender, Identity & Place: Understanding Feminist Geographies* (Minneapolis: University of Minnesota Press, 1999), 71.
3. McDowell, *Gender, Identity & Place*, 72.
4. While I do not discount the number of men who experience violence at home, statistically most abuse is directed by men toward women and children.
5. Gill Valentine, "The Geography of Women's Fear," *Area* 21 (1989): 385–390; at 386. See also Gill Valentine, "Images of Danger: Women's Sources of Information about the Spatial Distribution of Male Violence," *Area* 24 (1992): 22–29; Molly Warrington, "'I Must Get Out': The Geographies of Domestic Violence," *Transactions, Institute of British Geographers* 26 (2001): 365–382; and Barrie Levy, *Women and Violence* (Berkeley, CA: Seal Press, 2008).
6. Stanko, *Everyday Violence*, 35.
7. Liz Kelly and Jill Radford, "'Nothing Really Happened': The Invalidation of Women's Experiences of Sexual Violence," *Critical Social Policy* 39 (1991): 39–53; Patricia Tjaden and Nancy Thoennes, *Extent, Nature, and Consequences of Intimate Partner Violence: Findings from the National Violence Against Women Survey*

(Washington, DC: National Institute of Justice/Centers for Disease Control, 2000); Jeff Hearn and Antony Whitehead, "Collateral Damage: Men's 'Domestic' Violence to Women Seen Through Men's Relations with Men," *Probation Journal: The Journal of Community and Criminal Justice* 53 (2006): 38–56; Maureen C. McHugh and Irene Hanzon Frieze, "Intimate Partner Violence: New Directions," *Annals, New York Academy of Sciences* 1087 (2006): 121–141; Alex Alvarez and Ronet Bachman, *Violence: The Enduring Problem* (Los Angeles: Sage Publications, 2008); Angela J. Hattery, *Intimate Partner Violence* (Lanham, MD: Rowman & Littlefield, 2009).
8. Stanko, *Everyday Violence*, 9.
9. There now is a voluminous literature on home and its contested meanings. Good starting points include Peter Saunders and Peter Williams, "The Constitution of the Home: Towards a Research Agenda," *Housing Studies* 3 (1988): 81–93; Nicky Gregson and Michelle Lowe, "'Home-Making': On the Spatiality of Daily Social Reproduction in Contemporary Middle-Class Britain," *Transactions, Institute of British Geographers* 20 (1995): 224–235; Stuart C. Aitken, *Family Fantasies and Community Space* (New Brunswick, NJ: Rutgers University Press, 1998); Mona Domosh, "Geography and Gender: Home, Again?" *Progress in Human Geography* 22 (1998): 276–282; Mona Domosh and Joni Seager, *Putting Women in Place: Feminist Geographers Make Sense of the World* (New York: The Guilford Press, 2001); Shelley Mallett, "Understanding Home: A Critical Review of the Literature," *The Sociological Review* 52 (2004): 62–89.
10. Yi-Fu Tuan, "Geography, Phenomenology, and the Study of Human Nature," *Canadian Geographer* 15 (1971): 181–192.
11. Tuan, "Geography, Phenomenology," 189.
12. Mallett, "Understanding Home," 71.
13. Tuan, "Geography, Phenomenology," 181.
14. Mallett, "Understanding Home," 64.
15. Mallett, "Understanding Home," 68; see also Saunders and Williams, "Constitution of the Home."
16. McDowell, *Gender, Identity & Place*, 71.
17. Saunders and Williams, "Constitution of the Home," 82.
18. Gregson and Lowe, "'Home-Making,'" 226.
19. Mallett, "Understanding Home," 77.
20. John Rennie Short, *The Urban Order: An Introduction to Cities, Culture, and Power* (Cambridge, MA: Blackwell, 1996), 94.
21. Richard Peet, *Global Capitalism: Theories of Societal Development* (New York: Routledge, 1991), 59.
22. Henri Lefebvre, *The Production of Space* (Oxford, UK: Blackwell, 1991 [1974]), 46–47.
23. By convention, productive work refers to the provision of food, shelter, and clothing; reproductive work includes those tasks necessary to reproduce people, such as child-rearing and socialization.
24. Aitken, *Family Fantasies*, 39.
25. Aitken, *Family Fantasies*, 40.
26. Elizabeth Uy Eviota, *The Political Economy of Gender: Women and the Sexual Division of Labour in the Philippines* (London: Zed Books, 1992), 11.
27. Aitken, *Family Fantasies*, 39.
28. Paul Knox, John Agnew, and Linda McCarthy, *The Geography of the World Economy*, 4th ed. (London: Edward Arnold, 2003), 127.
29. Eviota, *Political Economy of Gender*, 12.
30. Eviota, *Political Economy of Gender*, 13.
31. Eviota, *Political Economy of Gender*, 13.
32. Saunders and Williams, "Constitution of the Home," 85.

33. Domosh and Seager, *Putting Women in Place*, 3–4.
34. Aitken, *Family Fantasies*, 27.
35. Aitken, *Family Fantasies*, 41.
36. Aitken, *Family Fantasies*, 46.
37. Domosh and Seager, *Putting Women in Place*, 5.
38. Aitken, *Family Fantasies*, 46.
39. Eviota, *Political Economy of Gender*, 14.
40. Andrew Sayer and Richard Walker, *The New Social Economy: Reworking the Division of Labor* (Cambridge, MA: Blackwell, 1992), 34–36.
41. McDowell, *Gender, Identity & Place*, 75.
42. Aitken, *Family Fantasies*, 47.
43. Sayer and Walker, *New Social Economy*, 43.
44. McDowell, *Gender, Identity & Place*, 75.
45. Wayne D. Myslik, "Renegotiating the Social/Sexual Identities of Places: Gay Communities as Safe Havens or Sites of Resistance?" in *BodySpace: Destabilizing Geographies of Gender and Sexuality*, edited by Nancy Duncan (London: Routledge, 1996), 156–169; at 159.
46. Domosh and Seager, *Putting Women in Place*, 4.
47. McDowell, Gender, *Identity & Place*, 73.
48. McDowell, Gender, *Identity & Place*, 88.
49. Hattery, *Intimate Partner Violence*, 4.
50. McDowell, *Gender, Identity & Place*, 89.
51. Sayer and Walker, *New Social Economy*, 36.
52. Maggie Wykes and Kirsty Welsh, *Violence, Gender and Justice* (Los Angeles: Sage Publications, 2009), 97.
53. From *Housekeeping Monthly*, "Guide to Being a Good Wife," 1955, quoted in Hattery, *Intimate Partner Violence*, 79.
54. Julia Wardhaugh, "The Unaccommodated Woman: Home, Homelessness and Identity," *The Sociological Review* 47 (1999): 91–109; at 94–95.
55. Wardhaugh, "Unaccommodated Woman," 96.
56. Warrington, "Geographies of Domestic Violence," 368.
57. Some studies indicate a presence of 'symmetry' in incidences of violence; that women are just as likely to become violent toward their male partners as men are to women. However, these studies have been called into question. Indeed, the interpretation that men and women are equally combative often ignores the physical and economic power disparities between men and women, and also fails to consider the motive for, or consequences of, aggressive acts. In fact, a more nuanced interpretation of female-on-male violence indicates that women are most often responding to male violence: women are more often defending themselves against hostile attacks. Thus, as McHugh and Frieze conclude, although many women acknowledge that they have initiated violence, "they generally did so in the context of a relationship in which the male partner initiated violence more often and was likely to have initiated the overall pattern of violence." See McHugh and Frieze, "Intimate Partner Violence," 131.
58. Hattery, *Intimate Partner Violence*, 14.
59. James E. Anderson, Mufiyda Abraham, Diane Michelle Bruessow, Robert David Coleman, Kelly C. McCarthy, Trisha Harris-Odimgbe, and Cindy K. Tong, "Cross-Cultural Perspectives on Intimate Partner Violence," *JAAPA* 21 (2008): 36–44; at 36.
60. McHugh and Frieze, "Intimate Partner Violence," 121.
61. McHugh and Frieze, "Intimate Partner Violence," 122.
62. Tjaden and Thoennes, *Intimate Partner Violence*, 5.
63. Tjaden and Thoennes, *Intimate Partner Violence*, 5.

64. McHugh and Frieze, "Intimate Partner Violence," 123.
65. Mary Ellsberg, Henrica A. F. M. Jansen, Lori Heise, Charlotte H. Watts, and Claudia García-Moreno, "Intimate Partner Violence and Women's Physical and Mental Health in the WHO Multi-Country Study on Women's Health and Domestic Violence: An Observational Study," *Lancet* 371 (2008): 1165–1172; at 1168. The 10 countries included Bangladesh, Brazil, Peru, Thailand, Tanzania, Ethiopia, Japan, Namibia, Samoa, and the former Union of Serbia and Montenegro.
66. Donna L. Ansara and Michelle J. Hindin, "Perpetration of Intimate Partner Aggression by Men and Women in the Philippines: Prevalence and Associated Factors," *Journal of Interpersonal Violence* 24 (2009): 1579–1590; and Manju Rani and Sekhar Bonu, "Attitudes Toward Wife Beating: A Cross-Country Study in Asia," *Journal of Interpersonal Violence* 24 (2009): 1371–1397.
67. Elizabeth Stanko, D. Crisp, C. Hale, and H. Lucraft, *Counting the Costs: Estimating the Impact of Domestic Violence in the London Borough of Hackney* (Swindon: Crime Concern, 1998).
68. McHugh and Frieze, "Intimate Partner Violence," 129. See also William L. Parish, Tianfu Wang, Edward O. Laumann, Suiming Pan, and Ye Luo, "Intimate Partner Violence in China: National Prevalence, Risk Factors and Associated Health Problems," *International Family Planning Perspectives* 30 (2004): 174–181; Manju Rani, Sekhar Bonu, and Nafissatou Diop-Sidibe, "An Empirical Investigation of Attitudes Towards Wife-Beating Among Men and Women in Seven Sub-Saharan African Countries," *African Journal of Reproductive Health* 8 (2004): 116–136; Nancy Luke, Sidney R. Schuler, Bui Thi Thanh Mai, Pham Vu Thien, and Tran Hung Minh, "Exploring Couple Attributes and Attitudes and Marital Violence in Vietnam," *Violence Against Women* 13 (2007): 5–27; Ursula Smartt and Helmut Kury, "Domestic Violence: Comparative Analysis of German and U.K. Research Findings," *Social Science Quarterly* 88 (2007): 1263–1280; Angie Boy and Andrzej Kulczycki, "What We Know About Intimate Partner Violence in the Middle East and North Africa," *Violence Against Women* 14 (2008): 53–70; and Stephen Lawoko, "Predictors of Attitudes Toward Intimate Partner Violence: A Comparative Study of Men in Zambia and Kenya," *Journal of Interpersonal Violence* 23 (2008): 1056–1074.
69. Levy, *Women and Violence*, 8.
70. Lawoko, "Attitudes Toward Intimate Partner Violence," 1057.
71. Luke et al., "Marital Violence in Vietnam," 14.
72. Boy and Kulczycki, "Intimate Partner Violence in the Middle East," 59.
73. Kelly and Radford, "'Nothing Really Happened,'" 39.
74. Quoted in Kelly and Radford, "'Nothing Really Happened,'" 43.
75. Kelly and Radford, "'Nothing Really Happened,'" 44–45.
76. Kelly and Radford, "'Nothing Really Happened,'" 51.
77. Kelly and Radford, "'Nothing Really Happened,'" 47.
78. Quoted in Kelly and Radford, "'Nothing Really Happened,'" 48.
79. Gwen Hunnicutt, "Varieties of Patriarchy and Violence Against Women: Resurrecting 'Patriarchy' as a Theoretical Tool," *Violence Against Women* 15 (2009): 553–573; at 554.
80. Hearn and Whitehead, "Collateral Damage," 43–44.
81. Hunnicutt, "Varieties of Patriarchy," 554–555.
82. Hearn and Whitehead, "Collateral Damage," 43.
83. Hunnicutt, "Varieties of Patriarchy," 560.
84. Hunnicutt, "Varieties of Patriarchy," 560.
85. Hearn and Whitehead, "Collateral Damage," 45.
86. Hearn and Whitehead, "Collateral Damage," 47.
87. Hunnicutt, "Varieties of Patriarchy," 561.
88. Hearn and Whitehead, "Collateral Damage," 47.

89. Judith Butler, *Gender Trouble: Feminism and the Subversion of Identity* (New York: Routledge, 1999), 173.
90. Sayer and Walker, *New Social Economy*, 43–44.
91. Kristin L. Anderson, "Gender, Status, and Domestic Violence: An Integration of Feminist and Family Violence Approaches," *Journal of Marriage and the Family* 59 (1997): 655–669.
92. Peter Jackson, "The Cultural Politics of Masculinity: Towards a Social Geography," *Transactions of the Institute of British Geographers* 16 (1991): 199–213; at 203.
93. Kristen Day, "Constructing Masculinity and Women's fear in Public Space in Irvine, California," *Gender, Place and Culture* 8 (2001): 109–127; at 110.
94. Valentine, "Images of Danger," 23.
95. Aitken, *Family Fantasies*, 27.
96. Jackson, "Cultural Politics," 201.
97. McDowell, *Gender, Identity & Place*, 92.
98. James Gilligan, *Violence: Reflections on a National Epidemic* (New York: Vintage, 1997), 5.
99. Butler, *Gender Trouble*, 179.
100. Peter Glick and Susan T. Fiske, "The Ambivalent Sexism Inventory: Differentiating Hostile and Benevolent Sexism," *Journal of Personality and Social Psychology* 70 (1996): 491–512; at 492.
101. Hattery, for example, explains that in some homes, female employment is perceived by the male 'breadwinner' as threatening. First, employment provides income that would allow an abused woman the resources to successfully escape her dependency upon the man. Second, working outside the home may be a source of friends and contacts for the woman, again creating a situation wherein the woman could potentially confide about the violence. Lastly, outside employment may also provide interactions with men of whom the male partner is jealous. See Hattery, *Intimate Partner Violence*, 59.
102. Hattery, *Intimate Partner Violence*, 57. See also Lawoko, "Attitudes Toward Intimate Partner Violence," 1057.
103. Anderson, "Gender, Status," 658.
104. Hattery, *Intimate Partner Violence*, 3.
105. An understanding of 'male' violence, according to Gilligan, is first necessary since most violence is committed by males. See Gilligan, Violence, 229.
106. Gilligan, *Violence*, 229.
107. Douglas Kellner, *Guys and Guns Amok: Domestic Terrorism and School Shootings from the Oklahoma City Bombing to the Virginia Tech Massacre* (Boulder, CO: Paradigm Publishers, 2008), 14–15, 28. See also Andrew J. Bacevich, *The New American Militarism: How Americans are Seduced by War* (Oxford: Oxford University Press, 2005) and Cynthia Enloe, *Globization and Militarism: Feminists Make the Link* (Lanham, MD: Rowman & Littlefield, 2007).
108. Gilligan, *Violence*, 233.
109. Hattery, *Intimate Partner Violence*, 89.
110. Quoted in Hattery, *Intimate Partner Violence*, 88.
111. Quoted in Hattery, *Intimate Partner Violence*, 87–88.
112. Jackson Tooby, "Violence and the Masculine Ideal: Some Qualitative Data," *Annals of the American Academy of Political and Social Science* 364 (1966): 19–27; see also Alan Rosenbaum, "Of Men, Macho, and Marital Violence," *Journal of Family Violence* 1 (1986): 121–129.
113. Luke et al., "Marital Violence in Vietnam," 14.
114. Rani and Bonu, "Attitudes Toward Wife Beating," 1394.
115. Rani et al., "Empirical Investigation of Attitudes Towards Wife-Beating," 119.
116. Hunnicutt, "Varieties of Patriarchy," 566.

117. Glick and Fiske, "Ambivalent Sexism," 491. See also Niwako Yamawaki, Joseph Ostenson, and C. Ryan Brown, "The Functions of Gender Role Traditionality, Ambivalent Sexism, Injury, and Frequency of Assault on Domestic Violence Perception: A Study Between Japanese and American College Students," *Violence Against Women* 15 (2009): 1126–1142.
118. Hunnicutt, "Varieties of Patriarchy," 565.
119. Glick and Fiske, "Ambivalent Sexism," 492.
120. Glick and Fiske, "Ambivalent Sexism," 491.
121. Glick and Fiske, "Ambivalent Sexism," 492.
122. Glick and Fiske, "Ambivalent Sexism," 494.
123. Glick and Fiske, "Ambivalent Sexism," 494. Glick and Fiske note the 'problems' that arise when a woman 'fits' into both types. They give the example of a man's attitudes toward his daughter, who is a radical feminist. We can extend this further. Consider, for example, a racist and sexist white man whose daughter is dating an African-American man, or consider a sexist man whose daughter is a lesbian.
124. Hattery, *Intimate Partner Violence*, 111.
125. The literature on 'same-sex' violence is increasing rapidly. Good starting points include K. Lobel (ed.), *Naming the Violence: Speaking Out About Lesbian Battering* (Seattle: Seal Press, 1986); Claire M. Renzetti, "Violence in Lesbian Relationships: A Preliminary Analysis of Causal Factors," *Journal of Interpersonal Violence* 3 (1988): 381–399; Claire M. Renzetti, "Building a Second Closet: Third Party Responses to Victims of Lesbian Partner Abuse," *Family Relations* 38 (1989): 157–163; Carolyn M. West, "Lesbian Intimate Partner Violence: Prevalence and Dynamics," *Journal of Lesbian Studies* 6 (2002): 121–127; Karen Corteen, "Lesbian Safety Talk: Problematizing Definitions and Experiences of Violence, Sexuality and Space," *Sexualities* 5 (2002): 259–280; Lori B. Girshick, "No Sugar, No Spice: Reflections on Research on Woman-to-Woman Sexual Violence," *Violence Against Women* 8 (2002): 1500–1520; Lori B. Girshick, *Woman-to-Woman Sexual Violence: Does She Call it Rape?* (Boston: Northeastern University Press, 2002); Kimberly F. Balsam and Dawn M. Szymanski, "Relationship Quality and Domestic Violence in Women's Same-Sex Relationships: The Role of Minority Stress," *Psychology of Women Quarterly* 29 (2005): 258–269; and Jude Irwin, "(Dis)Counted Stories: Domestic Violence and Lesbians," *Qualitative Social Work* 7 (2008): 199–215.
126. Gill Valentine, "(Hetero)sexing Space: Lesbian Perceptions and Experiences of Everyday Space," *Environment and Planning D: Society and Space* 11 (1993): 395–413; Lynda Johnston and Gill Valentine, "Wherever I Lay My Girlfriend, That's My Home: The Performance and Surveillance of Lesbian Identities in Domestic Environments," in *Mapping Desire: Geographies of Sexualities*, edited by David Bell and Gill Valentine (London: Routledge, 1995), 99–113; Stewart Kirby and Iain Hay, "(Hetero)sexing Space: Gay Men and 'Straight' Space in Adelaide, South Australia," *The Professional Geographer* 49 (1997): 295–305; Sarah A. Elwood, "Lesbian Living Spaces: Multiple Meanings of Home," *Journal of Lesbian Studies* 4 (2000): 11–27; Gill Valentine, Tracey Skelton, and Ruth Butler, "Coming Out and Outcomes: Negotiating Lesbian and Gay Identities With, and In, the Family," *Environment and Planning D: Society and Space* 21 (2003): 479–499; Andrew Gorman-Murray, "Homeboys: Uses of Home by Gay Australian Men," *Social & Cultural Geography* 7 (2006): 53–69; Andrew Gorman-Murray, "Reconfiguring Domestic Values: Meanings of Home for Gay Men and Lesbians," *Housing, Theory and Society* 24 (2007): 229–246; and Sue Kentlyn, "The Radically Subversive Space of the Queer Home: 'Safety House' and 'Neighborhood Watch,'" *Australian Geographer* 39 (2008): 327–337.
127. Diance Helene Miller, Kathryn Greene, Vickie Causby, Barbara W. White, and Lettie L. Lockhart, "Domestic Violence in Lesbian Relationships," *Women*

& *Therapy* 23 (2001): 107–127; at 108. See also Lettie L. Lockhart, Barbara W. White, Vickie Causby, and Alicia Isaac, "Letting Out the Secret: Violence in Lesbian Relationships," *Journal of Interpersonal Violence* 9 (1994): 469–492; Danica R. Bornstein, Jake Fawcett, Marianne Sullivan, Kirsten D. Senturia, and Sharyne Shui-Thornton, "Understanding the Experiences of Lesbian, Bisexual and Trans Survivors of Domestic Violence: A Qualitative Study," *Journal of Homosexuality* 51 (2006): 159–181; and Nicola Brown, "Stories from Outside the Frame: Intimate Partner Abuse in Sexual-Minority Women's Relationships with Transsexual Men," *Feminism & Psychology* 17 (2007): 373–393.
128. West, "Lesbian Intimate Partner Violence," 122.
129. Quoted in Irwin, "(Dis)Counted Stories," 206.
130. Irwin, "(Dis)Counted Stories," 206.
131. Renzetti, "Building a Second Closet," 160–161.
132. Brown, "Stories from Outside the Frame," 374.
133. West, "Lesbian Intimate Partner Violence," 123.
134. For reviews, see L. K. Burke and D. R. Follingstad, "Violence in Lesbian and Gay Relationships: Theory, Prevalence, and Correlational Factors," *Clinical Psychology Review* 19 (1999): 487–512 and L. K. Waldner-Haugrud, "Sexual Coercion in Lesbian and Gay Relationships: A Review and Critique," *Aggression and Violent Behavior* 4 (1999): 139–149.
135. Kirby and Hay, "(Hetero)sexing Space," 297.
136. Kentlyn, "Radically Subversive Space," 328.
137. Gorman-Murray, "Homeboys," 55.
138. Gorman-Murray, "Domestic Values," 231.
139. Valentine, "(Hetero)sexing Space," 399–400.
140. Valentine et al., "Coming Out," 485.
141. Kirby and Hay, "(Hetero)sexing Space," 298. See also Ritch C. Savin-Williams, "Verbal and Physical Abuse as Stressors in the Lives of Lesbian, Gay Male, and Bisexual Youths: Associations with School Problems, Running Away, Substance Abuse, Prostitution, and Suicide," *Journal of Consulting and Clinical Psychology* 62 (1994): 261–269.
142. Joyce Hunter, "Violence Against Lesbian and Gay Male Youths," *Journal of Interpersonal Violence* 5 (1990): 295–300; and A. D'Augelli, S. Hershberger, and N. Pilkington, "Lesbian, Gay and Bisexual Youth and Their Families: Disclosure of Sexual Orientation and its Consequences," *American Journal of Orthopsychiatry* 68 (1998): 361–371.
143. Valentine et al., "Coming Out," 488–489.
144. Gorman-Murray, "Homeboys," 53.
145. Gorman-Murray, "Domestic Values," 231.
146. A similar argument has been made by Black feminists when considering the meaning of 'home' for African-American women. See Patricia Hill Collins, *Black Feminist Thought: Knowledge, Conciousness, and the Politics of Empowerment* (New York: Routledge, 1990).
147. Kirby and Hay, "(Hetero)sexing Space," 296.
148. Myslik, "Renegotiating Social/Sexual Identities," 159.
149. Corteen, "Lesbian Safety Talk," 260.
150. Gorman-Murray, "Domestic Values," 240.
151. Kirby and Hay, "(Hetero)sexing Space," 296.
152. Gorman-Murray, "Domestic Values," 240.
153. Elwood, "Lesbian Living Spaces," 12.
154. Valentine, "(Hetero)sexing Space," 399.
155. Valentine, "(Hetero)sexing Space," 411.
156. Elwood, "Lesbian Living Spaces," 19.

157. Elwood, "Lesbian Living Spaces," 19.
158. Saunders and Williams, "Constitution of the Home," 83–84.
159. Domosh, "Geography and Gender," 280.
160. Elwood, "Lesbian Living Spaces," 14.
161. Gorman-Murray, "Domestic Values," 231.
162. Miller et al., "Domestic Violence," 109–110.
163. Balsam and Szymanski, "Relationship Quality and Domestic Violence," 259.
164. Kentlyn, "Radically Subversive Space," 331–332.
165. Miller et al., "Domestic Violence," 110.
166. Miller et al., "Domestic Violence," 111.
167. Johnston and Valentine, "Wherever I Lay My Girlfriend," 109.
168. Bornstein et al., "Experiences of Lesbians," 170.
169. Girshick, *Woman-to-Woman Sexual Violence*, 68.
170. Brown, "Stories from Outside the Frame," 377–378.
171. Balsam and Szymanski, "Relationship Quality and Domestic Violence," 259.
172. West, "Lesbian Intimate Partner Violence," 123.
173. Girshick, "No Sugar, No Spice," 1515.
174. James A. Tyner, "The Globalization of Transnational Labor Migration and the Filipino Family: A Narrative," *Asian and Pacific Migration Journal* 11 (2002): 95–116; at 98.
175. Pierrette Hondagneu-Sotelo, *Gendered Transitions: Mexican Experiences of Immigration* (Berkeley: University of California Press, 1994), 98.
176. Hondagneu-Sotelo, *Gendered Transitions*, 193.
177. Hondagneu-Sotelo, *Gendered Transitions*, 194.
178. Eleonore Kofman, "Foreword," in *Wife or Worker? Asian Women and Migration*, edited by Nicola Piper and Mina Roces (Lanham, MD: Rowman & Littlefield, 2003), ix–x.
179. Cecilia Menjívar and Olivia Salcido, "Immigrant Women and Domestic Violence: Common Experiences in Different Countries," *Gender & Society* 16 (2002): 898–920.
180. Uma Narayan, "'Mail-Order' Brides: Immigrant Women, Domestic Violence and Immigration Law," *Hypatia* 10 (1995): 104–119; at 105.
181. Menjívar and Salcido, "Immigrant Women," 903. These authors note also, though, that improvements in immigrant women's language abilities may exacerbate abusive behavior since male control is contested.
182. Kathleen Ferraro, "Policing Battered Women," *Social Problems* 36 (1989): 61–74.
183. See for example Chris Cunneen and Julie Stubbs, "Violence Against Filipino Women in Australia: Race, Class and Gender," *Waikato Law Review* 131 (1996): n.p.; Marie Crandall, Kirsten Senturia, Marianne Sullivan, and Sharyne Shiu-Thornton, "'No Way Out': Russian-Speaking Women's Experiences with Domestic Violence," *Journal of Interpersonal Violence* 20 (2005): 941–958; and Leonora Angeles and Sirijit Sunanta, "'Exotic Love at Your Fingertips': Intermarriage Websites, Gendered Representation, and the Transnational Migration of Filipino and Thai Women," *Kasarinlan: Philippine Journal of Third World Studies* 22 (2007): 3–31.
184. Cunneen and Stubbs, "Violence Against Filipino Women," n.p.
185. Angeles and Sunanta, "'Exotic Love,'" 4.
186. Narayan, "'Mail-Order' Brides," 107.
187. Angeles and Sunanta, "'Exotic Love,'" 18.
188. Cunneen and Stubbs, "Violence Against Filipino Women," n.p.
189. Venny Villapando, "The Business of Selling Mail-Order Brides," in *Making Waves: An Anthology By and About Asian American Women*, edited by Asian Women United of California (Boston: Beacon Press, 1989), 319–326; at 324.
190. Quoted in Villapando, "The Business of Selling Mail-Order Brides," 324.

191. Quoted in Michael Duenas, "Filipino Mail Order Brides," *Philippines Free Press*, July 25 (1987), pp. 18–19, 28, 30, and 32; at 19.
192. Quoted in Ernesto Parial, "RP Women Labeled as 'House Pets,'" *Philippine News* July 22–28 (1992), pp. 1 and 12.
193. Gina Marchetti, *Romance and the 'Yellow Peril': Race, Sex, and Discursive Strategies in Hollywood Fiction* (Berkeley: University of California Press, 1993), 179. For a different perspective, and one that stresses the agency among Asia/American female actors, see Celine Parreñas Shimizu, *The Hypersexuality of Race: Performing Asian/American Women on Screen and Scene* (Durham, NC: Duke University Press, 2007).
194. Cunneen and Stubbs, "Violence Against Filipino Women," n.p.
195. Cunneen and Stubbs, "Violence Against Filipino women," n.p.
196. Chris Cunneen and Julie Stubbs, "Male Violence, Male Fantasy and the Commodification of Women Through the Internet," *International Review of Victimology* 7 (2000): 5–22.
197. Narayan, "'Mail-Order' Brides," 108.
198. The following narrative is derived from Cunneen and Stubbs, "Violence Against Filipino Women," n.p.
199. Cunneen and Stubbs, "Violence Against Filipino Women," n.p.
200. Cunneen and Stubbs, "Violence Against Filipino Women," n.p.
201. Crandall et al., "'No Way Out,'" 947.
202. Narayan, "'Mail-Order' Brides," 106.
203. Menjívar and Salcido, "Immigrant Women," 906.
204. Crandall et al., "'No Way Out,'" 947.
205. Wykes and Welsh, *Violence, Gender and Justice*, 104.

Chapter 3

1. Anonymous adult male, quoted in Debby A. Phillips, "Punking and Bullying: Strategies in Middle School, High School, and Beyond," *Journal of Interpersonal Violence* 22 (2007): 158–178; at 159–160.
2. James Q. Wilson, quoted in Anne-Marie Cusac, *Cruel and Unusual: The Culture of Punishment in America* (New Haven, CT: Yale University Press, 2009), 174.
3. Glenn Muschert and Dawn Carr argue that school shootings were first recognized as a 'social problem' in 1997, although the 1999 Columbine shootings solidified the fears of many. See Glenn Muschert and Dawn Carr, "Media Salience and Frame Changing Across Events: Coverage of Nine School Shootings," *Journalism & Mass Communication Quarterly* 83 (2006): 747–766.
4. Stuart C. Aitken, "Schoolyard Shootings: Racism, Sexism, and Moral Panics over Teen Violence," *Antipode* (2001): 593–600; at 593–594.
5. Joel Wallman, "Disarming Youth," *The HFG Review* 2 (1997): 3–9.
6. Katherine Beckett and Theodore Sasson, *The Politics of Injustice: Crime and Punishment in America*, 2nd ed. (Thousand Oaks, CA: Sage Publications, 2004), 27.
7. Jonathan Fast, *Ceremonial Violence: A Psychological Explanation of School Shootings* (New York: the Overlook Press, 2008), 9.
8. Glenn W. Muschert, "Research in School Shootings," *Sociology Compass* 1 (2007): 60–80; at 60.
9. Fast, *Ceremonial Violence*, 9.
10. Muschert, "School Shootings," 60.
11. Muschert, "School Shootings," 65.
12. Mark R. Leary, Robin M. Kowalski, Laura Smith, and Stephen Phillips, "Teasing, Rejecting, and Violence: Case Studies of the School Shootings," *Aggressive Behavior* 29 (2003): 202–214; Michelle Newman, Andree Woodcock, and Philip Dunham,

"'Playtime in the Borderlands': Children's Representations of School, Gender and Bullying Through Photographs and Interview," *Children's Geographies* 4 (2006): 289–302; Jane Brown and Pamela Munn, "'School Violence' as a Social Problem: Charting the Rise of the Problem and the Emerging Specialist Field," *International Studies in Sociology of Education* 18 (2008): 219–230; Stuart Henry, "School Violence Beyond Columbine: A Complex Problem in Need of an Interdisciplinary Analysis," *American Behavioral Scientist* 52 (2009): 1–20; and Stacey Nofziger, "Deviant Lifestyles and Violent Victimization at School," *Journal of Interpersonal Violence* 24 (2009): 1494–1517.

13. Brown and Munn, "'School Violence,'" 225.
14. According to Stuart Aitken, this 'silence' is slowly being heard (personal communication).
15. In this book I do not consider the violence meted on school children by non-related adults (i.e., stranger violence) such as the 1989 shooting spree of Patrick Purdy, that left five children dead and 29 others (including one teacher) wounded at the Cleveland Elementary School in Stockton, California or the 1996 'Dunblane Massacre' in which Thomas Watt Hamilton killed 16 children (and one adult) at the Dunblane Primary School, in Dunblane, Scotland. My omission is, in part, one of limitations: I cannot cover all forms of violence within this book and thus had to make (hard) decisions as to inclusion. It is my hope that students and instructors will take this opportunity to more fully explore and consider how stranger violence toward school children—at schools—figures in our broader discussions of space, place, and violence.
16. There is, of course, no essential 'school' or school experience. While most Western children attend public or private schools, many other children are 'home' schooled. And in many countries, schooling for vast proportions of children is simply not feasible. Class or caste inequalities may preclude school attendance for children; likewise, gender restrictions may prevent girls from attending school. In war-torn countries, there may simply be no schools.
17. Julia Ellis, "Place and Identity for Children in Classrooms and School," *Journal of the Canadian Association for Curriculum Studies* 3 (2005): 55–73; Sarah Thomson, "'Territorialising' the Primary School Playground: Deconstructing the Geography of Playtime," *Children's Geographies* 3 (2005): 63–78; Prudence L. Carter, "Straddling Boundaries: Identity, Culture, and School," *Sociology of Education* 79 (2006): 304–328; Joseph S. Agbenyega, "Developing the Understanding of the Influence of School Place on Students' Identity, Pedagogy and Learning, Visually," *International Journal of Whole Schooling* 4 (2008): 52–66; Jennifer A. Tupper, Terry Carson, Ingrid Johnston, and Jyoti Mangat, "Building Place: Students' Negotiation of Spaces and Citizenship in Schools," *Canadian Journal of Education* 31 (2008): 1065–1092; Simon Catling, "Children's Personal Geographies and the English Primary School Geography Curriculum," *Children's Geographies* 3 (2005): 325–344; Ruyu Hung and Andrew Stables, "Lost in Space? Located in Place: Geo-Phenomenological Exploration and School," *Educational Philosophy and Theory* (2009): 1–11; and Cynthia L. Uline, Megan Tschannen-Moran, and Thomas DeVere Wolsey, "The Walls Still Speak: The Stories Occupants Tell," *Journal of Educational Administration* 47 (2009): 400–426.
18. Carter, "Straddling Boundaries," 304.
19. Catling, "Children's Personal Geographies," 325.
20. Uline et al., "Walls Still Speak," 404.
21. Paul J. Hirschfield, "Preparing for Prison? The Criminalization of School Discipline in the USA," *Theoretical Criminology* 12 (2008): 79–101; at 79.
22. Michael B. Katz, "The Origins of Public Education: A Reassessment," *History of Education Quarterly* 16 (1976): 381–407; Charles N. Glaab and A. Theodore Brown,

A History of Urban America, 2nd ed. (New York: Macmillan Publishing, 1976); Howard P. Chudacoff and Judith E. Smith, *The Evolution of American Urban Society*, 3rd ed. (Englewood Cliffs, NJ: Prentice Hall, 1988); and Tom Loveless, "Uneasy Allies: The Evolving Relationship of School and State," *Educational Evaluation and Policy Analysis* 20 (1998): 1–8.

23. Cusac, *Cruel and Unusual*, 6, 135.
24. Glaab and Brown, *History of Urban America*, 121. Approximately 30 percent of the new city residents were rural-to-urban migrants; the remainder of the growth in urban population was composed of natural increase (22 percent) or through the reclassification of rural areas into urban areas (8 percent).
25. See, for example, Paul L. Knox, *Urbanization: An Introduction to Urban Geography* (Englewood Cliffs, NJ: Prentice Hall, 1994), 25–26.
26. Katz, "Origins of Public Education," 391.
27. Katz, "Origins of Public Education," 392.
28. Katz, "Origins of Public Education," 395.
29. Glaab and Brown, *History of Urban America*, 132.
30. Katz, "Origins of Public Education," 399.
31. Diane B. Paul, *Controlling Human Heredity: 1865 to the Present* (Atlantic Highlands, NJ: Humanities Press, 1995), 78.
32. Katz, "Origins of Public Education," 386.
33. Katz, "Origins of Public Education," 386.
34. Glaab and Brown, *History of Urban America*, 132.
35. Glaab and Brown, *History of Urban America*, 133.
36. Chudacoff and Smith, *Evolution of American Urban Society*, 191.
37. Katz, "Origins of Public Education," 396–397.
38. Hirschfield, "Preparing for Prison," 80.
39. Catling, "Children's Personal Geographies," 327.
40. Thomson, "Primary School Playground," 63.
41. Katz, "Origins of Public Education," 389.
42. Katz, "Origins of Public Education," 388.
43. Katz, "Origins of Public Education," 386.
44. Katz, "Origins of Public Education," 389.
45. Katz, "Origins of Public Education," 384.
46. Katz, "Origins of Public Education," 384.
47. Chudacoff and Smith, *Evolution of American Urban Society*, 184.
48. Katz, "Origins of Public Education," 393.
49. John R. Commons, *Races and Immigrants in America* (New York: Macmillan, 1907), 70.
50. See, for example, Paul Popenoe and R. H. Johnson, *Applied Eugenics*, 2nd ed. (New York: Macmillan, 1918).
51. Madison Grant, *The Passing of the Great Race, or the Racial Basis of European History*, 2nd ed. (New York: Charles Scribner's, 1918); Lothrop Stoddard, *The Rising Tide of Color Against White World Supremacy* (New York: Charles Scribner's Sons, 1920); and James H. Curle, *Our Testing Time: Will the White Race Win Through?* (New York: George H. Doran, 1926).
52. Chudacoff and Smith, *Evolution of American Urban Society*, 191.
53. Quoted in Chudacoff and Smith, *Evolution of American Urban Society*, 191.
54. Glaab and Brown, *History of Urban America*, 132.
55. Chudacoff and Smith, *Evolution of American Urban Society*, 190.
56. Katz, "Origins of Public Education," 393. Interestingly, these same arguments remain in vogue as school districts attempt to justify continued educational programs to reluctant tax-payers.
57. Hirschfield, "Preparing for Prison," 81.

58. A. Troy Adams, "The Status of School Discipline and Violence," *Annals of the American Academy of Political and Social Science* 567 (2000): 140–156, at 144–45.
59. Adams, "School Discipline," 145.
60. Hirschfield, "Preparing for Prison," 80; Beckett and Sasson, *Politics of Injustice*.
61. Murray Edelman, *Political Language: Words that Succeed and Policies that Fail* (New York: Academic Press, 1977), 43–44.
62. Philip Jenkins, *Decade of Nightmares: The End of the Sixties and the Making of Eighties America* (Oxford: Oxford University Press, 2006).
63. Beckett and Sasson, *Politics of Injustice*, 58–59.
64. Beckett and Sasson, *Politics of Injustice*, 45.
65. Jenkins, *Decade of Nightmares*, 134.
66. Cusac, *Cruel and Unusual*, 123.
67. Cusac, *Cruel and Unusual*, 175.
68. Hirschfield, "Preparing for Prison," 85.
69. Tim Newburn, "Atlantic Crossings: 'Policy Transfer' and Crime Control in the USA and Britain," *Punishment & Society* 4 (2002): 165–194; Trevor Jones and Tim Newburn, "Policy Convergence and Crime Control in the USA and the UK: Streams of Influence and Levels of Impact," *Criminal Justice* 2 (2002): 173–203.
70. Hirschfield, "Preparing for Prison," 81–82.
71. Hirschfield, "Preparing for Prison," 80.
72. Cusac, *Cruel and Unusual*, 10.
73. Cusac, *Cruel and Unusual*, 227.
74. Joe Harris, "Kids Tasered in Classroom," *Courthouse News Service*, www.courthousenews.com/2010/01//22/23944.htm (accessed May 2011). The use of stun guns and related devices is extremely controversial. Supporters, such as the Cleveland-based 'National School Safety and Security Services' (www.schoolsecurity.org) consulting firm maintains that the mis-use of these "hand-held weapons" is statistically rare and the "inappropriate use" is resultant from "situations involving poor individual judgment." This firm provides a listing of school-related incidents wherein the use of tasers prevented other, more violent acts to occur. Opponents, however, question the overall wisdom of shocking children with upwards of 50,000 volts of electricity.
75. Hirschfield, "Preparing for Prison," 83.
76. C. J. Pascoe, *Dude, You're a Fag: Masculinity and Sexuality in High School* (Berkeley: University of California Press, 2007), 4.
77. Tupper et al., "Building Place," 1068.
78. Stephen Waterhouse, "Deviant and Non-Deviant Identities in the Classroom: Patrolling the Boundaries of the Normal Social World," *European Journal of Special Needs Education* 19 (2004): 69–84; at 72–73.
79. Hirschfield, "Preparing for Prison," 80.
80. See, for example, Gill Valentine, "Angels and Devils: Moral Landscapes of Childhood," *Environment and Planning D: Society and Space* 14 (1996): 581–599 and Stuart C. Aitken and Randi C. Marchant, "Memories and Miscreants: Teenage Tales of Terror," *Children's Geographies* 1 (2003): 151–164.
81. Waterhouse, "Deviant and Non-Deviant Identities," 73.
82. Waterhouse, "Deviant and Non-Deviant Identities," 74.
83. Waterhouse, "Deviant and Non-Deviant Identities," 74.
84. Wolfgang Natter and John Paul Jones, "Identity, Space, and Other Uncertainties," in *Space and Social Theory: Intepreting Modernity and Postmodernity*, edited by Georges Benko and Ulf Strohmayer (Oxford: Blackwell, 1997), 141–161; at 142.
85. Edward Soja, *Postmodern Geographies: The Reassertion of Space in Critical Social Theory* (London: Verso, 1989), 81.
86. Ellis, "Place and Identity," 60.
87. Ellis, "Place and Identity," 64.

88. Catling, "Children's Personal Geographies," 327.
89. Emma Renold, "Learning the 'Hard' Way: Boys, Hegemonic Masculinity and the Negotiation of Learner Identities in the Primary School," *British Journal of Sociology and Education* 22 (2001): 369–385, at 372.
90. Dónal O Donoghue, "'James Always Hangs Out Here': Making Space for Place in Studying Masculinities at School," *Visual Studies* 22 (2007): 62–73, at 66.
91. Thomson, "Primary School Playground," 74.
92. Tupper et al., "Building Place," 1066.
93. Tupper et al., "Building Place," 1078.
94. Thomson, "Primary School Playground," 69, 71–73.
95. Catling, "Children's Personal Geographies," 328–330.
96. Bullying, in fact, is spectacular in that it is primarily conducted in the *public spaces* of the school. As public performances, these practices are used to position one's self within society. This is why most bullies do not tease or harm children in isolation, but instead do so in front of an audience. As a performance, the bully must humiliate his or her victim in public.
97. Carter, "Straddling Boundaries," 307.
98. Phillips, "Punking and Bullying," 163.
99. Renold, "Learning the 'Hard' Way," 373.
100. Catherine Belsey, *Post-Structuralism: A Very Short Introduction* (Oxford: Oxford University Press, 2002), 51–52.
101. Belsey, *Post-Structuralism*, 52.
102. Gill Valentine, "Boundary Crossing: Transitions from Childhood to Adulthood," *Children's Geographies* 1 (2003): 37–52.
103. Chris Weedon, *Feminist Practice and Poststructuralist Theory*, 2nd ed. (Malden, MA: Blackwell, 1997), 3. See also Judith Butler, *Gender Trouble: Feminism and the Subversion of Identity* (New York: Routledge, 1999) and Judith Butler, *Bodies that Matter: On the Discursive Limits of "Sex"* (New York: Routledge, 1993).
104. Belsey, *Post-Structuralism*, 52.
105. Butler, *Gender Trouble*, 173.
106. Mary E. Thomas, "The Identity Politics of School Life: Territoriality and the Racial Subjectivity of Teen Girls in LA," *Children's Geographies* 7 (2009): 7–19; at 8.
107. Thomas, "Identity Politics," 12.
108. Thomas, "Identity Politics," 12.
109. Pascoe, *Dude, You're a Fag*.
110. O Donoghue, "Making Space for Place," 62–63.
111. Nofziger, "Deviant Lifestyles," 1499.
112. Pascoe, *Dude, You're a Fag*, 13; emphasis added.
113. Sandra Lee Bartky, *Femininity and Domination: Studies in the Phenomenology of Oppression* (New York: Routledge, 1990), 75.
114. Pascoe, *Dude, You're a Fag*, 26–27.
115. Pascoe, *Dude, You're a Fag*, 26.
116. Pascoe, *Dude, You're a Fag*, 5.
117. Douglas Kellner, *Guys and Guns Amok: Domestic Terrorism and School Shootings from the Oklahoma City Bombing to the Virginia Tech Massacre* (Boulder, CO: Paradigm Publishers, 2008), 18.
118. Aimee Allison and David Solnit, *Army of None: Strategies to Counter Military Recruitment, End War, and Build a Better World* (New York: Seven Stories Press, 2007), 9–10.
119. Andrew J. Bacevich, *The New American Militarism: How Americans Are Seduced by War* (Oxford: Oxford University Press, 2005), 2. See also Chris Hedges, *War is a Force That Gives Us Meaning* (New York: Anchor Books, 2003).
120. Nick Turse, *The Complex: How the Military Invades Our Everyday Lives* (New York: Metropolitan Books, 2008), 151–152.

121. Cynthia Enloe, *Globalization & Militarism: Feminists Make the Link* (Lanham, MD: Rowman & Littlefield, 2007), 4.
122. Newman et al., "Playtime in the Borderlands," 294. See also Phillips, "Punking and Bullying," 169.
123. Phillips, "Punking and Bullying," 160.
124. Elizabeth Stanko, *Everyday Violence: How Women and Men Experience Sexual and Physical Danger* (San Francisco, CA: Pandora, 1990), 112.
125. Newman et al., "Playtime in the Borderlands," 298.
126. Phillips, "Punking and Bullying," 168.
127. Becky Francis, "Discussing Discrimination: Children's Construction of Sexism Between Pupils in Primary School," *British Journal of Sociology of Education* 18 (1997): 519–532; at 523.
128. Joyce Hunter, "Violence Against Lesbian and Gay Male Youths," *Journal of Interpersonal Violence* 5 (1990): 295–300; Andi O'Conor, "Who Gets Called Queer in School? Lesbian, Gay and Bisexual Teenagers, Homophobia and High School," *The High School Journal* 77 (1994): 7–12; Anthony R. D'Augelli, Neil W. Pilkington, and Scott Hershberger, "Incidence and Mental Health Impact of Sexual Orientation Victimization of Lesbian, Gay, and Bisexual Youths in High School," *School Psychology Quarterly* 17 (2002): 148–167; Dorothy L. Espelage, Steven R. Aragon, Michelle Birkett, and Brian W. Koenig, "Homophobic Teasing, Psychological Outcomes, and Sexual Orientations Among High School Students: What Influences do Parents and High Schools Have?" *School Psychology Review* 37 (2008): 202–216.
129. Hunter, "Violence Against Lesbian and Gay Male Youths," 299.
130. O'Conor, "Who Gets Called Queer," 11.
131. D'Augelli et al., "Incidence and Mental Health Impact," 161.
132. Hunter, "Violence Against Lesbian and Gay Male Youths," 299.
133. O'Conor, "Who Gets Called Queer," 11.
134. Stanko, *Everyday Violence*, 113.
135. Espelage et al., "Homophobic Teasing," 203. Homophobic victimization has emerged as one of the strongest predictors of school disengagement by gay, lesbian, and bisexual youth; drug and alcohol abuse; and suicide.
136. O'Conor, "Who Gets Called Queer," 11.
137. D. Davis, "The Production of Crime Policies," *Crime and Social Justice* 20 (1983): 121–137; at 127. See also Beckett and Sasson, *Politics of Injustice*, 58.
138. Nancy D. Brener, Thomas R. Simon, Etienne G. Krug, and Richard Lowry, "Recent Trends in Violence-Related Behaviors Among High School Students in the United States," *Journal of the American Medical Association* 281 (1999): 440–446; at 440.
139. Stanko, *Everyday Violence*, 113.

Chapter 4

1. Alex Alvarez and Ronet Bachman, *Violence: The Enduring Problem* (Los Angeles: Sage Publications, 2008), 158.
2. See, for example, Gill Valentine, "The Geography of Women's Fear," *Area* 21 (1989): 385–390; Rachel Pain, "Space, Sexual Violence and Social Control: Integrating Geographical and Feminist Analysis of Women's Fear of Crime," *Progress in Human Geography* 15 (1991): 415–431; Gill Valentine, "Images of Danger: Women's Source of Information about the Spatial Distribution of Male Violence," *Area* 24 (1992): 22–29; Kristen Day, "Strangers in the Night? Women's Fear of Sexual Assault on Urban College Campuses," *Journal of Architectural and Planning Research* 16 (1999): 289–312; and Kristen Day, "Being Feared: Masculinity and Race in Public Space," *Environment and Planning A* 38 (2006): 569–586.

3. Brenda R. Lewis, *Mapping the Trail of a Serial Killer: How the World's Most Infamous Murderers Were Tracked Down* (Guilford, CT: Lyons Press, 2009), 7. Emphasis added.
4. Lewis, *Mapping the Trail*, 7.
5. See, for example, Darrell Y. Hamamoto, "Empire of Death: Militarized Society and the Rise of Serial Killing and Mass Murder," *New Political Science* 24 (2002): 105–120; Harold Schecter, *The Serial Killer Files: The Who, What, Where, How, and Why of the World's Most Terrifying Murderers* (New York: Ballantine Books, 2003); Peter Vronsky, *Serial Killers: The Method and Madness of Monsters* (New York: Berkeley Books, 2004); David M. Buss, *The Murderer Next Door: Why the Mind is Designed to Kill* (New York: Penguin Books, 2005); Kevin D. Haggerty, "Modern Serial Killers," *Crime, Media, Culture* 5 (2009): 168–187; Tom Philbin and Michael Philbin, *The Killer Book of Serial Killers: Incredible Stories, Facts, and Trivia from the World of Serial Killers* (Naperville, IL: Sourcebooks, Inc., 2009); and Ronald M. Holmes and Stephen T. Holmes, *Serial Murder*, 3rd ed. (Los Angeles: Sage Publications, 2010). For more cultural approaches, see Philip Jenkins, *Using Murder: The Social Construction of Serial Homicide* (New York: Aldine de Gruyter, 1994); Mark Seltzer, *Serial Killers: Death and Life in America's Wound Culture* (New York: Routledge, 1998); David Schmid, *Natural Born Celebrities: Serial Killers in American Culture* (Chicago: The University of Chicago Press, 2005); Alexandria Warwick, "The Scene of the Crime: Inventing the Serial Killer," *Social & Legal Studies* 15 (2006): 552–569; and Brian Jarvis, "Monsters Inc.: Serial Killers and Consumer Culture," *Crime, Media, Culture* 3 (2007): 326–344.
6. Lawrence H. Keely, *War Before Civilization: The Myth of the Peaceful Savage* (Oxford: Oxford University Press, 1996), 37. See also David Livingstone Smith, *The Most Dangerous Animal: Human Nature and the Origins of War* (New York: St. Martin's Griffin, 2007).
7. See, for example, Martin Daly and Margo Wilson, *Homicide* (London: Transaction Publishers, 2008) and Eric W. Hickey, *Serial Murders and Their Victims*, 5th ed. (Belmont, CA: Wadsworth, 2010).
8. Daly and Wilson, *Homicide*, 1–2.
9. Smith, *Most Dangerous Animal*, xvi.
10. Alex Alvarez, *Genocidal Crimes* (London: Routledge, 2010), 104.
11. Schecter, *Serial Killer Files*, 122.
12. A useful parallel may be drawn with current debates surrounding the historicity of genocide. The term 'genocide' was coined in 1944 by Raphael Lemkin. Since then, there has been extensive and, at times, acrimonious debate as to the 'correct' definition and interpretation of genocide. Most importantly, for our current discussion of serial murder, has been the question as to whether genocide is a twentieth-century phenomenon or instead a continual feature of 'civilization'. Hence, while some scholars (such as Frank Chalk and Kurt Jonassohn) have found examples of genocide in earlier periods, others (such as Zygmung Bauman) maintain that genocide is a condition of modernity. Chalk and Jonassohn (p. 33) explain that while the "evidence from antiquity is often contradictory, ambiguous, or missing," it becomes clear that genocides most likely originated both with the domestication of agriculture and the process of urbanization. Early examples of genocide would thus include the destruction of Carthage during the Punic Wars (264–146 BC) and the massive slaughters enacted by the Mongols under Genghis Khan. Significantly, though, even Chalk and Jonassohn's argument entails a structural parameter: certain preconditions, namely settled populations, the promotion of distinct communal identities (e.g., nationalism) and so forth. Consequently, as broader political, economic, and societal conditions changed, so too did the motivation for, and understanding of, mass violence. Genocide, thus, may in fact be a product of

modernity. According to Martin Shaw (pp. 133–134), therefore, "although mass killing is hardly novel, it is only in modernity that we get *systematic* policies to destroy social groups 'as such', distinct from policies to defeat armed enemies in war." For further discussion, see Frank Chalk and Kurt Jonassohn, *The History and Sociology of Genocide: Analyses and Case Studies* (New Haven, CT: Yale University Press, 1990); Benjamin A. Valentino, *Final Solutions: Mass Killings and Genocide in the 20th Century* (Ithaca, NY: Cornell University Press, 2004); Martin Shaw, *What is Genocide* (Malden, MA: Polity, 2007); and Samuel Totten and William S. Parsons (eds.), *Century of Genocide: Critical Essays and Eyewitness Accounts*, 3rd ed. (New York: Routledge, 2009).
13. Elliott Leyton, *Hunting Humans: The Rise of the Modern Multiple Murderer* (Toronto: McClelland and Stewart, 1995).
14. Haggerty, "Modern Serial Killers," 176. This argument, of course, counters the prevalence of non-urban based serial killers. Nevertheless, the connection between supposed social anonymity and serial killing is worth considering.
15. Haggerty, "Modern Serial Killers," 177.
16. Very few serial killers have been found to be legally insane at the time of their crimes. Criminologists and psychologists both lean to the conclusion that only a small fraction, perhaps 1 or 2 percent, of all serial killers actually suffer from some form of mental illness or brain injury. In other words, nearly all serial homicides are pre-meditated.
17. Steven A. Egger, *The Killers Among Us: An Examination of Serial Murder and its Investigation* (Paramus, NJ: Prentice Hall, 1998).
18. Vronsky, *Serial Killers*, 37.
19. Haggerty, "Modern Serial Killers," 180.
20. Vronsky, *Serial Killers*, 37.
21. Jenkins, *Using Murder*, 171.
22. Jenkins, *Using Murder*, 160.
23. Jenkins, *Using Murder*, 173.
24. Jenkins, *Using Murder*, 173. Albert Fish was active between 1910 and 1935.
25. Jenkins, *Using Murder*, 171.
26. Vronsky, *Serial Killers*, 12.
27. Vronsky, *Serial Killers*, 14.
28. Haggerty, "Modern Serial Killers," 183.
29. See, for example, Barry Bluestone and Bennett Harrison, *The Deindustrialization of America: Plant Closings, Community Abandonment, and the Dismantling of Basic Industry* (New York: Basic Books, 1982); David Harvey, *The Condition of Postmodernity: An Enquiry into the Origins of Cultural Change* (Cambridge, MA: Blackwell, 1989); Paul Knox and John Agnew, *The Geography of the World Economy*, 2nd ed. (London: Edward Arnold, 1994); Neil Smith, *The New Urban Frontier: Gentrification and the Revanchist City* (London: Routledge, 1996); Andy Merrifield, "The Dialectics of Dystopia: Disorder and Zero Tolerance in the City," *International Journal of Urban and Regional Research* 24 (2000): 474–489; Steven Flusty, "The Banality of Interdiction: Surveillance, Control and the Displacement of Diversity," *International Journal of Urban and Regional Research* 25 (2001): 658–664; Gordon MacLeod and Kevin Ward, "Spaces of Utopia and Dystopia: Landscaping the Contemporary City," *Geografiska Annaler* 84B (2002): 153–170; Neil Smith, "New Globalism, New Urbanism: Gentrification as Global Urban Strategy," *Antipode* 34 (2002): 434–457; and Phil Hubbard, "Revenge and Injustice in the Neoliberal City: Uncovering Masculinist Agendas," *Antipode* 36 (2004): 665–686.
30. Knox and Agnew, *World Economy*, 209–210.
31. Lisa Benton-Short and John Rennie Short, "Cities of the United States and Canada," in *Cities of the World: World Regional Urban Development*, edited by Stanley

D. Brunn, Maureen Hays-Mitchell, and Donald J. Ziegler (Boulder, CO: Rowman & Littlefield, 2008), 53–101; at 61.
32. Bluestone and Harrison, *Deindustrialization*, 9.
33. Bluestone and Harrison, *Deindustrialization*, 9–10.
34. Harvey, *Condition of Postmodernity*, 142.
35. MacLeod and Ward, "Spaces of Utopia," 155.
36. David Wilson, *Inventing Black-on-Black Violence: Discourse, Space, and Representation* (Syracuse: Syracuse University Press, 2005), 29.
37. Knox and Agnew, *World Economy*, 246.
38. MacLeod and Ward, "Spaces of Utopia," 155.
39. John Rennie Short and Yeong-Hyun Kim, *Globalization and the City* (New York: Addison Wesley Longman, 1999), 117.
40. MacLeod and Ward, "Spaces of Utopia," 155; see also Sharon Zukin, "Space and Symbols in an Age of Decline," in *Re-Presenting the City: Ethnicity, Capital and Culture in the 21st-Century Metropolis*, edited by Anthony D. King (New York: New York University Press, 1996), 43–59; at 47.
41. Zukin, "Space and Symbols," 47.
42. MacLeod and Ward, "Spaces of Utopia," 155.
43. Hubbard, "Revenge and Injustice," 681.
44. John Rennie Short, Lisa M. Benton, W. B. Luce, and Judy Walton, "Reconstructing the Image of an Industrial City," *Annals of the Association of American Geographers* 83 (1993): 207–224; at 208.
45. Short et al., "Reconstructing the Image," 221.
46. Philip Jenkins, *Decade of Nightmares: The End of the Sixties and the Making of Eighties America* (Oxford: Oxford University Press, 2006), 66.
47. Wilson, *Inventing Black-on-Black Violence*, 4, 39.
48. Schmid, *Natural Born Celebrities*, 71.
49. Schmid, *Natural Born Celebrities*, 80.
50. Schmid, *Natural Born Celebrities*, 77.
51. It is worth noting that other special interest groups have also placed serial killers on their political platforms. Feminist groups, advocates of black rights, white supremacists, both gay and anti-gay rights supporters, nativists, fundamentalists: All have used the 'serial killer' as vehicle to promote their own political and/or financial agendas. See Jenkins, *Using Murder*, 3.
52. Jenkins, *Using Murder*, 22.
53. Jenkins, *Using Murder*, 28–29.
54. As David Schmid calculates, these killers would have had to drive an average of 550 miles each day, every day, for an entire year. See Schmid, *Natural Born Celebrities*, 81.
55. MacLeod and Ward, "Spaces of Utopia," 154.
56. MacLeod and Ward, "Spaces of Utopia," 159.
57. Neil Smith, *The New Urban Frontier: Gentrification and the Revanchist City* (London: Routledge, 1996), 45.
58. Jenkins, *Using Murder*, 8.
59. Don Mitchell, "Postmodern Geographical Praxis? Post-Modern Impulse and the War Against Homeless People in the Post-Justice City," in *Postmodern Geography: Theory and Praxis*, edited by C. Minca (Oxford: Blackwell, 2001), 57–92; at 71.
60. Marilyn A. Papayanis, "Sex and the Revanchist City: Zoning Out Pornography in New York," *Environment and Planning D: Society and Space* 18 (2000): 341–353; at 342.
61. MacLeod and Ward, "Spaces of Utopia," 163.
62. Katherine Beckett and Theodore Sasson, *The Politics of Injustice: Crime and Punishment in America*, 2nd ed. (Thousand Oaks, CA: Sage Publications, 2004), 134.

63. Tim Newburn, "Atlantic Crossings: 'Policy Transfer' and Crime Control in the USA and Britain," *Punishment & Society* 4 (2002): 165–194.
64. Beckett and Sasson, *Politics of Injustice*, 134.
65. Holmes and Holmes, *Serial Murder*, 222.
66. Schecter, *Serial Killer Files*, 288.
67. Vronsky, *Serial Killers*, 14.
68. Anonymous serial killer, quoted in Holmes and Holmes, *Serial Murder*, 95.
69. Gary Ridgway, quoted in Vronsky, *Serial Killers*, 38.
70. Phil Hubbard and Teela Sanders, "Making Space for Sex Work: Female Street Prostitution and the Production of Urban Space," *International Journal of Urban and Regional Research* 27 (2003): 75–89; at 75.
71. Hubbard, "Revenge and Injustice," 682.
72. See, for example, Phil Hubbard, "Red-Light Districts and Toleration Zones: Geographies of Female Street Prostitution in England and Wales," *Area* 29 (1997): 129–140; Hubbard and Sanders, "Making Space"; Phil Hubbard, "Cleansing the Metropolis: Sex Work and the Politics of Zero Tolerance," *Urban Studies* 41 (2004): 1687–1702; and Maggie O'Neill, Rose Campbell, Phil Hubbard, Jane Pitcher, and Jane Scoular, "Living with the Other: Street Sex Work, Contingent Communities and Degrees of Tolerance," *Crime, Media, Culture* 4 (2008): 73–93.
73. Hubbard, "Cleansing the Metropolis," 1689.
74. Papayanis, "Sex and the Revanchist City," 342.
75. Hubbard, "Cleansing the Metropolis," 1698.
76. Hubbard, "Cleaning the Metropolis," 1698.
77. Hubbard, "Revenge and Injustice," 682.
78. Hubbard, "Cleansing the Metropolis," 1692.
79. Hubbard, "Red-Light Districts," 136.
80. Vronsky, *Serial Killers*, 41.
81. Hubbard and Sanders, "Making Space," 75.
82. Hubbard, "Red-Light Districts," 129.
83. And in a further irony, it was not uncommon for protestors of street prostitution to mistakenly target *any* woman who was walking alone at night—actions that parallel those of serial killers.
84. Philbin and Philbin, *Killer Book of Serial Killers*, 210–211.
85. Holmes and Holmes, *Serial Murder*, 101.
86. Holmes and Holmes, *Serial Murder*, 93–95. Significantly, Simmons' ex-girlfriend was a prostitute.
87. Vronsky, *Serial Killers*, 38.
88. Andy Merrifield, "The Dialectics of Dystopia: Disorder and Zero Tolerance in the City," *International Journal of Urban and Regional Research* 24 (2000): 473–489; at 473.
89. Hubbard, "Revenge and Injustice," 677.
90. Schmid, *Natural Born Celebrities*, 105. Interestingly, Schmid also notes that one of Thomas Edison's earliest phonograph recordings featured an actor reading the confession of American serial killer H. H. Holmes; furthermore, one of Edison's first kinetoscopes showed the execution of Mary, Queen of Scots.
91. Schmid, *Natural Born Celebrities*, 108–109.
92. Hickey, *Serial Murders*, 3.
93. Jenkins, *Using Murder*, 85.
94. Jenkins, *Using Murder*, 103.
95. Jenkins, *Using Murder*, 9.
96. To be sure, many serial killers came from 'broken' families and many were the offspring of prostitute mothers and delinquent fathers. But a remarkable number of serial murders (e.g., Ted Bundy) did not come from dysfunctional families. These

killers, by and large, have not received the notoriety of their more (in)famous celebrity brethren.
97. Cited in Carol Mueller, Michelle Hansen, and Karen Qualtire, "Femicide on the Border and New Forms of Protest: The International Caravan for Justice," in *Human Rights Along the U.S.–Mexico Border: Gendered Violence and Insecurity*, edited by Kathleen Staudt, Tony Payan, and Z. Anthony Kruszewski (Tucson: University of Arizona Press, 2009), 125–149; at 126.
98. Melissa W. Wright, "The Dialectics of Still Life: Murder, Women, and Maquiladoras," *Public Culture* 11 (1999): 453–474; Verónica Zebadúa-Yañez, "Killing as Performance: Violence and the Shaping of Community," *e-misférica* 2 (2005): 1–22; Melissa W. Wright, "From Protests to Politics: Sex Work, Women's Worth, and Ciudad Juárez Modernity," *Annals of the Association of American Geographers* 94 (2004): 369–386; Melissa W. Wright, "Public Women, Profit, and Femicide in Northern Mexico," *South Atlantic Quarterly* 105 (2006): 681–698; Diana Washington Valdez, *The Killing Fields: Harvest of Women; The Truth About Mexico's Bloody Border Legacy* (Burbank, CA: Peace at the Border, 2006).
99. Mueller et al., "Femicide on the Border," 126.
100. Wright, "Dialectics of Still Life," 471.
101. See also Olga Aikin Arluce, "Transnational Advocacy Networks, International Norms, and Political Change in Mexico: The Murdered Women of Ciudad Juárez," in *Human Rights Along the U.S.–Mexico Border: Gendered Violence and Insecurity*, edtied by Kathleen Staudt, Tony Payan, and Z. Anthony Kruszewski (Tucson: University of Arizona Press, 2009), 150–167.
102. Justin Akers Chacón and Mike Davis, *No One is Illegal: Fighting Racism and State Violence on the U.S.–Mexico Border* (Chicago: Haymarket Books, 2006), 115.
103. Altha J. Cravey, *Women and Work in Mexico's Maquiladoras* (Lanham, MD: Rowman and Littlefield, 1998), 15; see also Susan Tiano, "Maquiladora Women: A New Category of Workers?" in *Women Workers and Global Restructuring*, edited by Kathryn Ward (Ithaca, NY: Cornell University Press, 1990), 193–223.
104. Chacón and Davis, *No One is Illegal*, 117.
105. Wright, "Dialectics of Still Life," 461–462.
106. Tiano, "Maquiladora Women," 213.
107. Cynthia H. Enloe, "Women Textile Workers in the Militarization of Southeast Asia," in *Women, Men and the International Division of Labor*, edited by June Nash and Maria Patricia Fernández-Kelly (Albany: State University of New York Press, 1983), 194–206; Annette Fuentes and Barbara Ehrenreich, "The New Factory Girls," *Multinational Monitor* 4 (1983): 5–9, 22; Linda Y. C. Lim, "Capitalism, Imperialism, and Patriarchy: The Dilemma of Third World Women Workers in Multinational Factories," in *Women, Men and the International Division of Labor*, edited by June Nash and Maria Patricia Fernández-Kelly (Albany: State University of New York Press, 1983), 70–91; Noeleen Neyzer, "The Internationalization of Women's Work," *Southeast Asian Journal of Social Sciences* 17 (1989): 25–40; Jean L. Pyle, "Export-Led Development and the Underemployment of Women: The Impact of Discriminatory Development Policy in the Republic of Ireland," in *Women Workers and Global Restructuring*, edited by Kathryn Ward (Ithaca, NY: Cornell University Press, 1990), 85–112.
108. Wright, "Dialectics of Still Life," 465.
109. Wright, "Dialectics of Still Life," 455.
110. Valdez, *The Killing Fields*, 33.
111. Wright, "Public Women," 682.
112. Wright, "Public Women," 686.
113. Quoted in Arluce, "Transnational Advocacy Networks," 157.
114. Wright, "Public Women," 682.

115. Wright, "Public Women," 686.
116. Wright, "Public Women," 682.
117. Wright, "From Protests to Politics," 370.
118. Wright, "From Protests to Politics," 370.
119. Wright, "From Protests to Politics," 379.
120. Wright, "Dialectics of Still Life," 469.
121. Zebadúa-Yañez, "Killing as Performance," 6.

Chapter 5

1. William A. V. Clark, *The California Cauldron: Immigration and the Fortunes of Local Communities* (New York: The Guilford Press, 1998), 12–13.
2. James DeFilippis, Robert Fisher, and Eric Shragge, "Neither Romance Nor Regulation: Re-Evaluating Community," *International Journal of Urban and Regional Research* 30 (2006): 673–689; William Sites, Robert J. Chaskin, and Virginia Parks, "Reframing Community Practice for the 21st Century: Multiple Traditions, Multiple Challenges," *Journal of Urban Affairs* 29 (2007): 519–541; Robert E. Thibault, "Between Survival and Revolution: Another Community System is Possible," *Antipode* 39 (2007): 874–895; and Joshua F. J. Inwood, "Searching for the Promised Land: Examining Dr. Martin Luther King's Concept of the Beloved Community," *Antipode* 41 (2009): 487–508.
3. Christopher Adair-Toteff, "Ferdinand Tönnies: Utopian Visionary," *Sociological Theory* 13 (1995): 58–65.
4. David M. Smith, *Moral Geographies: Ethics in a World of Difference* (Edinburgh: Edinburgh University Press, 2000), 33.
5. Adair-Toteff, "Ferdinand Tönnies," 60.
6. Smith, *Moral Geographies*, 33.
7. Smith, *Moral Geographies*, 33.
8. Philip Jenkins, *Decade of Nightmares: The End of the Sixties and the Making of Eighties America* (Oxford: Oxford University Press, 2006), 27.
9. DeFilippis et al., "Neither Romance Nor Regulation," 675.
10. Lynn Staheli, "Citizenship and the Problem of Community," *Political Geography* 27 (2008): 5–21; at 18.
11. Staheli, "Citizenship," 8.
12. Inwood, "Searching for the Promised Land," 493.
13. Iris Marion Young, *Justice and the Politics of Difference* (Princeton, NJ: Princeton University Press, 1990), 235.
14. Smith, *Moral Geographies*, 35.
15. Young, *Justice and the Politics of Difference*, 234.
16. DeFilippis et al., "Neither Romance Nor Regulation," 681.
17. Linda McDowell, *Gender, Identity & Place: Understanding Feminist Geographies* (Minneapolis: University of Minnesota Press, 1999), 101.
18. DeFilippis et al., "Neither Romance Nor Regulation," 674.
19. McDowell, *Gender, Identity & Place*, 100.
20. Young, *Justice and the Politics of Difference*, 234.
21. McDowell, *Gender, Identity & Place*, 100.
22. Stuart C. Aitken, *Family Fantasies and Community Space* (New Jersey: Rutgers University Press, 1998), 133–134.
23. Aitken, *Family Fantasies*, 134.
24. David Sibley, *Geographies of Exclusion: Society and Difference in the West* (London: Routledge 1995), 3.
25. Amartya Sen, *Identity and Violence: The Illusion of Destiny* (New York: W. W. Norton & Company, 2006), 2.

26. Both the Ku Klux Klan and the Guardian Angels, for example, may be considered 'vigilante' groups. So too are lynch mobs and neighborhood watch patrols. See H. Jon Rosenbaum and Peter C. Sederberg, "Vigilantism: An Analysis of Establishment Violence," *Comparative Politics* 6 (1974): 541–570; Robert M. Brown, *Strain of Violence* (New York: Oxford University Press, 1975); Les Johnston, "What is Vigilantism?" *British Journal of Criminology* 36 (1996): 220–236; Ray Abrahams, *Vigilante Citizens: Vigilantism and the State* (Malden, MA: Polity Press, 1998); Roxanne Lynn Doty, *The Law Into Their Own Hands: Immigration and the Politics of Exceptionalism* (Tucson: University of Arizona Press, 2009).
27. Doty, *Law Into Their Own Hands*, 15.
28. Abrahams, *Vigilante Citizens*, 4.
29. Doty, *Law Into Their Own Hands*, 23.
30. Abrahams, *Vigilante Citizens*, 76.
31. Abrahams, *Vigilante Citizens*, 78.
32. Doty, *Law Into Their Own Hands*, 11.
33. Abrahams, *Vigilante Citizens*, 78.
34. Rosenbaum and Sederberg, "Vigilantism," 542.
35. Johnston, "What is Vigilantism?" 222.
36. Johnston, "What is Vigilantism?" 226.
37. Johnston, "What is Vigilantism?" 229.
38. Sen, *Identity and Violence*, 10.
39. The Mexican–American War was initiated, in part, by southern slave and northern industrial interests and must be seen as part of the on-going Western expansion of the United States. Southern states, for example, sought territories in the northern tier of Mexico to expand slavery, while northern-based private corporations sought new areas of natural resources. The ratification of the Treaty of Guadalupe Hildalgo was a requirement for the removal of U.S. troops from Mexican territory.
40. Justin Akers Chacón and Mike Davis, *No One is Illegal: Fighting Racism and State Violence on the U.S.–Mexico Border* (Chicago: Haymarket Books, 2006), 99–100. See also Pierrette Hondagneu-Sotelo, *Gendered Transitions: Mexican Experiences of Immigration* (Berkeley: University of California Press, 1994); Peter Andreas, *Border Games: Policing the U.S.–Mexico Divide* (Ithaca: Cornell University Press, 2000); Joseph Nevins, *Dying to Live: A Story of U.S. Immigration in an Age of Global Apartheid* (San Francisco: City Lights Books, 2008); Joseph Nevins, *Operation Gatekeeper and Beyond: The War on 'Illegals' and the Remaking of the U.S.–Mexico Boundary* (New York: Routledge, 2010).
41. Nevins, *Dying to Live*, 67.
42. Andreas, *Border Games*, 86.
43. Andreas, *Border Games*, 32.
44. Andreas, *Border Games*, 33.
45. Marta Tienda, "Looking to the 1990s: Mexican Immigration in Sociological Perspective," in *Mexican Migration to the United States: Origins, Consequences, and Policy Options*, edited by W. Cornelius and J. A. Bustamante (San Diego: Center for U.S.–Mexican Studies, University of California San Diego, 1989), 109–150; at 115.
46. Chacón and Davis, *No One is Illegal*, 104.
47. Hondagneu-Sotelo, *Gendered Transitions*, 20–21.
48. Chacón and Davis, *No One is Illegal*, 110.
49. Chacón and Davis, *No One is Illegal*, 110.
50. Patricia Zamudio, "Mexico: Mexican International Migration," in *Migration and Immigration: A Global View*, edited by Marua I. Toro-Morn and Marixsa Alicea (Westport, CT: Greenwood Press, 2004), 129–145; at 133.
51. Hondagneu-Sotelo, *Gendered Transitions*, 22.

52. Hondagneu-Sotelo, *Gendered Transitions*, 23.
53. Zamudio, "Mexico," 133.
54. Hondagneu-Sotelo, *Gendered Transitions*, 23.
55. It came under attack, not so much because of the presence of Mexican workers per se, but rather (and somewhat ironically) out of a liberal concern about the working conditions of the Mexicans.
56. Zamudio, "Mexico," 134.
57. Andreas, *Border Games*, 35.
58. Zamudio, "Mexico," 134.
59. Andreas, *Border Games*, 5–6.
60. Chacón and Davis, *No One is Illegal*, 201.
61. Ironically, conservative right-wing appeals for border protection actually undermine the fiscal intentions of American business interests.
62. Nevins, *Dying to Live*, 103.
63. Andreas, *Border Games*, 86.
64. Philip Martin, "Proposition 187 in California," *International Migration Review* 29 (1995): 255–263; and Marcelo M. Suárez-Orozco, "California Dreaming: Proposition 187 and the Cultural Psychology of Racial and Ethnic Exclusion," *Anthropology & Education Quarterly* 27 (1996): 151–167.
65. Suárez-Orozco, "California Dreaming," 154.
66. Martin, "Proposition 187," 256.
67. Chacón and Davis, *No One is Illegal*, 201.
68. Quoted in Andreas, *Border Games*, 87.
69. Andreas, *Border Games*, 87.
70. Suárez-Orozco, "California Dreaming," 153.
71. Andreas, *Border Games*, 89.
72. Chacón and Davis, *No One is Illegal*, 205.
73. Andreas, *Border Games*, 89.
74. Chacón and Davis, *No One is Illegal*, 205.
75. Andreas, *Border Games*, 95; see also his discussion, on pages 96–100.
76. Maria Jimenez, *Humanitarian Crisis: Migrant Deaths at the U.S.–Mexico Border* (San Diego, CA: American Civil Liberties Union and Mexico's National Commission of Human Rights, 2009), 21.
77. Jimenez, *Humanitarian Crisis*, 21.
78. Jimenez, *Humanitarian Crisis*, 14.
79. Nevins, *Dying to Live*.
80. Nevins, *Dying to Live*, 21; see also Jimenez, *Humanitarian Crisis*, 17.
81. Jimenez, *Humanitarian Crisis*, 21.
82. See, for example, Lisa A. Flores, "Constructing Rhetorical Borders: Peons, Illegal Aliens, and Competing Narratives of Immigration," *Critical Studies in Media Communication* 20 (2003): 362–387; Gilberto Rosas, "The Managed Violence of the Borderlands: Treacherous Geographies, Policeability, and the Politics of Race," *Latino Studies* 4 (2006): 401–418; Stephen R. Vina, Blas Nunez-Neto, and Alyssa Barlett Weir, "Civilian Patrols Along the Border: Legal and Policy Issues," *CRS Report for Congress*, Congressional Research Service: The Library of Congress, Washington, D.C. (2006); Robert F. Castro, "Busting the Bandito Boyz: Militarism, Masculinity, and the Hunting of Undocumented Persons in the U.S.–Mexico Borderlands," *Journal of Hate Studies* 6 (2007/8): 7–30; J. David Cisneros, "Contaminated Communities: the Metaphor of 'Immigrant as Pollutant' in Media Representations of Immigration," *Rhetoric & Public Affairs* 11 (2008): 569–602; Monica Varsanyi, "Immigration Policing through the Backdoor: City Ordinances, the 'Right to the City,' and the Exclusion of Undocumented Day Laborers," *Urban*

Geography 29 (2008): 29–52; D. Robert DeChaine, "Bordering the Civic Imaginary: Alienization, Fence Logic, and the Minuteman Civil Defense Corps," *Quarterly Journal of Speech* 95 (2009): 43–65; Sang H. Kil, Cecilia Menjivar, and Roxanne L. Doty, "Securing Borders: Patriotism, Vigilantism and the Brutalization of the US American Public," *Sociology of Crime, Law and Deviance* 13 (2009): 297–312; Luis Cabrera and Sonya Glavac, "Minutemen and Desert Samaritans: Mapping the Attitude of Activists on the United States' Immigration Front Lines," *Journal of Ethnic and Migration Studies* 36 (2010): 673–695; and Bridget Hayden, "Impeach the Traitors: Citizenship, Sovereignty and Nation in Immigration Control Activism in the United States," *Social Semiotics* 20 (2010): 155–174.

83. Doty, *Law Into Their Own Hands*, 28.
84. Castro, "Busting the Bandito Boyz," 13. See also Doty, *Law Into Their Own Hands*, 30–32.
85. Vina et al., "Civilian Patrols," 9.
86. Cabrera and Glavac, "Minutement and Desert Samaritans," 678.
87. Kil et al., "Securing Borders," 305. Gilchrist's Minuteman Project would establish chapters in California, Florida, New Jersey, Illinois, Maine, Massachusetts, North Carolina, Texas, and Oregon.
88. Kil et al., "Securing Borders," 304. See also the Southern Poverty Law Center, "'Nativist Extremist' Group List," at www.splcenter.org. Members of these groups are often portrayed as 'authorities' on immigration, and regularly appear as guests on cable newscasts, including Fox New's Sean Hannity and CNN's Lou Dobbs.
89. See, for example, Hayden, "Impeach the Traitors," 159.
90. Andreas, *Border Games*, 7.
91. Chacón and Davis, *No One is Illegal*, 120.
92. Chacón and Davis, *No One is Illegal*, 120.
93. Chacón and Davis, *No One is Illegal*, 120–121.
94. Andreas, *Border Games*, 7–8.
95. Nevins, *Dying to Live*, 68.
96. Sen, *Identity and Violence*, 1–2.
97. Sen, *Identity and Violence*, 4–5.
98. Michel Foucault, *The Archaeology of Knowledge and the Discourse on Language*, translated by A. M. Sheridan Smith (New York: Pantheon Books, 1972), 17.
99. Sen, *Identity and Violence*, 23–24.
100. Sen, *Identity and Violence*, 11.
101. Sen, *Identity and Violence*, 7.
102. Castro, "Busting the Bandito Boyz," 11.
103. Nevins, *Dying to Live*, 120.
104. Hayden, "Impeach the Traitors," 161.
105. Castro, "Busting the Bandito Boyz," 12.
106. Hayden, "Impeach the Traitors," 160.
107. Chacón and Davis, *No One is Illegal*, 253.
108. Quoted in Hayden, "Impeach the Traitors," 163.
109. George T. Winston, "The Relation of the Whites to the Negros," *Annals of the American Academy of Political and Social Science* 18 (1901): 103–118; at 109.
110. Susan Opotow, "Reconciliation in Time of Impunity: Challenges for Social Justice," *Social Justice Research* 14 (2001): 149–170; at 156.
111. Sen, *Identity and Violence*, 45.
112. Sen, *Identity and Violence*, 7.
113. Nevins, *Dying to Live*, 77.
114. Castro, "Busting the Bandito Boyz," 9.

Chapter 6

1. Eviatar Zerubavel, *The Elephant in the Room: Silence and Denial in Everyday Life* (Oxford: Oxford University Press, 2006).
2. Zerubavel, *The Elephant in the Room*, 13.
3. Elizabeth A. Stanko, "The Day to Count: Reflections on a Methodology to Raise Awareness about the Impact of Domestic Violence in the UK," *Criminology and Criminal Justice* 1 (2001): 215–226.
4. For a discussion on her methodology, see page 217.
5. Stanko, "Day to Count," 219–222. Stanko notes that there was no report of a domestic killing in the UK on that day; however, other surveys indicate that two women a week are killed by their partners in England and Wales (p. 224).
6. See Barrie Levy, *Women and Violence* (Berkeley: Seal Press, 2008), 95. The estimates from the Center for Disease Control and Prevention, as well as the Department of Justice, are quoted from Levy, p. 95.
7. Zerubavel, *The Elephant in the Room*, 20.
8. Friedrich Nietzsche, *Beyond Good & Evil: Prelude to a Philosophy of the Future*, translated by Walter Kaufmann (New York: Vintage Books, 1989 [1886]), 89.
9. Harald Bauder, "Learning to Become a Geographer: Reproduction and Transformation in Academia," *Antipode* 38 (2006): 671–679.
10. See Bauder, "Learning to Become a Geographer," 672; see also Noel Castree, "Professionalisation, Activism, and the University: Whither 'Critical geography'?" *Environment and Planning A* 32 (2000): 955–970; Ron Johnston, "Authors, Editors, and Authority in the Postmodern Academy," *Antipode* 32 (2000): 271–291; Susan Roberts, "Realizing Critical Geographies of the University," *Antipode* 32 (2000): 230–244; David Smith, "On Performing Geography," *Antipode* 33 (2001): 141–146; Don Mitchell, "Between Books and Streets, Between Home, Mall and Battlefield: The Politics and Pleasure of Cultural Geography," *Antipode* 34 (2002): 335–339; and Eric Sheppard, "Practicing Geography," *Annals of the Association of American Geographers* 94 (2004): 744–747.
11. Bauder, "Learning to Become a Geographer," 675.
12. Michael Solem and Kenneth Foote, "Concerns, Attitudes, and Abilities of Early-Career Geography Faculty," *Annals of the Association of American Geographers* 94 (2004): 889–912.
13. Bauder, "Learning to Become a Geographer," 676.
14. Zerubavel, *The Elephant in the Room*, 23.
15. Ruth Wilson Gilmore, "Globalisation and US Prison Growth: From Military Keynesianism to Post-Keynesian Militarism," *Race & Class* 40 (1998/1999): 171–188; Lawrence Di Bartolo, "The Geography of Reported Domestic Violence in Brisbane: A Social Justice Perspective," *Australian Geographer* 32 (2001): 321–341; Ruth Wilson Gilmore, *Golden Gulag: Prisons, Surplus, Crisis, and Opposition in Globalizing California* (Berkeley: University of California Press, 2007); Lauren L. Martin and Matthew L. Mitchelson, "Geographies of Detention and Imprisonment: Interrogating Spatial Practices of Confinement, Discipline, Law and State Power," *Geography Compass* 3 (2009): 459–477; Katherine Brickell, "'Fire in the House': Gendered Experiences of Drunkenness and Violence in Siem Reap, Cambodia," *Geoforum* 39 (2008): 1667–1675.
16. Joseph Nevins, *Operation Gatekeeper and Beyond: The War on 'Illegals' and the Remaking of the U.S.–Mexico-Boundary* (New York: Routledge, 2010); *Dying to Live: A Story of U.S. Immigration in an Age of Global Apartheid* (San Francisco: City Lights Books, 2008); and *A Not-So-Distant Horror: Mass Violence in East Timor* (Ithaca, NY: Cornell University Press, 2005).

17. David Harvey, "Revolutionary and Counter Revolutionary Theory in Geography and the Problem of Ghetto Formation," *Antipode* 4 (1972): 1–12; at 11.
18. Johnston, "Authors, Editors, and Authority," 272.
19. Don Mitchell, *Cultural Geography: A Critical Introduction* (Malden, MA: Blackwell Publishing, 2000), xv.
20. Peggy McIntosh, "White Privilege: Unpacking the Invisible Knapsack," *Peace and Freedom* July/August (1989): 10–12; at 10.

BIBLIOGRAPHY

Abrahams, Ray. *Vigilante Citizens: Vigilantism and the State* (Malden, MA: Polity Press, 1998).

Adair-Toteff, Christopher. "Ferdinand Tönnies: Utopian Visionary," *Sociological Theory* 13 (1995): 58–65.

Adams, A. Troy. "The Status of School Discipline and Violence," *Annals of the American Academy of Political and Social Science* 567 (2000): 140–156.

Adams, Paul C., Steven Hoelscher, and Karen E. Till. "Place in Context: Rethinking Humanist Geographies," in *Textures of Place: Exploring Humanist Geographies*, edited by Paul C. Adams, Steven Hoelscher, and Karen E. Till (Minneapolis: University of Minnesota Press, 2001).

Agbenyega, Joseph S. "Developing the Understanding of the Influence of School Place on Students' Identity, Pedagogy and Learning, Visually," *International Journal of Whole Schooling* 4 (2008): 52–66.

Aitken, Stuart C. "Schoolyard Shootings: Racism, Sexism, and Moral Panics over Teen Violence," *Antipode* (2001): 593–600.

Aitken, Stuart C. *Family Fantasies and Community Space* (New Brunswick, NJ: Rutgers University Press, 1998).

Aitken, Stuart C. and Randi C. Marchant. "Memories and Miscreants: Teenage Tales of Terror," *Children's Geographies* 1 (2003): 151–164.

Allison, Aimee and David Solnit. *Army of None: Strategies to Counter Military Recruitment, End War, and Build a Better World* (New York: Seven Stories Press, 2007).

Alvarez, Alex. *Genocidal Crimes* (London: Routledge, 2010).

Alvarez, Alex and Ronet Bachman. *Violence: The Enduring Problem* (Los Angeles: Sage Publications, 2008).

Anderson, James E., Mufiyda Abraham, Diane Michelle Bruessow, Robert David Coleman, Kelly C. McCarthy, Trisha Harris-Odimgbe, and Cindy K. Tong.

"Cross-Cultural Perspectives on Intimate Partner Violence," *JAAPA* 21 (2008): 36–44.

Anderson, Kristin L. "Gender, Status, and Domestic Violence: An Integration of Feminist and Family Violence Approaches," *Journal of Marriage and the Family* 59 (1997): 655–669.

Andreas, Peter. *Border Games: Policing the U.S.–Mexico Divide* (Ithaca, NY: Cornell University Press, 2000).

Angeles, Leonora and Sirijit Sunanta. "'Exotic Love at Your Fingertips': Intermarriage Websites, Gendered Representation, and the Transnational Migration of Filipino and Thai Women," *Kasarinlan: Philippine Journal of Third World Studies* 22 (2007): 3–31.

Ansara, Donna L. and Michelle J. Hindin. "Perpetration of Intimate Partner Aggression by Men and Women in the Philippines: Prevalence and Associated Factors," *Journal of Interpersonal Violence* 24 (2009): 1579–1590.

Arluce, Olga Aikin. "Transnational Advocacy Networks, International Norms, and Political Change in Mexico: The Murdered Women of Ciudad Juárez," in *Human Rights Along the U.S.–Mexico Border: Gendered Violence and Insecurity*, edited by Kathleen Staudt, Tony Payan, and Z. Anthony Kruszewski (Tucson: University of Arizona Press, 2009), 150–167.

Bacevich, Andrew J. *The New American Militarism: How Americans are Seduced by War* (Oxford: Oxford University Press, 2005).

Balsam, Kimberly F. and Dawn M. Szymanski. "Relationship Quality and Domestic Violence in Women's Same-Sex Relationships: The Role of Minority Stress," *Psychology of Women Quarterly* 29 (2005): 258–269.

Bartky, Sandra Lee. *Femininity and Domination: Studies in the Phenomenology of Oppression* (New York: Routledge, 1990).

Bauder, Harald. "Learning to Become a Geographer: Reproduction and Transformation in Academia," *Antipode* 38 (2006): 671–679.

Beckett, Katherine and Theodore Sasson. *The Politics of Injustice: Crime and Punishment in America*, 2nd ed. (Thousand Oaks, CA: Sage Publications, 2004).

Belsey, Catherine. *Post-Structuralism: A Very Short Introduction* (Oxford: Oxford University Press, 2002).

Benton-Short, Lisa and John Rennie Short. "Cities of the United States and Canada," in *Cities of the World: World Regional Urban Development*, edited by Stanley D. Brunn, Maureen Hays-Mitchell, and Donald J. Ziegler (Boulder, CO: Rowman & Littlefield, 2008), 53–101.

Blomley, Nicholas. "The Spaces of Critical Geography," *Progress in Human Geography* 32 (2008): 285–293.

Blomley, Nicholas. "Uncritical Critical Geography," *Progress in Human Geography* 30 (2006): 87–94.

Bluestone, Barry and Bennett Harrison. *The Deindustrialization of America: Plant Closings, Community Abandonment, and the Dismantling of Basic Industry* (New York: Basic Books, 1982).

Bornstein, Danica R., Jake Fawcett, Marianne Sullivan, Kirsten D. Senturia, and Sharyne Shui-Thornton. "Understanding the Experiences of Lesbian, Bisexual and Trans Survivors of Domestic Violence: A Qualitative Study," *Journal of Homosexuality* 51 (2006): 159–181.

Boy, Angie and Andrzej Kulczycki. "What We Know About Intimate Partner Violence in the Middle East and North Africa," *Violence Against Women* 14 (2008): 53–70.

Brener, Nancy D., Thomas R. Simon, Etienne G. Krug, and Richard Lowry. "Recent Trends in Violence-Related Behaviors Among High School Students in the United States," *Journal of the American Medical Association* 281 (1999): 440–446.

Brickell, Katherine. "'Fire in the House': Gendered Experiences of Drunkenness and Violence in Siem Reap, Cambodia," *Geoforum* 39 (2008): 1667–1675.

Brown, Jane and Pamela Munn. "'School Violence' as a Social Problem: Charting the Rise of the Problem and the Emerging Specialist Field," *International Studies in Sociology of Education* 18 (2008): 219–230.

Brown, Nicola. "Stories from Outside the Frame: Intimate Partner Abuse in Sexual-Minority Women's Relationships with Transsexual Men," *Feminism & Psychology* 17 (2007): 373–393.

Brown, Robert M. *Strain of Violence* (New York: Oxford University Press, 1975).

Brownlow, Alec. "A Geography of Men's Fear," *Geoforum* 36 (2005): 581–592.

Burke, L. K. and D. R. Follingstad. "Violence in Lesbian and Gay Relationships: Theory, Prevalence, and Correlational Factors," *Clinical Psychology Review* 19 (1999): 487–512.

Buss, David M. *The Murderer Next Door: Why the Mind is Designed to Kill* (New York: Penguin, 2005).

Butler, Judith. *Gender Trouble: Feminism and the Subversion of Identity* (New York: Routledge, 1999).

Butler, Judith. *Bodies that Matter: On the Discursive Limits of "Sex"* (New York: Routledge, 1993).

Cabrera, Luis and Sonya Glavac. "Minutemen and Desert Samaritans: Mapping the Attitude of Activists on the United States' Immigration Front Lines," *Journal of Ethnic and Migration Studies* 36 (2010): 673–695.

Carter, Prudence L. "Straddling Boundaries: Identity, Culture, and School," *Sociology of Education* 79 (2006): 304–328.

Castree, Noel. "Professionalisation, Activism, and the University: Whither 'Critical Geography'?" *Environment and Planning A* 32 (2000): 955–970.

Castro, Robert F. "Busting the Bandito Boyz: Militarism, Masculinity, and the Hunting of Undocumented Persons in the U.S.–Mexico Borderlands," *Journal of Hate Studies* 6 (2007/8): 7–30.

Catling, Simon. "Children's Personal Geographies and the English Primary School Geography Curriculum," *Children's Geographies* 3 (2005): 325–344.

Chacón, Justin Akers and Mike Davis. *No One is Illegal: Fighting Racism and State Violence on the U.S.–Mexico Border* (Chicago: Haymarket Books, 2006).

Chalk, Frank and Kurt Jonassohn. *The History and Sociology of Genocide: Analyses and Case Studies* (New Haven, CT: Yale University Press, 1990).

Chudacoff, Howard P. and Judith E. Smith. *The Evolution of American Urban Society*, 3rd ed. (Englewood Cliffs, NJ: Prentice Hall, 1988).

Cisneros, J. David. "Contaminated Communities: The Metaphor of 'Immigrant as Pollutant' in Media Representations of Immigration," *Rhetoric & Public Affairs* 11 (2008): 569–602.

Clark, William A. V. *The California Cauldron: Immigration and the Fortunes of Local Communities* (New York: The Guilford Press, 1998).

Collins, Patricia Hill. *Black Feminist Thought: Knowledge, Consciousness, and the Politics of Empowerment* (New York: Routledge, 1990).

Collins, Randall. *Violence: A Micro-Sociological Theory* (Princeton, NJ: Princeton University Press, 2008).

Commons, John R. *Races and Immigrants in America* (New York: Macmillan, 1907).

Corteen, Karen. "Lesbian Safety Talk: Problematizing Definitions and Experiences of Violence, Sexuality and Space," *Sexualities* 5 (2002): 259–280.

Crandall, Marie, Kirsten Senturia, Marianne Sullivan, and Sharyne Shiu-Thornton. "'No Way Out': Russian-Speaking Women's Experiences with Domestic Violence," *Journal of Interpersonal Violence* 20 (2005): 941–958.

Cravey, Altha. *Women and Work in Mexico's Maquiladoras* (Lanham, MD: Rowman & Littlefield, 1998).

Cresswell, Tim. *Place: A Short Introduction* (Malden, MA: Blackwell, 2004).

Cresswell, Tim. *In Place/Out of Place: Geography, Ideology and Transgression* (Minneapolis: University of Minnesota Press, 1996).

Cunneen, Chris and Julie Stubbs. "Male Violence, Male Fantasy and the Commodification of Women Through the Internet," *International Review of Victimology* 7 (2000): 5–22.

Cunneen, Chris and Julie Stubbs. "Violence Against Filipino Women in Australia: Race, Class and Gender," *Waikato Law Review* 131 (1996): n.p.

Curle, James H. *Our Testing Time: Will the White Race Win Through?* (New York: George H. Doran, 1926).

Cusac, Anne-Marie. *Cruel and Unusual: The Culture of Punishment in America* (New Haven, CT: Yale University Press, 2009).

Cutter, Susan L., Douglas B. Richardson, and Thomas J. Wilbanks. "The Changing Landscape of Fear," in *The Geographical Dimensions of Terrorism*, edited by Susan L. Cutter, Douglas B. Richardson, and Thomas J. Wilbanks (New York: Routledge, 2002), 1–5.

Daly, Martin and Margo Wilson. *Homicide* (London: Transaction Publishers, 2008).

D'Augelli, Anthony R., Neil W. Pilkington, and Scott Hershberger. "Incidence and Mental Health Impact of Sexual Orientation Victimization of Lesbian, Gay, and Bisexual Youth in High School," *School Psychology Quarterly* 17 (2002): 148–167.

D'Augelli, Anthony R., Scott Hershberger, and Neil W. Pilkington. "Lesbian, Gay and Bisexual Youth and Their Families: Disclosure of Sexual Orientation and its Consequences," *American Journal of Orthopsychiatry* 68 (1998): 361–371.

Davis, D. "The Production of Crime Policies," *Crime and Social Justice* 20 (1983): 121–137.

Day, Kristen. "Being Feared: Masculinity and Race in Public Space," *Environment and Planning A* 38 (2006): 569–586.

Day, Kristen. "Constructing Masculinity and Women's Fear in Public Space in Irvine, California," *Gender, Place and Culture* 8 (2001): 109–127.

Day, Kristen. "Strangers in the Night? Women's Fear of Sexual Assault on Urban College Campuses," *Journal of Architectural and Planning Research* 16 (1999): 289–312.

DeChaine, D. Robert. "Bordering the Civic Imaginary: Alienization, Fence Logic, and the Minuteman Civil Defense Corps," *Quarterly Journal of Speech* 95 (2009): 43–65.

DeFilippis, James, Robert Fisher, and Eric Shragge. "Neither Romance Nor Regulation: Re-Evaluating Community," *International Journal of Urban and Regional Research* 30 (2006): 673–689.
Di Bartolo, Lawrence. "The Geography of Reported Domestic Violence in Brisbane: A Social Justice Perspective," *Australian Geographer* 32 (2001): 321–341.
Domosh, Mona. "Geography and Gender: Home, Again?" *Progress in Human Geography* 22 (1998): 276–282.
Domosh, Mona. "Those 'Gorgeous Incongruities': Polite Politics and Public Space on the Streets of Nineteenth-Century New York City," *Annals of the Association of American Geographers* 88 (1998): 209–226.
Domosh, Mona and Joni Seager. *Putting Women in Place: Feminist Geographers Make Sense of the World* (New York: The Guilford Press, 2001).
Doty, Roxanne Lynn. *The Law Into Their Own Hands: Immigration and the Politics of Exceptionalism* (Tucson: University of Arizona Press, 2009).
Duenas, Michael. "Filipino Mail Order Brides," *Philippines Free Press*, July 25 (1987), pp. 18–19, 28, 30, and 32.
Edelman, Murray. *Political Language: Words that Succeed and Politics that Fail* (New York: Academic Press, 1977).
Egger, Steven A. *The Killers Among Us: An Examination of Serial Murder and its Investigation* (Paramus, NJ: Prentice Hall, 1998).
Ellis, Julia. "Place and Identity for Children in Classrooms and School," *Journal of the Canadian Association for Curriculum Studies* 3 (2005): 55–73.
Ellsberg, Mary, Henrica A. F. M. Jansen, Lori Heise, Charlotte H. Watts, and Claudia García-Moreno. "Intimate Partner Violence and Women's Physical and Mental Health in the WHO Multi-Country Study on Women's Health and Domestic Violence: An Observational Study," *The Lancet* 371 (2008): 1165–1172.
Elwood, Sarah A. "Lesbian Living Spaces: Multiple Meanings of Home," *Journal of Lesbian Studies* 4 (2000): 11–27.
Enloe, Cynthia. *Globalization and Militarism: Feminists Make the Link* (Lanham, MD: Rowman & Littlefield, 2007).
Enloe, Cynthia. "Women Textile Workers in the Militarization of Southeast Asia," in *Women, Men and the International Division of Labor*, edited by June Nash and Maria Patricia Fernández-Kelly (Albany: State University of New York Press, 1983), 194–206.
Espelage, Dorothy L., Steven R. Aragon, Michelle Birkett, and Brian W. Koenig. "Homophobic Teasing, Psychological Outcomes, and Sexual Orientations Among High School Students: What Influences do Parents and High Schools Have?" *School Psychology Review* 37 (2008): 202–216.
Eviota, Elizabeth Uy. *The Political Economy of Gender: Women and the Sexual Division of Labour in the Philippines* (London: Zed Books, 1992).
Fast, Jonathan. *Ceremonial Violence: A Psychological Explanation of School Shootings* (New York: The Overlook Press, 2008).
Ferraro, Kathleen. "Policing Battered Women," *Social Problems* 36 (1989): 61–74.
Flannery, Daniel J. *Violence and Mental Health in Everyday Life: Prevention and Intervention Strategies for Children and Adolescents* (Lanham, MD: AltaMira Press, 2006).

Flores, Lisa A. "Constructing Rhetorical Borders: Peons, Illegal Aliens, and Competing Narratives of Immigration," *Critical Studies in Media Communication* 20 (2003): 362–387.

Flusty, Steven. "The Banality of Interdiction: Surveillance, Control and the Displacement of Diversity," *International Journal of Urban and Regional Research* 25 (2001): 658–664.

Foucault, Michel. *Discipline and Punish: The Birth of the Prison*, translated by Alan Sheridan (New York: Vintage Books, 1979).

Foucault, Michel. *The Archaeology of Knowledge and the Discourse on Language*, translated by A. M. Sheridan Smith (New York: Pantheon Books, 1972).

Francis, Becky. "Discussing Discrimination: Children's Construction of Sexism Between Pupils in Primary School," *British Journal of Sociology of Education* 18 (1997): 519–532.

Fuentes, Annette and Barbara Ehrenreich. "The New Factory Girls," *Multinational Monitor* 4 (1983): 5–9, 22.

Fuller, Duncan and Rob Kitchin. "Radical Theory/Critical Praxis: Academic Geography Beyond the Academy," in *Radical Theory/Critical Praxis: Making a Difference Beyond the Academy*, edited by Duncan Fuller and Rob Kitchin (Praxis (e)Press, 2004), 1–20.

Gilligan, James. *Violence: Reflections on a National Epidemic* (New York: Vintage Books, 1996).

Gilmore, Ruth Wilson. *Golden Gulag: Prisons, Surplus, Crisis, and Opposition in Globalizing California* (Berkeley: University of California Press, 2007).

Gilmore, Ruth Wilson. "Globalisation and US Prison Growth: From Military Keynesianism to Post-Keynesian Militarism," *Race & Class* 40 (1998/1999): 171–188.

Girschick, Lori B. "No Sugar, No Spice: Reflections on Research on Woman-to-Woman Sexual Violence," *Violence Against Women* 8 (2002): 1500–1520.

Girschick, Lori B. *Woman-to-Woman Sexual Violence: Does She Call it Rape?* (Boston: Northeastern University Press, 2002).

Glaab, Charles N. and A. Theodore Brown. *A History of Urban America*, 2nd ed. (New York: Macmillan Publishing, 1976).

Glick, Peter and Susan T. Fiske. "The Ambivalent Sexism Inventory: Differentiating Hostile and Benevolent Sexism," *Journal of Personality and Social Psychology* 70 (1996): 491–512.

Gorman-Murray, Andrew. "Reconfiguring Domestic Values: Meanings of Home for Gay Men and Lesbians," *Housing, Theory and Society* 24 (2007): 229–246.

Gorman-Murray, Andrew. "Homeboys: Uses of Home by Gay Australian Men," *Social & Cultural Geography* 7 (2006): 53–69.

Grant, Madison. *The Passing of the Great Race, or the Racial Basis of European History*, 2nd ed. (New York: Charles Scriber's, 1918).

Gregory, Derek and Allan Pred (eds.). *Violent Geographies: Fear, Terror, and Political Violence* (New York: Routledge, 2007).

Gregson, Nicky and Michelle Lowe. "'Home-Making': On the Spatiality of Daily Social Reproduction in Contemporary Middle-Class Britain," *Transactions, Institute of British Geographers* 20 (1995): 224–235.

Haggerty, Kevin D. "Modern Serial Killers," *Crime, Media, Culture* 5 (2009): 168–187.

Hamamoto, Darrell Y. "Empire of Death: Militarized Society and the Rise of Serial Killing and Mass Murder," *New Political Science* 24 (2002): 105–120.
Hartnagel, Timothy F., James J. Teevan, Jr., and Jennie J. McIntyre. "Television Violence and Violent Behavior," *Social Forces* 54 (1975): 341–351.
Harvey, David. "The Geographies of Critical Geography," *Transactions, Institute of British Geographers* 31 (2006): 409–412.
Harvey, David. *The Condition of Postmodernity: An Enquiry into the Origins of Cultural Change* (Cambridge, MA: Blackwell, 1989).
Harvey, David. "Revolutionary and Counter-Revolutionary Theory in Geography and the Problem of Ghetto Formation," *Antipode* 4 (1972): 1–12.
Hattery, Angela J. *Intimate Partner Violence* (Lanham, MD: Rowman & Littlefield, 2009).
Hayden, Bridget. "Impeach the Traitors: Citizenship, Sovereignty and Nation in Immigration Control Activism in the United States," *Social Semiotics* 20 (2010): 155–174.
Hearn, Jeff and Anthony Whitehead. "Collateral Damage: Men's 'Domestic' Violence to Women Seen Through Men's Relations with Men," *Probation Journal: The Journal of Community and Criminal Justice* 53 (2006): 38–56.
Hedges, Chris. *War is a Force that Gives Us Meaning* (New York: Anchor books, 2003).
Henry, Stuart. "School Violence Beyond Columbine: A Complex Problem in Need of an Interdisciplinary Analysis," *American Behavioral Scientist* 52 (2009): 1–20.
Hickey, Eric W. *Serial Murders and Their Victims*, 5th ed. (Belmont, CA: Wadsworth, 2010).
Hirschfield, Paul J. "Preparing for Prison? The Criminalization of School Discipline in the USA," *Theoretical Criminology* 12 (2008): 79–101.
Holmes, Ronald M. and Stephen T. Holmes. *Serial Murder*, 3rd ed. (Los Angeles: Sage Publications, 2010).
Holt-Jensen, Arild. *Geography: History and Concepts*, 4th ed. (Los Angeles: Sage Publications, 2009).
Hondagneu-Sotelo, Pierrette. *Gendered Transitions: Mexican Experiences of Immigration* (Berkeley: University of California Press, 1994).
Hubbard, Phil. "Cleansing the Metropolis: Sex Work and the Politics of Zero Tolerance," *Urban Studies* 41 (2004): 1687–1702.
Hubbard, Phil. "Revenge and Injustice in the Neoliberal City: Uncovering Masculinist Agendas," *Antipode* 36 (2004): 665–686.
Hubbard, Phil. "Red-Light Districts and Toleration Zones: Geographies of Female Street Prostitution in England and Wales," *Area* 29 (1997): 129–140.
Hubbard, Phil and Teela Sanders. "Making Space for Sex Work: Female Street Prostitution and the Production of Urban Space," *International Journal of Urban and Regional Research* 27 (2003): 75–89.
Hung, Ruyu and Andrew Stables. "Lost in Space? Located in Place: Geo-Phenomenological Exploration and School," *Educational Philosophy and Theory* 2009: 1–11.
Hunnicutt, Gwen. "Varieties of Patriarchy and Violence Against Women: Resurrecting 'Patriarchy' as a Theoretical Tool," *Violence Against Women* 15 (2009): 553–573.
Hunter, Joyce. "Violence Against Lesbian and Gay Male Youths," *Journal of Interpersonal Violence* 5 (1990): 295–300.

Iadicola, Peter and Anson Shupe. *Violence, Inequality, and Human Freedom* (Lanham, MD: Rowman & Littlefield, 2003).
Inwood, Joshua F. J. "Searching for the Promised Land: Examining Dr. Martin Luther King's Concept of the Beloved Community," *Antipode* 41 (2009): 487–508.
Irwin, Jude. "(Dis)Counted Stories: Domestic Violence and Lesbians," *Qualitative Social Work* 7 (2008): 199–215.
Jackson, Peter. "The Cultural Politics of Masculinity: Towards a Social Geography," *Transactions of the Institute of British Geographers* 16 (1991): 199–213.
Janelle, Donald G., Barney Warf, and Kathy Hansen (eds.). *WorldMinds: Geographical Perspectives on 100 Problems* (Boston: Kluwer Academic Publishers, 2004).
Jarvis, Brian. "Monsters, Inc.: Serial Killers and Consumer Culture," *Crime, Media, Culture* 3 (2007): 326–344.
Jenkins, Philip. *Decade of Nightmares: The End of the Sixties and the Making of Eighties America* (Oxford: Oxford University Press, 2006).
Jenkins, Philip. *Using Murder: The Social Construction of Serial Homicide* (New York: Aldine de Gruyter, 1994).
Jimenez, Maria. *Humanitarian Crisis: Migrant Deaths at the U.S.–Mexico Border* (San Diego, CA: American Civil Liberties Union and Mexico's National Commission on Human Rights, 2009).
Johnston, Les. "What is Vigilantism?" *British Journal of Criminology* 36 (1996): 220–236.
Johnston, Lynda and Gill Valentine. "Wherever I Lay My Girlfriend, That's My Home: The Performance and Surveillance of Lesbian Identities in Domestic Environments," in *Mapping Desire: Geographies of Sexualities*, edited by David Bell and Gill Valentine (London: Routledge, 1995): 99–113.
Johnston, Ron. "Authors, Editors, and Authority in the Postmodern Academy," *Antipode* 32 (2000): 271–291.
Johnston, Ron. *Philosophy and Human Geography: An Introduction to Contemporary Approaches*, 2nd ed. (London: Edward Arnold, 1986).
Jones, Trevor and Tim Newburn. "Policy Convergence and Crime Control in the USA and the UK: Streams of Influence and Levels of Impact," *Criminal Justice* 2 (2002): 173–203.
Katz, Michael B. "The Origins of Public Education: A Reassessment," *History of Education Quarterly* 16 (1976): 381–407.
Keely, Lawrence H. *War Before Civilization: The Myth of the Peaceful Savage* (Oxford: Oxford University Press, 1996).
Kellner, Douglas. *Guys and Guns Amok: Domestic Terrorism and School Shootings from the Oklahoma City Bombing to the Virginia Tech Massacre* (Boulder, CO: Paradigm Publishers, 2008).
Kelly, Liz and Jill Radford. "'Nothing Really Happened': The Invalidation of Women's Experiences of Sexual Violence," *Critical Social Policy* 39 (1991): 39–53.
Kentlyn, Sue. "The Radically Subversive Space of the Queer Home: 'Safety House' and 'Neighborhood Watch,'" *Australian Geographer* 39 (2008): 327–337.
Kil, Sang H., Cecilia Menjívar, and Roxanne L. Doty. "Securing Borders: Patriotism, Vigilantism and the Brutalization of the US American Public," *Sociology of Crime, Law and Deviance* 13 (2009): 297–312.
Kirby, Stewart and Iain Hay. "(Hetero)sexing Space: Gay Men and 'Straight' Space in Adelaide, South Australia," *The Professional Geographer* 49 (1997): 295–305.

Kitchin, Rob M. and Phil J. Hubbard. "Research, Action, and 'Critical' Geographies," *Area* 31 (1999): 195–198.
Knox, Paul. *Urbanization: An Introduction to Urban Geography* (Englewood Cliffs, NJ: Prentice Hall, 1994).
Knox, Paul and John Agnew. *The Geography of the World Economy*, 2nd ed. (London: Edward Arnold, 1994).
Knox, Paul, John Agnew, and Linda McCarthy. *The Geography of the World Economy*, 4th ed. (London: Edward Arnold, 2003).
Kofman, Eleonore. "Foreword," in *Wife or Worker? Asian Women and Migration*, edited by Nicola Piper and Mina Roces (Lanham, MD: Rowman & Littlefield, 2003), ix–x.
Koskela, Hille. "'Gendered Exclusions': Women's Fear of Violence and Changing Relations to Space," *Geografiska Annaler* 81B (1999): 111–124.
Koskela, Hille. "'Bold Walk and Breakings': Women's Spatial Confidence Versus Fear of Violence," *Gender, Place and Culture* 4 (1997): 301–319.
Krug, Etienne G., James A. Mercy, Linda L. Dahlberg, and Anthony B. Zwi. "The World Report on Violence and Health," *The Lancet* 360 (2002): 1083–1088.
Lawoko, Stephen. "Predictors of Attitudes Toward Intimate Partner Violence: A Comparative Study of Men in Zambia and Kenya," *Journal of Interpersonal Violence* 23 (2008): 1056–1074.
Leary, Mark R., Robin M. Kowalski, Laura Smith, and Stephen Phillips. "Teasing, Rejecting, and Violence: Case Studies of the School Shootings," *Aggressive Behavior* 29 (2003): 202–214.
Lefebvre, Henri. *The Production of Space* (Oxford: Blackwell, 1991 [1974]).
Levy, Barrie. *Women and Violence* (Berkeley, CA: Seal Press, 2008).
Lewis, Brenda R. *Mapping the Trail of a Serial Killer: How the World's Most Infamous Murderers Were Tracked Down* (Guilford, CT: Lyons Press, 2009).
Leyton, Elliott. *Hunting Humans: The Rise of the Modern Multiple Murderer* (Toronto: McClelland and Stewart, 1995).
Lim, Linda Y. C. "Capitalism, Imperialism, and Patriarchy: The Dilemma of Third World Women Workers in Multinational Factories," in *Women, Men and the International Division of Labor*, edited by June Nash and Maria Patricia Fernández-Kelly (Albany: State University of New York Press, 1983), 70–91.
Lobel, K. (ed.). *Naming the Violence: Speaking Out About Lesbian Battering* (Seattle: Seal Press, 1986).
Lockhart, Lettie L., Barbara W. White, Vickie Causby, and Alicia Isaac. "Letting Out the Secret: Violence in Lesbian Relationships," *Journal of Interpersonal Violence* 9 (1994): 469–492.
Loveless, Tom. "Uneasy Allies: The Evolving Relationship of School and State," *Educational Evaluation and Policy Analysis* 20 (1998): 1–8.
Luke, Nancy, Sidney R. Schuler, Bui Thi Thanh Mai, Pham Vu Thien, and Tran Hung Minh. "Exploring Couple Attributes and Attitudes and Marital Violence in Vietnam," *Violence Against Women* 13 (2007): 5–27.
MacLeod, Gordon and Kevin Ward. "Spaces of Utopia and Dystopia: Landscaping the Contemporary City," *Geografiska Annaler* 84B (2002): 153–170.
Mallett, Shelley. "Understanding Home: A Critical Review of the Literature," *The Sociological Review* 52 (2004): 62–89.

Marchetti, Gina. *Romance and the 'Yellow Peril': Race, Sex, and Discursive Strategies in Hollywood Fiction* (Berkeley: University of California Press, 1993).
Martin, Lauren L. and Matthew L. Mitchelson. "Geographies of Detention and Imprisonment: Interrogating Spatial Practices of Confinement, Discipline, Law and State Power," *Geography Compass* 3 (2009): 459–477.
Martin, Philip. "Proposition 187 in California," *International Migration Review* 29 (1995): 255–263.
Massey, Doreen. *Space, Place, and Gender* (Minneapolis: University of Minnesota Press, 1994).
Matthews, Roger. *Doing Time: An Introduction to the Sociology of Imprisonment*, 2nd ed. (New York: Palgrave Macmillan, 2009).
McDowell, Linda. *Gender, Identity & Place: Understanding Feminist Geographies* (Minneapolis: University of Minnesota Press, 1999).
McHugh, Maureen C. and Irene Hanson Frieze. "Intimate Partner Violence: New Directions," *Annals, New York Academy of Sciences* 1087 (2006): 121–141.
McIntosh, Peggy. "White Privilege: Unpacking the Invisible Knapsack," *Peace and Freedom* July/August (1989): 10–12.
Menjívar, Cecilia and Olivia Salcido. "Immigrant Women and Domestic Violence: Common Experiences in Different Countries," *Gender & Society* 16 (2002): 898–920.
Merrifield, Andy. "The Dialectics of Dystopia: Disorder and Zero Tolerance in the City," *International Journal of Urban and Regional Research* 24 (2000): 474–489.
Miller Diane Helene, Kathryn Greene, Vickie Causby, Barbara W. White, and Lettie L. Lockhart. "Domestic Violence in Lesbian Relationships," *Women & Therapy* 23 (2001): 107–127.
Mitchell, Don. "Between Books and Streets, Between Home, Mall and Battlefield: The Politics and Pleasure of Cultural Geography," *Antipode* 34 (2002): 335–339.
Mitchell, Don. "Postmodern Geographical Praxis? Post-Modern Impulse and the War Against Homeless People in the Post-Justice City," in *Postmodern Geography: Theory and Praxis*, edited by C. Minca (Oxford: Blackwell, 2001), 57–92.
Mitchell, Don. *Cultural Geography: A Critical Introduction* (Malden, MA: Blackwell, 2000).
Mizen, Richard. "A Contribution Towards an Analytic Theory of Violence," *Journal of Analytical Psychology* 48 (2003): 285–305.
Mueller, Carol, Michelle Hansen, and Karen Qualtire. "Femicide on the Border and New Forms of Protest: The International Caravan for Justice," in *Human Rights Along the U.S.–Mexico Border: Gendered Violence and Insecurity*, edited by Kathleen Staudt, Tony Payan, and Z. Anthony Kruszewski (Tucson: University of Arizona Press, 2009), 125–149.
Muschert, Glenn. "Research in School Shootings," *Sociology Compass* 1 (2007): 60–80.
Muschert, Glenn and Dawn Carr. "Media Salience and Frame Changing Across Events: Coverage of Nine School Shootings," *Journalism & Mass Communication Quarterly* 83 (2006): 747–766.
Myslik, Wayne D. "Renegotiating the Social/Sexual Identities of Places: Gay Communities as Safe Havens or Sites of Resistance?" in *BodySpace: Destabilizing Geographers of Gender and Sexuality*, edited by Nancy Duncan (London: Routledge, 1996), 156–169.

Narayan, Uma. "'Mail-Order' Brides: Immigrant Women, Domestic Violence and Immigration Law," *Hypatia* 10 (1995): 104–119.
Natter, Wolfgang and John Paul Jones. "Identity, Space, and Other Uncertainties," in *Space and Social Theory: Interpreting Modernity and Postmodernity*, edited by Georges Benko and Ulf Strohmayer (Oxford: Blackwell, 1997), 141–161.
Nevins, Joseph. *Operation Gatekeeper and Beyond: The War on 'Illegals' and the Remaking of the U.S.–Mexico-Boundary* (New York: Routledge, 2010).
Nevins, Joseph. *Dying to Live: A Story of U.S. Immigration in an Age of Global Apartheid* (San Francisco: City Lights Books, 2008).
Nevins, Joseph. *A Not-So-Distant Horror: Mass Violence in East Timor* (Ithaca, NY: Cornell University Press, 2005).
Newburn, Tim. "Atlantic Crossings: 'Policy Transfer' and Crime Control in the USA and Britain," *Punishment & Society* 4 (2002): 165–194.
Newman, Michelle, Andree Woodcock, and Philip Dunham. "'Playtime in the Borderlands': Children's Representations of School, Gender and Bullying Through Photographs and Interview," *Children's Geographies* 4 (2006): 289–302.
Neyzer, Noeleen. "The Internationalization of Women's Work," *Southeast Asian Journal of Social Sciences* 17 (1989): 25–40.
Nietzsche, Friedrich. *Beyond Good & Evil: Prelude to a Philosophy of the Future*, translated by Walter Kaufman (New York: Vintage Books, 1989 [1886]).
Nofziger, Stacey. "Deviant Lifestyles and Violent Victimization at School," *Journal of Interpersonal Violence* 24 (2009): 1494–1517.
O'Conor, Andi. "Who Gets Called Queer in School? Lesbian, Gay and Bisexual Teenagers, Homophobia and High School," *The High School Journal* 77 (1994): 7–12.
O Donoghue, Dónal, "'James Always Hangs Out Here': Making Space for Place in Studying Masculinities at School," *Visual Studies* 22 (2007): 62–73.
Olson, Elizabeth and Andrew Sayer. "Racial Geography and its Critical Standpoints: Embracing the Normative," *Antipode* 41 (2009): 180–198.
O'Neill, Maggie, Rose Campbell, Phil Hubbard, Jane Pitcher, and Jane Scoular. "Living With the Other: Street Sex Work, Contingent Communities and Degrees of Tolerance," *Crime, Media, Culture* 4 (2008): 73–93.
Opotow, Susan. "Reconciliation in Time of Impunity: Challenges for Social Justice," *Social Justice Research* 14 (2001): 149–170.
Pain, Rachel. "Elderly Women and Fear of Violent Crime: The Least Likely Victims?" *British Journal of Criminology* 35 (1995): 584–598.
Pain, Rachel. "Space, Sexual Violence and Social Control: Integrating Geographical and Feminist Analyses of Women's Fear of Crime," *Progress in Human Geography* 15 (1991): 415–431.
Papayanis, Marilyn A. "Sex and the Revanchist City: Zoning Out Pornography in New York," *Environment and Planning D: Society and Space* 18 (2000): 341–353.
Parial, Ernesto. "RP Women Labeled as 'House Pets,'" *Philippine News* July 22–28 (1992), pp. 1 and 12.
Parish, William L., Tianfu Wang, Edward O. Laumann, Suiming Pan, and Ye Luo. "Intimate Partner Violence in China: National Prevalence, Risk Factors and Associated Health Problems," *International Family Planning Perspectives* 30 (2004): 174–181.

Pascoe, C. J. *Dude, You're a Fag: Masculinity and Sexuality in High School* (Berkeley: University of California Press, 2007).
Paul, Diane B. *Controlling Human Heredity: 1865 to the Present* (Atlantic Highlands, NJ: Humanities Press, 1995).
Peet, Richard. *Global Capitalism: Theories of Societal Development* (New York: Routledge, 1991).
Philbin, Tom and Michael Philbin. *The Killer Book of Serial Killers: Incredible Stories, Facts, and Trivia from the World of Serial Killers* (Naperville, IL: Sourcebooks, Inc., 2009).
Phillips, Debby A. "Punking and Bullying: Strategies in Middle School, High School, and Beyond," *Journal of Interpersonal Violence* 22 (2007): 158–178.
Popenoe, Paul and R. H. Johnson. *Applied Eugenics*, 2nd ed. (New York: Macmillan, 1918).
Pyle, Jean L. "Export-Led Development and the Underemployment of Women: the Impact of Discriminatory Development Policy in the Republic of Ireland," in *Women Workers and Global Restructuring*, edited by Kathryn Ward (Ithaca, NY: Cornell University Press, 1990), 85–112.
Rani, Manju and Sekhar Bonu. "Attitudes Toward Wife Beating: A Cross-Country Study in Asia," *Journal of Interpersonal Violence* 24 (2009): 1371–1397.
Rani, Manju, Sekhar Bonu, and Nafissatou Diop-Sidibe. "An Empirical Investigation of Attitudes Towards Wife-Beating Among Men and Women in Seven Sub-Saharan African Countries," *African Journal of Reproductive Health* 8 (2004): 116–136.
Razack, Sherene H. "Gendered Racial Violence and Spatialized Justice: The Murder of Pamela George," *Canadian Journal of Law and Society* 15 (2000): 91–130.
Reiss, Albert and Jeffrey A. Roth (eds.). *Understanding and Preventing Violence* (Washington, DC: National Academy Press, 1993).
Renold, Emma, "Learning the 'Hard' Way: Boys, Hegemonic Masculinity and the Negotiation of Learner Identities in the Primary School," *British Journal of Sociology and Education* 22 (2001): 369–385.
Renzetti, Claire M. "Building a Second Closet: Third Party Responses to Victims of Lesbian Partner Abuse," *Family Relations* 38 (1989): 157–163.
Renzetti, Claire M. "Violence in Lesbian Relationships: A Preliminary Analysis of Causal Factors," *Journal of Interpersonal Violence* 3 (1988): 381–399.
Roberts, Susan M. "Realizing Critical Geographies of the University," *Antipode* 32 (2000): 230–244.
Rosas, Gilberto. "The Managed Violence of the Borderlands: Treacherous Geographies, Policeability, and the Politics of Race," *Latino Studies* 4 (2006): 401–418.
Rosenbaum, Alan. "Of Men, Macho, and Marital Violence," *Journal of Family Violence* 1 (1986): 121–129.
Rosenbaum, H. Jon and Peter C. Sederberg. "Vigilantism: An Analysis of Establishment Violence," *Comparative Politics* 6 (1974): 541–570.
Saunders, Peter and Peter Williams. "The Constitution of the Home: Towards a Research Agenda," *Housing Studies* 3 (1988): 81–93.
Savin-Williams, Ritch C. "Verbal and Physical Abuse as Stressors in the Lives of Lesbian, Gay Male, and Bisexual Youth: Associations with School Problems, Running Away, Substance Abuse, Prostitution, and Suicide," *Journal of Consulting and Clinical Psychology* 62 (1994): 261–269.

Sayer, Andrew and Richard Walker. *The New Social Economy: Reworking the Division of Labor* (Cambridge, MA: Blackwell, 1992).
Schecter, Harold. *The Serial Killer Files: The Who, What, Where, How, and Why of the World's Most Terrifying Murderers* (New York: Ballantine Books, 2003).
Schmid, David. *Natural Born Celebrities: Serial Killers in American Culture* (Chicago: The University of Chicago Press, 2005).
Seltzer, Mark. *Serial Killers: Death and Life in America's Wound Culture* (New York: Routledge, 1998).
Sen, Amartya. *Identity and Violence: The Illusion of Destiny* (New York: W. W. Norton & Company, 2006).
Shaw, Martin. *What is Genocide?* (Malden, MA: Polity, 2007).
Sheppard, Eric. "Practicing Geography," *Annals of the Association of American Geographers* 94 (2004): 744–747.
Shimizu, Celine Parrañas. *The Hypersexuality of Race: Performing Asian/American Women on Screen and Scene* (Durham, NC: Duke University Press, 2007).
Short, John Rennie. *The Urban Order: An Introduction to Cities, Culture, and Power* (Cambridge, MA: Blackwell, 1996).
Short, John Rennie, Lisa M. Benton, W. B. Luce, and Judy Walton. "Reconstructing the Image of an Industrial City," *Annals of the Association of American Geographers* 83 (1993): 207–224.
Short, John Rennie and Yeong-Hyun Kim. *Globalization and the City* (New York: Addison Wesley Longman, 1999).
Sibley, David. *Geographies of Exclusion: Society and Difference in the West* (London: Routledge, 1995).
Sites, William, Robert J. Chaskin, and Virginia Parks. "Reframing Community Practice for the 21st Century: Multiple Traditions, Multiple Challenges," *Journal of Urban Affairs* 29 (2007): 519–541.
Smartt, Ursula and Helmut Kury. "Domestic Violence: Comparative Analysis of German and U.K. Research Findings," *Social Sciences Quarterly* 88 (2007): 1263–1280.
Smith, David Livingstone. *The Most Dangerous Animal: Human Nature and the Origins of War* (New York: St. Martin's Griffin, 2007).
Smith, David M. "On Performing Geography," *Antipode* 33 (2001): 141–146.
Smith, David M. *Moral Geographies: Ethics in a World of Difference* (Edinburgh: Edinburgh University Press, 2000).
Smith, Neil. "New Globalism, New Urbanism: Gentrification as Global Urban Strategy," *Antipode* 34 (2002): 434–457.
Smith, Neil. *The New Urban Frontier: Gentrification and the Revanchist City* (London: Routledge, 1996).
Soja, Edward. *Postmodern Geographies: The Reassertion of Space in Critical Social Theory* (London: Verso, 1989).
Solem, Michael and Kenneth Foote. "Concerns, Attitudes, and Abilities of Early-Career Geography Faculty," *Annals of the Association of American Geographers* 94 (2004): 889–912.
Staheli, Lynn. "Citizenship and the Problem of Community," *Political Geography* 27 (2008): 5–21.
Stanko, Elizabeth. "The Day to Count: Reflections on a Methodology to Raise Awareness about the Impact of Domestic Violence in the UK," *Criminology and Criminal Justice* 1 (2001): 215–226.

Stanko, Elizabeth. *Everyday Violence: How Women and Men Experience Sexual and Physical Danger* (San Francisco: Pandora, 1990).
Stanko, Elizabeth, D. Crisp, C. Hale, and H. Lucraft. *Counting the Costs: Estimating the Impact of Domestic Violence in the London Borough of Hackney* (Swindon: Crime Concern, 1998).
Stoddard, Lothrop. *The Rising Tide of Color Against White World Supremacy* (New York: Charles Scribner's Sons, 1920).
Suárez-Orozco, Marcelo. "California Dreaming: Proposition 187 and the Cultural Psychology of Racial and Ethnic Exclusion," *Anthropology & Education Quarterly* 27 (1996): 151–167.
Thibault, Robert E. "Between Survival and Revolution: Another Community System is Possible," *Antipode* 39 (2007): 874–895.
Thomas, Mary E. "The Identity Politics of School Life: Territoriality and the Racial Subjectivity of Teen Girls in LA," *Children's Geographies* 7 (2009): 7–19.
Thomson, Sarah. "'Territorialising' the Primary School Playground: Deconstructing the Geography of Playtime," *Children's Geographies* 3 (2005): 63–78.
Thrift, Nigel. "Space: The Fundamental Stuff of Human Geography," in *Key Concepts in Geography*, edited by Sarah L. Holloway, Stephen P. Rice, and Gill Valentine (Los Angeles: Sage Publications, 2003), 95–107.
Tiano, Susan. "Maquiladora Women: A New Category of Workers?" in *Women Workers and Global Restructuring*, edited by Kathryn Ward (Ithaca, NY: Cornell University Press, 1990), 193–223.
Tienda, Marta. "Looking to the 1990s: Mexican Immigration in Sociological Perspective," in *Mexican Migration to the United States: Origins, Consequences, and Policy Options*, edited by Wayne Cornelius and Jorge A. Bustamante (San Diego: Center for U.S.–Mexican Studies, University of California San Diego, 1989), 109–115.
Tjaden, Patricia and Nancy Thoennes. *Extent, Nature, and Consequences of Intimate Partner Violence: Findings from the National Violence Against Women Survey* (Washington, DC: National Institute of Justice/Center for Disease Control, 2000).
Tooby, Jackson. "Violence and the Masculine Ideal: Some Qualitative Data," *Annals of the American Academy of Political and Social Science* 364 (1966): 19–27.
Totten, Samuel and William S. Parsons (eds.). *Century of Genocide: Critical Essays and Eyewitness Accounts*, 3rd ed. (New York: Routledge, 2009).
Tuan, Yi-Fu. "Geography, Phenomenology, and the Study of Human Nature," *Canadian Geographer* 15 (1971): 181–192.
Tupper, Jennifer A., Terry Carson, Ingrid Johnston, and Jyoti Mangat. "Building Place: Students' Negotiation of Spaces and Citizenship in Schools," *Canadian Journal of Education* 31 (2008): 1065–1092.
Turse, Nick. *The Complex: How the Military Invades Our Everyday Lives* (New York: Metropolitan Books, 2008).
Tyner, James A. "The Globalization of Transnational Labor Migration and the Filipino Family: A Narrative," *Asian and Pacific Migration Journal* 11 (2002): 95–116.
Uline, Cynthia, Megan Tschannen-Moran, and Thomas DeVere Wolsey. "The Walls Still Speak: The Stories Occupants Tell," *Journal of Educational Administration* 47 (2009): 400–426.

Valdez, Diana Washington. *The Killing Fields: Harvest of Women; The Truth About Mexico's Bloody Border Legacy* (Burbank, CA: Peace at the Border, 2006).
Valentine, Gill. "Boundary Crossing: Transitions from Childhood to Adulthood," *Children's Geographies* 1 (2003): 37–52.
Valentine, Gill. "Angels and Devils: Moral Landscapes of Childhood," *Environment and Planning D: Society & Space* 14 (1996): 581–599.
Valentine, Gill. "(Hetero)sexing Space: Lesbian Perceptions and Experiences of Everyday Space," *Environment and Planning D: Society and Space* 11 (1993): 395–413.
Valentine, Gill. "Images of Danger: Women's Sources of Information about the Spatial Distribution of Male Violence," *Area* 24 (1992): 22–29.
Valentine, Gill. "The Geography of Women's Fear," *Area* 21 (1989): 385–390.
Valentine, Gill, Tracey Skelton, and Ruth Butler. "Coming Out and Outcomes: Negotiating Lesbian and Gay Identities With, and In, the Family," *Environment and Planning D: Society and Space* 21 (2003): 479–499.
Valentino, Benjamin A. *Final Solutions: Mass Killings and Genocide in the 20th Century* (Ithaca, NY: Cornell University Press, 2004).
Varsanyi, Monica. "Immigration Policing Through the Backdoor: City Ordinances, the 'Right to the City,' and the Exclusion of Undocumented Day Laborers," *Urban Geography* 29 (2008): 29–52.
Villapando, Venny. "The Business of Selling Mail-Order Brides," in *Making Waves: An Anthology By and About Asian American Women*, edited by Asian Women United of California (Boston: Beacon Press, 1989), 319–326.
Vina, Stephen R., Blas Nunez-Neto, and Alyssa Bartlett Weir. "Civilian Patrols Along the Border: Legal and Policy Issues," *CRS Report for Congress* (Washington DC: Congressional Research Service, Library of Congress, 2006).
Vronsky, Peter. *Serial Killers: The Method and Madness of Monsters* (New York: Berkeley Books, 2004).
Waldner-Haugrud, L. K. "Sexual Coercion in Lesbian and Gay Relationships: A Review and Critique," *Aggression and Violent Behavior* 4 (1999): 139–149.
Waller, James. *Becoming Evil: How Ordinary People Commit Genocide and Mass Killing* (New York: Oxford University Press, 2002).
Wallman, Joel. "Disarming Youth," *The HFG Review* 2 (1997): 3–9.
Wander, Philip. "Introduction to the Transaction Edition," in Henri Lefebvre, *Everyday Life in the Modern World*, translated by Sacha Rabinovitch (London: Transaction Publishers, 2002), vii–xxiii.
Wardhaugh, Julia. "The Unaccommodated Woman: Home, Homelessness and Identity," *The Sociological Review* 47 (1999): 91–109.
Warf, Barney, Donald G. Janelle, and Kathy Hansen, "Introducing *WorldMinds*," in *WorldMinds: Geographical Perspectives on 100 Problems*, edited by Donald Janelle, Barney Warf, and Kathy Hansen (Boston: Kluwer Academic Publishers, 2004), xvii–xxii.
Warrington, Molly. "'I Must Get Out': The Geographies of Domestic Violence," *Transactions, Institute of British Geographers* 26 (2001): 365–382.
Warwick, Alexandra. "The Scene of the Crime: Inventing the Serial Killer," *Social & Legal Studies* 15 (2006): 552–569.
Waterhouse, Stephen. "Deviant and Non-Deviant Identities in the Classroom: Patrolling the Boundaries of the Normal Social World," *European Journal of Special Needs Education* 19 (2004): 69–84.

Weedon, Chris. *Feminist Practice and Poststructuralist Theory*, 2nd ed. (Malden, MA: Blackwell, 1997).
Weiner, Neil A., Margaret A. Zahn, and Rita J. Sagi. *Violence: Patterns, Causes, Public Policy* (San Diego, CA: Harcourt Brace Jovanovich, 1990).
West, Carolyn M. "Lesbian Intimate Partner Violence: Prevalence and Dynamics," *Journal of Lesbian Studies* 6 (2002): 121–127.
Widom, Cathy S. "Does Violence Beget Violence? A Critical Examination of the Literature," *Psychological Bulletin* 106 (1989): 3–28.
Wilson, David. *Inventing Black-on-Black Violence: Discourse, Space, and Representation* (Syracuse, NY: Syracuse University Press, 2005).
Winston, George T. "The Relation of the Whites to the Negros," *Annals of the American Academy of Political and Social Science* 18 (1901): 103–118.
Wright, Melissa W. "Public Women, Profit, and Femicide in Northern Mexico," *South Atlantic Quarterly* 105 (2006): 681–698.
Wright, Melissa W. "From Protests to Politics: Sex Work, Women's Worth, and Ciudad Juárez Modernity," *Annals of the Association of American Geographers* 94 (2004): 369–386.
Wright, Melissa W. "The Dialectics of Still Life: Murder, Women, and Maquiladoras," *Public Culture* 11 (1999): 453–474.
Wykes, Maggie and Kirsty Welsh. *Violence, Gender and Justice* (Los Angeles: Sage Publications, 2009).
Yamawaki, Niwako, Joseph Ostenson, and C. Ryan Brown. "The Functions of Gender Role Traditionality, Ambivalent Sexism, Injury, and Frequency of Assault on Domestic Violence Perception: A Study Between Japanese and American College Students," *Violence Against Women* 15 (2009): 1126–1142.
Young, Iris. *Justice and the Politics of Difference* (Princeton, NJ: Princeton University Press, 1990).
Zamudio, Patricia. "Mexico: Mexican International Migration," in *Migration and Immigration: A Global View*, edited by Marua I. Toro-Morn and Marixsa Alicea (Westport, CT: Greenwood Press, 2004), 129–145.
Zebadúa-Yañez, Verónica. "Killing as Performance: Violence and the Shaping of Community," *e-misférica* 2 (2005): 1–22.
Zerubavel, Eviatar. *The Elephant in the Room: Silence and Denial in Everyday Life* (Oxford: Oxford University Press, 2006).
Zukin, Sharon. "Space and Symbols in an Age of Decline," in *Re-Presenting the City: Ethnicity, Capital and Culture in the 21st-Century Metropolis*, edited by Anthony D. King (New York: New York University Press, 1996), 43–59.

INDEX

Adams, Paul 18
African-Americans 77, 92, 102–03, 116, 159
Agnew, John 104–105
Aitken, Stuart 30, 31, 32, 44, 69–70, 136, 167
alienation 52–53, 68, 93
Allison, Aimee 91
Alvarez, Alex 7, 8–9, 21
Andreas, Peter 141, 144, 152
anti-immigrant groups 147, 150–52
Asian women: representations 62–66, 88
Atkinson, Patricia 112

Bacevich, Andrew 91
Bachman, Ronet 7, 8–9, 21
Balsam, Kimberly 59
Bartky, Sandra Lee 89
battered woman 35 *see also* intimate partner violence
Bauder, Harald 166
Beckett, Katherine 79
belonging 18, 65, 84, 128, 136, 140, 150–60
Belsey, Catherine 87–88
Berkowitz, David 118
Bianci, Kenneth 118
bisexual 50–59, 93–94, 140
'black-on-black' violence 107

blaming the victim 35, 111–12, 125
Blomley, Nicholas 22
Bluestone, Barry 105
body, bodies 6–8, 41, 80, 87–88, 95, 101
Border Industrialization Program 121–22
Bracero Program 143–44
Brandehoft, Joseph 112
Brener, Nancy 95
Brickell, Katherine 167
Brophy, John 107–108
Brown, Nicola 52, 58
bullying 13, 71, 86, 92, 164, 169–70
Bundy, Ted 103, 118
Buono, Angelo 118
Buss, David 10
Butler, Judith 43, 45

capitalism 4, 26–27, 30–33, 45, 67, 72–74, 101, 104–13, 122–29, 135
Carter, Prudence 72
Castree, Noel 166
Castro, Robert 156
Catling, Simon 75
Chacón, Justin 121–22, 144, 146, 158
charged attributions 156
child abuse 68
children 2, 8–9, 16, 19, 26–27, 31–33, 37, 44, 47, 52–55, 59, 61, 67, 70–76, 91–92, 95, 97, 103, 118, 136, 139,

217

155, 160, 165; as criminal 79–82; as deviant 83–84, 107; as normal 83–84
Ciudad Juárez 99, 120–129
Civil Homeland Defense 151
Civil Rights movement 80, 110, 133
Clark, Douglas 112
Clark, William 131
class 11, 29, 31, 40, 67, 77, 86, 88–89, 100, 102–03, 109–10, 112–14, 146, 155, 166, 170–71
Coleman, Alton 103
Collins, Randall 4, 9, 21
community 6, 169; controlling 150–55; making of 140–50; meanings of 132–35, 155–60; and sovereignty 135–40
Corteen, Karen 55
Crandall, Marie 67
Cresswell, Tim 18, 19, 20
culture of impunity 164
culture of silence 163
culture of violence 9
Cunneen, Chris 64–66
Cusac, Anne-Marie 72, 82
cycle of violence 9

D'Augelli, Anthony 93
Dahmer, Jeffrey 103, 112
Daly, Martin 7, 99
Davis, Mike 121–22, 144, 146, 158
Day, Kristen 43
DeFilippis, James 134
deindustrialization 104–06, 122, 129
Department of Homeland Security 147
deviancy, 83–84
deviant, 67, 78, 83–84, 114, 135, 160
Di Bartolo, Lawrence 167
Dickson, Grierson 107
Dilthey, Wilhelm 4
disability 89
discipline 18–22, 26, 32, 34–36, 45–46, 53–54, 57, 59, 67–68, 71–72, 78–85, 88–89, 92, 95, 99, 134–36, 140, 154, 156, 159–61, 169
disempowered 61, 65, 134
domestic violence 6, 28, 34–35, 37, 50–52, 54, 61, 65, 92, 95, 98, 164, 167 *see also* intimate partner violence
Domosh, Mona 32, 56
Doty, Roxanne 137–38

Edelman, Murray 80
Egger, Steven 102
elder abuse 68

Elwood, Sarah 55–56
embody, embodied 18, 20, 22, 41, 45, 56, 76, 88, 95, 101, 110, 128, 134
enacted fantasies 43, 64–65
Enloe, Cynthia 92
Espelage, Dorothy 94
ethical relativism 134
ethnic, ethnicity 4, 88, 94, 133, 168
European Observatory of Violence 71
everyday 1–2, 12–14, 16, 27–28, 32–34, 36, 54–55, 60, 71, 85–87, 91, 101, 116, 154, 157, 163–66, 168, 170
Eviota, Elizabeth 32

familialism 32
family 6, 25, 30–34, 37, 44–45, 48, 51–54, 56, 60–61, 63, 67–68, 76, 93, 110, 114, 119, 170; transnational 60–61
fear 11–12, 43, 55–56, 69, 75, 77–78, 80–83, 93, 95, 97–98, 100, 107–10, 114–15, 119, 158, 167, 171
Federal Bureau of Investigation 107–109
femicide 99, 124–28
feminism, femininity 32, 43, 44, 57, 68, 76, 122–24, 170
feminist movement 80, 110, 133, 140
Ferraro, Kathleen 61
Filipina, Filipinas 62–66, 88
Fiske, Susan 49
Flannery, Dan 4
Foote, Ken 166
Foucault, Michel 19, 156

Gacy, John Wayne 103
gated community 109, 129
gay, gay men 50–59, 93–94, 109, 112, 140
gay liberation movement 80, 133
Gemeinschaft 132–33, 138
gender: expectations 67, 88–94, 122–128, 169; gender hierarchy 42, 45; gender roles 32–33, 37, 40–50, 51, 61–62, 68, 76, 88–94, 122–28
gentrification 109, 120
geographic perspective 3–4, 11, 21
geography 3, 12, 14–15, 28, 43, 75, 85–86, 125, 149, 163–71; critical 22, 168–69
George, Pamela 7–8
Gesellschaft 132–33, 138
Gilchrist, James 151–52
Gilligan, James 45, 46

Gilmore, Ruth Wilson 167
Girshick, Lori 59
Glick, Peter 49
globalization 60
Gorman-Murray, Andrew 53, 56
Gregson, Nicky 29
group identity 10
gun culture 9–10, 46, 90
gun violence 70

Haggerty, Kevin 100–102
Harris, Eric 69
Harris, William 74–75
Harrison, Bennett 105
Harvey, David 105, 168
Hattery, Angela 47
Hay, Iain 52, 54
Hayden, Bridget 157
Hearn, Jeff 41, 42
hetero-normativity 56, 67, 89–90, 169
hetero-patriarchy 33, 34, 51–53
heterosexism 57
heterosexual, heterosexuality 26, 29, 33–36, 41, 44, 50–59, 83–84, 89, 93–94, 96, 102, 110, 112, 135
Hirschfield, Paul 72, 79
Holmes, Ronald 111
home: constructions of 29–34; meanings of 26–27, 28–29, 34–35, 54; as place 26, 44; as prison 66; as safe place 26, 54; as refuge 27–29, 67; spatial practice 25–26
homeless 3, 100, 102, 109–12, 114, 136, 140, 169
homophobia 56–57, 90, 94
homophobic violence 55–59, 94
homosexual, homosexuality 56, 59, 102, 110, 112, 119
Hondagneu-Sotelo, Pierrette 60
Hubbard, Phil 22, 113–115
Hunnicutt, Gwen 40–43, 48
Hunter, Joyce 53, 93–94

identity, identities 10, 29, 33, 38, 42–45, 47, 49, 52–59, 67–68, 71, 83–95, 129, 132–33, 136–37, 155, 160, 168
'illegal' migrants 144–50, 154–55, 156–61, 169
Immigration and Naturalization Service 147
Immigration Reform and Control Act 144–45
individual rights 138

industrialization 121–23
intimate partner violence 22, 26, 27, 34–50; definitions 35–36; levels of 35
Inwood, Josh 133
Irwin, Jude 51

Jackson, Calvin 103
Jenkins, Philip 100, 105, 133
Jimenez, Maria 149–50
Johnson, Milton 103
Johnston, Les 139
Johnston, Lynda 58
Johnston, Ron 166, 169
Jordan, Jean 112
justice 10, 14, 126, 133, 138–40, 154, 159, 161, 165
juvenile training 75–76

Katz, Michael 76
Kellner, Douglas 46, 90
Kelly, Liz 37–39
Kentlyn, Sue 52, 57
Kim, Yeong-Hyun 106
Kirby, Stewart 52, 54
Kitchin, Rob 22
Klebold, Dylan 69
Knox, Paul 104–105
Kofman, Eleonore 60
Koskela, Hille 1, 12
Krug, Etienne 6
Kummerfield, Steven 7–8

Lacy, Oliver 112
'language of illegality' 156–57
Latino 94
Lefebvre, Henri 16, 25, 72
lesbian, lesbians 27, 35, 49, 50–59, 93–94, 109, 140
Levy, Barrie 36
Lewis, Brenda 98
Leyton, Elliot
Lowe, Michelle 29

Macdonald, Jayne 112
MacLeod, Gordon 106, 110
mail-order brides 27, 59–67
male dominance 42, 48, 59
male privilege 170
Manson, Charles 118
Maquiladoras 121–28
Marchetti, Gina 64
marriage 33–35, 39; gay 55; transnational 59–67

masculinism, masculinity 28, 32, 34, 42–43, 57, 68, 90–94, 169; crisis of 46
Massey, Doreen 15
Matthews, Roger 16
McDowell, Linda 25, 26, 28, 33, 134
McIntosh, Peggy 170
Merrifield, Andy 117
Mexican 60, 127, 142–50
militarism 46, 90–92, 147–49, 157
Miller, Diane 57
minorities 102, 109
Minuteman Project 151–52
misogyny 57, 169
Mitchell, Don 110, 166, 169–70
Mitchelson, Matthew 167
Mizen, Richard 5
mode of production 29, 31
modernity 99–104, 128, 132
moral conservative 110
moral exclusion 10–11, 57, 136, 159, 164
moral inclusion 10–11, 159
Muschert, Glenn 70
Myslik, Wayne 55

Narayan, Uma 61, 63, 65
nationalism 4, 134, 154
National Rifle Association 70
National Violence Against Women Survey 36
neighborhood 25, 78, 136, 139, 169
neoconservatism 109–110
neoliberalism 113, 121–22, 126, 133, 138
Nevins, Joseph 141, 149, 161, 167
Newburn, Tim 111
Nietzsche, Friedrich 166

O'Conor, Andi 93–94
Olson, Elizabeth 23
Operation Gatekeeper 147, 149, 150
Operation Hold the Line 147, 150
Operation Rio Grande 147
Operation Safeguard 147
Operation Wetback 143
Opotow, Susan 10, 164

Pain, Rachel 12, 167
Papayanis, Marilyn 114
Pascoe, C.J. 89–90
patriarchy 4, 26, 27, 34, 37, 40–45, 52, 56, 60, 67, 84, 89, 92, 97, 120, 123, 135
Pearson, Yvonne 112

pedagogy of impunity 165, 167–69
Peet, Richard 29
Phillips, Debby 92, 93
place 3, 14–18; as disciplined space 18–20, 34 137; production of 43, 85–86, 134–35, 160–61
power 5, 11, 19, 20–21, 40–43, 45, 47, 52, 57–58, 61, 64–65, 75, 86, 90, 92, 108, 134–35
private spaces 12, 39, 55–59, 85
Proposition 187 146–47
prostitute, prostitution 100, 102–03, 111–12, 113–17, 125, 129
public schools 72–82, 133
public spaces 27–28, 39, 54–56, 85, 97–98, 110–11, 114–16, 118, 120, 124, 127, 129, 137
'public woman' 124–28
punishment: in schools 78–82

race 7, 20, 29, 40, 61, 67, 87–89, 95, 155, 166, 170–71
racism 11, 27, 63, 71, 94, 103, 158–59
Radford, Jill 37–39
Ramirez, Richard 118
Ranch Rescue 151
Rani, Manju 48
Renzetti, Claire 51–52
resistance 17, 19–20, 29, 54, 57
Ressler, Robert 107
revanchist city 109–10, 111, 113–17, 119–20, 121, 126–27, 138
Ridgway, Gary 103–04, 112, 117, 119
Roberts, Sue 166
Rule, Ann 109
runaways 100, 102, 111–12, 127
Rytka, Helen 112

safe privilege 170–71
same-sex 7, 36, 68
same-sex violence 27, 50–59; levels of 52
Sasson, Theodore 79
Saunders, Peter 28, 31, 56
'Save Our State' initiative 146–47
Sayer, Andrew 23, 32–33
Schecter, Harold 100, 111
school: constructions of 72–83; discipline in 71–83; level of 81; as place 84–86; punishment in 78–82; violence in 83–94
school rampage shootings 69–71, 94, 163
Seager, Joni 32

Sen, Amartya 136–37, 155–56, 160
serial killing 98, 99–104, 105, 107–13; 113–17, 128–29, 138, 152; statistics on 108, 128
sexism 4, 11, 37, 49, 57, 59, 63, 71, 94; ambivalent sexism 48–50, 63
sexuality 29, 53, 56, 64, 67, 86, 89–90, 95, 98, 166
sex work, sex workers 113–117, 125, 129
Sheppard, Eric 166
Short, John 106, 107
Sibley, David 136
Simcox, Chris 151–52
Simmons, Beoria 116–117, 119
singular affiliation 155–56, 159–60
slasher films 118–119, 129
Smith, David 21, 132, 166
Smith, Neil 109
social categorization 11
social conservatives 80, 95, 112, 119, 133
social control 11, 21–22, 72, 75, 80, 97, 133
Social Darwinism 77–78
social group 10, 86
social learning theory 8–9
social relations 8, 29–30, 34, 67, 135, 160
social reproduction 31, 44
social welfare 9, 80, 150
Soja, Edward 84
Sokol, Rowena 65–66
Solem, Michael 166
Solnit, David 91
sovereignty 135–40, 154
space 3, 14–18; absolute 14; of opportunity 115; production of 16–18, 168; relational 15, 17; relative 14–15; representational 16–17; representations of 16–17, 33; spatiality 22, 50, 84, 113
spatial isolation 61, 66, 94
spatial practice 11, 16–17, 23, 25–26, 59, 72, 73, 75
Stanko, Elizabeth 1, 12, 27, 92, 95–96, 164
stranger violence 27, 35, 97, 163
Stubbs, Julie 64–66
students *see* children
subjectivities 43, 83–94
Suff, William Lester 115
Sutcliffe, Peter 112, 116, 119
Szymanski, Dawn 59

Tale-Yax, Hugo Alfredo 3
target of opportunity 111, 115
temporary workers 123–125
Ternowetsky, Alex 7–8
Thomas, Mary 88
Thrift, Nigel 14, 20
Tönnies, Ferdinand 132
transgression 17, 20, 37, 44–45, 54, 58, 79, 85, 89, 127, 140
transsexual, transexuality 50–59, 93–94; and violence 58–59
Tuan, Yi-Fu 28
Tupper, Jennifer 85
Turder, Matt 112

undocumented immigrants 141–50, 150–60; deaths of 149–50
United States–Mexico border 140–50, 167
universal human rights 138
universalism 134
urban 73, 75–76, 81, 98, 101, 104
urban redevelopment 104–113, 113–120, 128–29
us–them thinking 11, 157

Valdez, Diana 124
Valentine, Gill 12, 44, 53, 56, 87, 167
verstehen 4–5, 18
vigilantes 137–38; and justice 138; and violence 139–40, 150–55
violence: capacity for 21, 99–100; causes of 6–10; costs of 165; definitions of 5; direct 4–5, 12, 20–21; exposure to 2, 9; geographic understanding 11–14, 14–18, 28; interpersonal 2, 4, 6, 12–13, 20, 26, 27, 34, 97, 163; levels of 2, 164; as rational behavior 21, 37, 47, 102, 139; as role enforcement 45; structural 4, 12, 21, 165, 167; as subject 5–11; and television 2; *see also specific types*
Vronsky, Peter 102, 111, 115

Walker, Richard 32–33
Waller, James 11
Wallman, Joel 70
Wander, Philip 1
Ward, Kevin 105, 110
Waterhouse, Stephen 83
Watts, Coral
Weedon, Chris 87–88
Weinberger, Jeremiah 112

Welsh, Kirsty 34, 67
West, Carolyn 59
Whitehead, Antony 41, 42
white privilege 170
wife abuse 35 *see also* intimate partner violence
Williams, Peter 28, 31, 56
Wilson, David 107
Wilson, Margo 7, 99
World Health Organization 2, 5, 6, 36
Wright, Melissa 123–28, 167
Wykes, Maggie 34, 67

Young, Iris 10, 134, 135
youth 52–54, 70–72, 75, 78–79, 88, 89, 91, 93–95, 102, 107, 111–12, 133, 159, 160; criminalization of 79–83, 95, 107, 133

Zamudio, Patricia 143
Zebadúa-Yañez, Verónica 128
'zero-tolerance' 81, 110–11, 115, 133
Zerubavel, Eviator 163–65
zones of opportunity 111, 115
Zukin, Sharon 106

Taylor & Francis
eBooks
FOR LIBRARIES

ORDER YOUR FREE 30 DAY INSTITUTIONAL TRIAL TODAY!

Over 23,000 eBook titles in the Humanities, Social Sciences, STM and Law from some of the world's leading imprints.

Choose from a range of subject packages or create your own!

Benefits for you
- Free MARC records
- COUNTER-compliant usage statistics
- Flexible purchase and pricing options

Benefits for your user
- Off-site, anytime access via Athens or referring URL
- Print or copy pages or chapters
- Full content search
- Bookmark, highlight and annotate text
- Access to thousands of pages of quality research at the click of a button

For more information, pricing enquiries or to order a free trial, contact your local online sales team.

UK and Rest of World: **online.sales@tandf.co.uk**
US, Canada and Latin America:
e-reference@taylorandfrancis.com

www.ebooksubscriptions.com

ALPSP Award for BEST eBOOK PUBLISHER 2009 Finalist

Taylor & Francis eBooks
Taylor & Francis Group

A flexible and dynamic resource for teaching, learning and research.

University Readers
Reading Materials Evolved.

Introducing the

SOCIAL ISSUES COLLECTION

A Routledge/University Readers Custom Library for Teaching

Customizing course material for innovative and excellent teaching in sociology has never been easier or more effective!

Choose from a collection of more than 300 readings from Routledge, Taylor & Francis, and other publishers to make a custom anthology that suits the needs of your social problems/ social inequality, and social issues courses.

All readings have been aptly chosen by academic editors and our authors and organized by topic and author.

Online tool makes it easy for busy instructors:

1. Simply select your favorite Routledge and Taylor & Francis readings, and add any other required course material, including your own.

2. Choose the order of the readings, pick a binding, and customize a cover.

3. One click will post your materials for students to buy. They can purchase print or digital packs, and we ship direct to their door within two weeks of ordering!

More information at www.socialissuescollection.com

Contact information: Call your Routledge sales rep, or
Becky Smith at University Readers, 800-200-3908 ext. 18, bsmith@universityreaders.com
Steve Rutter at Routledge, 207-434-2102, Steve.Rutter@taylorandfrancis.com.

Routledge
Taylor & Francis Group
an **informa** business